MW00581878

¡VINO!

AT TABLE

¡VINO!

The History and Identity of Spanish Wine

KARL J. TRYBUS

UNIVERSITY OF NEBRASKA PRESS   LINCOLN

© 2023 by the Board of Regents of
the University of Nebraska

All rights reserved

The University of Nebraska Press is part of a land-grant institution with campuses and programs on the past, present, and future homelands of the Pawnee, Ponca, Otoe-Missouria, Omaha, Dakota, Lakota, Kaw, Cheyenne, and Arapaho Peoples, as well as those of the relocated Ho-Chunk, Sac and Fox, and Iowa Peoples.

Library of Congress Cataloging-in-Publication Data
Names: Trybus, Karl J., author.
Title: ¡Vino! : the history and identity of Spanish wine / Karl J. Trybus, University of Nebraska Press.
Description: Lincoln : University of Nebraska Press, 2023. | Series: At table | Includes bibliographical references and index.
Identifiers: LCCN 2023015921
ISBN 9781496203625 (hardback)
ISBN 9781496237132 (epub)
ISBN 9781496237149 (pdf)
Subjects: LCSH: Wine and wine making—Spain—History. | Wine industry—Political aspects—Spain—History. | BISAC: COOKING / Beverages / Alcoholic / Wine | HISTORY / Europe / Spain
Classification: LCC TP559.S7 T79 2023 | DDC 663/.200946—dc23/eng/20230421
LC record available at https://lccn.loc.gov/2023015921

Set and designed in Garamond Premier by N. Putens.

For my mom, Margaret

Dime lo qué bebes y te diré quién eres.

Tell me what you drink, and I'll tell you who you are.

—SPANISH PROVERB

CONTENTS

ILLUSTRATIONS

ACKNOWLEDGMENTS

I am extremely grateful that I had the opportunity to write about a topic I enjoy. To complete a project on wine and Spain, I needed to meet and interact with numerous individuals in a variety of locations, and they all have helped me so much to complete this work. I hope they all understand that they have been invaluable to my research, but, most importantly, they helped me have the strength to complete this project.

I want to thank my institution, Limestone University, for the ability to research and for their help funding my trips to Spain and the many conferences I have attended over the years to share my work. My history colleagues have also assisted me during my years of writing. Many of these conferences—full of academics willing to assist learning and growth—were sponsored by the Association for Spanish and Portuguese Historical Studies (ASPHS), a tremendous organization that I must thank. In the ASPHS I would like to specifically thank Sandie Holguín, Jessica Davidson, Wayne Bowen, Clinton Young, Alejandro Gomez del Moral, Kathryn Mahaney, Charles Nicholas Saenz, Samuel Pierce, and Adrian Shubert. I also owe a deep debt of gratitude to Montserrat Miller, who has been a constant support and has helped me in so many ways, especially introducing me to her amazing family in Catalonia: Elizabeth Chambers, Marc Martí, Ángels Homs, and Josep Carbo. Without Montserrat's help, I am not sure if this project could have been completed.

In the world of wine, there are so many amazing people and organizations who have helped me over the years. In the United States, I must thank Juan Carlos Rodriguez, Olea Restaurant in New Haven, and Bond Street Wines in

Spartanburg. In Spain the list of people to thank is enormous, and I hope to acknowledge as many as I can here: Francesc de P. Valls Junyent, Josep Colomé Ferrer, Miryam Ochoa Arróniz, Rosa Ruíz Pula, Jordina Escala, Lorena Deibe, Manuel Raventós Negra, Rosa Mitjans, Lídia Pelejá, Josep Mata Caldú, Vinyet Almirall Bertran, Miguel Torres, María del Carmen Borrego Plá and her mother Doña Pilar, Ana Cabestrero Ortega, Manuel Marín Gil, Borja Leal, Marina Ramos, Javier Maldonado Rosso, Cristóbal Orellana González, and Jesús Anguita. I must also thank all the employees of the bodegas, restaurants, wine shops, and archives who assisted on my way through this exploration and adventure in Spain.

When it comes to Jerez de la Frontera, two people have helped me more than anyone could have ever imagined. José Luis Jiménez García, my guide through the archives and bodegas of the city, has introduced me to a number of fabulous people, and he has been an immeasurable help and good friend over the years. I must also thank Tomoko Kimura for her friendship and assistance over the years. She has been a wonderful person to visit bodegas with, and I enjoy talking with her about sherry and international markets. Over my many visits to Jerez, they have both been so kind to me and have taken me on many wonderful adventures, especially to the Tabanco El Pasaje for tapas, sherry, and flamenco.

To complete this book, I must thank the University of Nebraska Press for its professionalism, with special thanks to Bridget Barry, Emily Casillas, Haley Mendlik, Courtney Ochsner, and copyeditor Emily Shelton. I also want to thank Alisa Plant for her original interest in my project at the preliminary stages. Erin Greb has made wonderful maps for this work that show the important regions needed to understand the geography of the vine in Spain. I also thank the organizations that have allowed me to use their copywritten photos with acknowledgment: Fundación González Byass, Bodegas Maestro Sierra, Bodegas Raventós i Blanc, Bodegas Sánchez Romate, and Caves Blancher.

All projects, to be completed, need the support of friends and family, and I have an excellent group I want to thank. My best friend for over thirty years, Justin Morgatto, has been a wonderful support due to his knowledge of the alcohol business and his willingness to listen to my research when he did not have to. I also want to thank Alison Porpora for all our adventures over wine. Giusi Russo's friendship and professional advice has helped me for years. Jane Watkins, Jack Knipe, Dale Guffey, Gena Poovey, and Brian Holcomb are wonderful colleagues who have helped me along the way. Ellen Long has been a great sounding board for all my issues over the years, and it is wonderful to have a friend who sees things just like I do. I also want to thank Patricia Hoskins, who has been an amazing colleague and friend. She, her husband, Ray, and her son, Hank, have been so kind and always helped me when I needed it, and their friendships are key to my happiness. I must also thank my cat, Don Pedro Ximénez, who is named after sherry. He has been immensely helpful by sitting on my lap and sometimes my research when I was writing. He always knew when it was time to take a break. Finally, I want to thank my mother, Margaret Trybus. She has heard me read these chapters dozens of times, always telling me her favorite (and least favorite) parts of the work. During my travels to Spain, she has been a wonderful caregiver for my cat, even though when I return from Europe they seem to disagree on some things, including who broke the television in 2017. Without this support from my mom, none of this work could have been completed. I am so grateful to all these people, and I am a better person for knowing all of them.

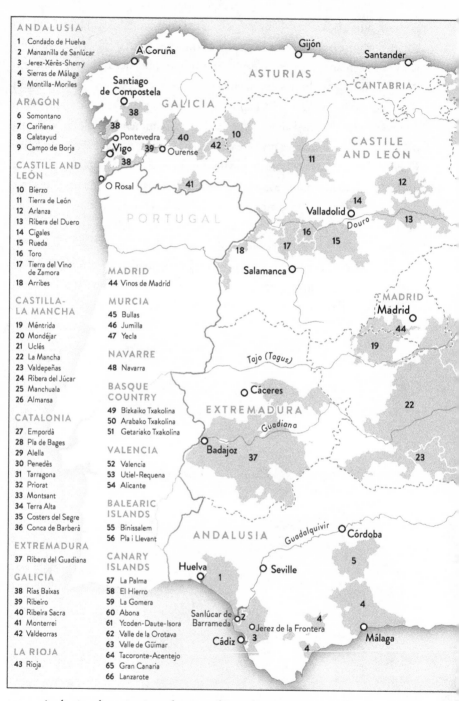

ANDALUSIA
1   Condado de Huelva
2   Manzanilla de Sanlúcar
3   Jerez-Xérès-Sherry
4   Sierras de Málaga
5   Montilla-Moriles

ARAGÓN
6   Somontano
7   Cariñena
8   Calatayud
9   Campo de Borja

CASTILE AND
LEÓN
10 Bierzo
11 Tierra de León
12 Arlanza
13 Ribera del Duero
14 Cigales
15 Rueda
16 Toro
17 Tierra del Vino
    de Zamora
18 Arribes

CASTILLA-
LA MANCHA
19 Méntrida
20 Mondéjar
21 Uclés
22 La Mancha
23 Valdepeñas
24 Ribera del Júcar
25 Manchuela
26 Almansa

CATALONIA
27 Empordà
28 Pla de Bages
29 Alella
30 Penedès
31 Tarragona
32 Priorat
33 Montsant
34 Terra Alta
35 Costers del Segre
36 Conca de Barberà

EXTREMADURA
37 Ribera del Guadiana

GALICIA
38 Rías Baixas
39 Ribeiro
40 Ribeira Sacra
41 Monterrei
42 Valdeorras

LA RIOJA
43 Rioja

MADRID
44 Vinos de Madrid

MURCIA
45 Bullas
46 Jumilla
47 Yecla

NAVARRE
48 Navarra

BASQUE
COUNTRY
49 Bizkaiko Txakolina
50 Arabako Txakolina
51 Getariako Txakolina

VALENCIA
52 Valencia
53 Utiel-Requena
54 Alicante

BALEARIC
ISLANDS
55 Binissalem
56 Pla i Llevant

CANARY
ISLANDS
57 La Palma
58 El Hierro
59 La Gomera
60 Abona
61 Ycoden-Daute-Isora
62 Valle de la Orotava
63 Valle de Güímar
64 Tacoronte-Acentejo
65 Gran Canaria
66 Lanzarote

MAP 1. A selection *denominaciones de origen* of Spanish wines. Map created by Erin Greb.

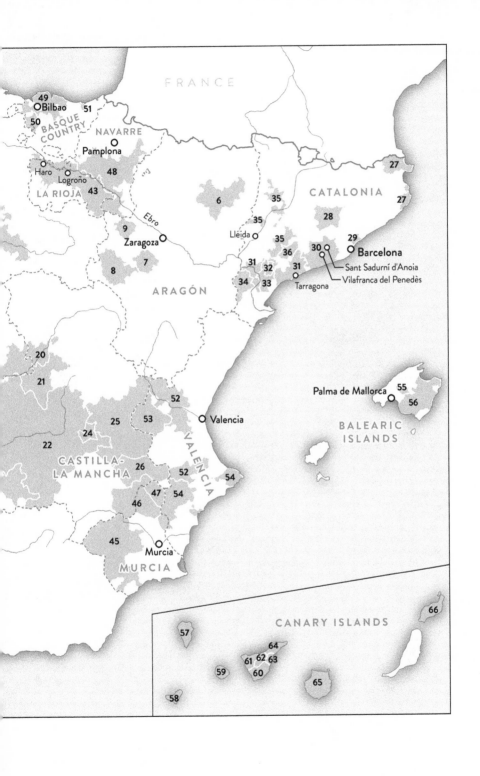

¡VINO!

Introduction

This project began with my personal interest in wine and a love of Spanish history. On trips to Spain I would enjoy the local wines with my meals, but I would often see native Spaniards drinking beer or cocktails at a higher rate. Often I would be the only foreigner drinking wine, as the others ordered the large ubiquitous pitchers of sangria for the tables. I always found this strange, as Spain was noted for its wines by both locals and visitors. Following my trips to Spain, I would return to the United States and look to purchase the Spanish products I had enjoyed. One product that often—and surprisingly—eluded me was Spanish wine. Unless I visited a Spanish restaurant, such as the spectacular Olea in New Haven, Connecticut, there was likely to be no more than one Spanish wine on the menu, and it was usually a tempranillo from Rioja. Even a visit to a package, liquor, or wine store would mean finding hardly any Spanish wines. If the store did have them, they were often relegated to a far back corner past the large selections of French, American, Italian, Chilean, Argentine, Australian, and New Zealand wines. If real Spanish sherry is available, it is often intermixed with cheap knockoffs. Although Spain is an annually top-three wine-producing nation, and it has the most land devoted to vineyards in the world, their wines did not seem to make it across the Atlantic unless they were destined for specialty locations. Even conversations with my best friend of over thirty years, Justin Morgatto, who works for a liquor distribution company, would lead to no clear determinations as to why.

As a historian I began to think about why these wines were so difficult to find in the United States and often excluded in conversations about wine generally, with the exception of true aficionados. I wanted to explore a few things concerning wine: why Spanish wine seemed to be a true mystery outside of Spain, and why Spanish wine seemed so underrepresented in Spain itself. Clearly Spanish winemakers and the Spanish government must have made attempts to make their products better known; greater knowledge about wines from Spain could result in more sales. Today Spanish wine regional authorities, *denominaciones de origen*, maintain dozens of websites about wine history. Even with these marketing attempts, something must not be working—or, more importantly, other influences must have prevented Spanish producers from becoming better known, and these could have historical roots. From there I embarked on three research trips to Spain to explore its archives, bodegas, wine shops, and museums to try to understand better the relationship between Spanish wine and the history of Spain.

To study the place of wine in Spanish history, I first needed to explore what Spanish wine meant to the country. In recent years food studies and food history have become growing fields, with scholars wanting to research one of the most human of all needs: what we eat. Food history is also clearly connected to the history of alcohol and, by extension, wine. While today wine is not viewed as a necessary foodstuff, this was not always the case, as it previously provided calories before improved agriculture and allowed better storage for agricultural goods before refrigeration. Clearly, these represent major shifts for the importance of wine as a product throughout modern history. Grape wine has been a part of Western societies for millennia, and, as Rachel Black and Robert Ulin explain, "wine has long been and continues to be an important commodity that generates significant interest because of its commercial, symbolic, cultural, and aesthetic value."[1] Wine has meanings associated with who buys it, what they buy, who drinks which types, when they drink, and where they drink it, among many other considerations. Wine has developed multiple identities, from the expensive and decanted pricey reds at a fine restaurant to wine in cans now available at some stores. As Mack Holt writes, "The culture of consumption of alcohol cannot be unilaterally dictated to masses from above. . . . The culture of the drink in the West has always been the product of negotiation between the ruling elites and the drinking population at large . . . [and] alcohol consumption has been so ubiquitous in our past that no single group or institution, no matter how powerful, has been able to control the meaning and culture of drinking."[2] No one can force a consumer to think of wine as cool, trendy, or stylish; its assessment depends upon time, place, product, and person. The Chablis craze of the 1980s and the Pinot Noir explosion after the popular 2004 film *Sideways* are proof of this. Therefore, the meaning of wine (and alcohol) in all societies is fluid, so a study of Spanish wines will show these historical adaptations over time.

As the purchaser often buys wine for their own consumption, this work also fits with conversations about the meaning of food and its change over time for the shopper. As renowned anthropologist Sidney Mintz explains, "Our relationships between production and consumption are still constrained, once market forces penetrate social relationships on the level of everyday life. Because of the changes those forces make possible, our understanding of the consumption of food in modern society confronts conundrums, apparent contradictions, contrasts, and polarities of a kind."[3] As new products emerge or old goods ship to more locations, new interactions occur between consumer and product. One of these conundrums, Mintz notes, is that, even though food is simply needed for human survival, it "is also a symbolic marker of membership (or nonmembership) in practically any sort of social grouping. Whether it is ceremonial or every day, public or private, kin-based or not, at work or at play, religious or secular, social groups characteristically employ food to draw lines, confirm statuses, and separate those who do, and do not, belong."[4] For example, some choose to drink Spanish sherry because they believe this indicates something about them as a group (possibly English, higher class, or older). In the nineteenth century, because sherry was sometimes viewed as a dangerous product, its sales collapsed. The French have always seemed to be successful marketing their foodstuffs, as they are better at eating their locally produced commodities and advertised the uniqueness of their products more effectively than any other Western state. Julia Child introduced American home chefs to the class and panache of French food in the 1960s, making these meals and products cool. Americans associate New Year's Eve and special occasions with French champagne, even though they might not buy the real stuff. These triumphs have had important outcomes for French agriculture, making it central to French identity in the minds of those both at home and abroad.

While food distinguishes groups, Mintz notes, food serves as a means of communication: "As with language, on many occasions people define themselves with food; at the same time, food consistently defines and redefines *them*."[5] Therefore, the choices made by the consumer say something about the individual as well as about the product they choose to purchase. Consumers of champagne and caviar may believe that these products present the appearance of an identity of wealth and class. In her captivating work on Barcelona food market history, Montserrat Miller writes, "The fact that consumption, habits, and tastes have changed over time shows that the system of food symbols is not a closed one; rather, it has responded to a multiplicity of outside forces."[6] Therefore, the meaning of a particular item—in this case, Spanish wine—is not stagnant, but changes due to a slew of issues. Miller continues, "Religion, technological and organization change, public policy, medicine, and the construction of sometimes competing cultural discourses produced by its dominant classes also shaped culinary practices."[7] Each of these issues had direct effects on how people saw and therefore purchased Spanish wines both in the country and outside. The ever-changing identity of Spanish wines was not made by just one group; producers, consumers, state agencies, and foreign actors all play a role.

While the upper classes and governmental controls have an effect on the cultural significance of particular products consumed in societies, the interactions at the ground level between food producers, consumers, and sellers modify cultural understanding of the meanings of different foods. As Montserrat Miller highlights, "How, where, and from whom we buy our food matters."[8] The personal preferences of the consumer, along with the choices and attitudes of the vendors, work together to create an expression of their identities through their food purchasing. By looking at food vendors and consumers, Miller underscores the key areas for exploring this interaction. While small-scale Barcelona food vendors achieved economic growth while remaining individually owned, "ultimately the success of Barcelona's markets has in very large part been due to the tenacity of the vendor population itself, which individually and collectively exercised tremendous agency in the consolidation and profitability of their small-scale firms. . . . Vendors exhibited tremendous capacity and inclination for adaptation."[9] These sellers, therefore, frequently acted as powerful food negotiators throughout Barcelona's history. With this power and adaptability, they "experienced upward social mobility in the early twentieth century and became part of the city's new lower middle class, which tended to own limited capital and employ little labor outside the family or household unit."[10] These vendors were able to negotiate and act as a unified group to gain influence in the city—through the sale of and interaction with food. Those who sold food, therefore, made a significant impact on the life of the everyday city dweller.

In addition, Miller notes the active participation of women in the development and success of these markets even as they were excluded from the political life in Franco's Spain. "The evidence of widespread and ongoing female market-stall license acquisition," Miller writes, "serves as further proof that industrialization did not bring an end to women's work in the formal economy. . . . Women's work in markets contributed to family well-being over the long run and the viability of small-scale commerce in food even after the appearance of supermarkets and other more highly capitalized competitors in the sector."[11] As women vendors actively participated in the selling of food, they interacted with women customers and recommended products to them. As this work will show, advertising agencies and state organizations specifically targeted Spanish women to buy more wine, with the clear understanding that they set the tables at home. Overall, as Miller shows, the level and interaction between consumer and vendor made a difference in terms of what food was purchased and from whom it was bought, therefore meaningfully influencing which foods became popular. If wine sellers or state agencies could make these connections with the consumers, either in Spain or internationally, then sales could maybe increase. Therefore, sellers (or, in this case, vineyards and state agencies) needed to establish these trustworthy connections with the purchasers if they hoped to market their product appropriately.

As consumers purchased food at the market, there comes the question of how that food was discussed. The discourses on food come from many points between consumers and society at large. In her exploration of the multidimensional conversation about food, *Word of Mouth*, sociologist Priscilla Parkhurst Ferguson writes, "Instead of focusing on people as individuals, sociologists look to the relationships that bring people together. In other words, we look at what people do when they are with other people, and we pay attention to how people talk and write about what they do—in this case, about the many ways they think about food."[12] Thus, the discourse of consumers, producers, sellers, and the state exert power over how people's ideas of what they eat change. One can also ask, then, How do people speak about wine? With regard to discourse around food, Parkhurst Ferguson explains, "Crucial to understanding this strikingly assertive food world is food talk. In every culture, people talk about, write about, and portray food for all sorts of reasons. . . . New modes of production and consumption, new requirements of supply and demand, and new forms of dining push us to think about food both more often and more intensely than before."[13] Therefore, as technology and discourse changed, ideas about food modified, leading to adaptations in what one might eat or prefer to buy at various class levels. As this book will show, numerous actors—those from the highest levels of government to the person on the street—all discussed the role of Spanish wines in society and culture, whether they knew it or not. At the same time, food has moved away from the arena of pure sustenance to that of pleasure: "Food talk—the right kind, the kind that we want to listen to— equates food with pleasure. A culinary paradise is ours for the eating. It is also, it seems, ours for the talking. For it is here that we find a sense of the pleasures that attend our encounters with food. Speaking about food both before and after the event sharpens our pleasures."[14] As the discourse about and variety of food became more commonplace, the idea of food and eating changed for each consumer. "For some," Parkhurst Ferguson writes, "food became a social issue; for others, a fashion; and still for others, a lens through which to examine and imagine the new world coming into being around them."[15] Because wine is no longer considered part of a required diet, it stands as a clear example of a product that has moved away from the necessity and has found itself at the center of a conversation of pleasure—and Spanish wine is the perfect place to view these adaptations in communication around food.

As Parkhurst Ferguson suggests, as more writers and gastronomes spoke about food, more consumers at numerous levels would become aware of these food differences.[16] As conversations about wine shifted from the simply red or white to questions about region, grape varietal, and vintage, the consumer could be more aware of what they could buy, and they could develop their own opinions. By the start of the twenty-first century, Parkhurst Ferguson asserts, the consumer had become more educated about and interested in their own pleasure, eschewing old rules of dining as the

> food world disdains, disregards, and largely dispenses with many of the forms that once made dining—whether at home or outside. . . . Meals were scripted and governed by an array of rules, conventions, and norms, both explicit and implicit. More often today, diners sit down at tables with no script at all. The rise of culinary individualism, the loss of the communal

forms that once presided over meals, and the substitution of familiarity for formality have unsettled contemporary dining. The excitement of adventure triumphs over the security of the known (or, for outsiders, the anxiety of the unknown).[17]

The individual could not only make a choice but also had many more options from which to choose and what to do with those choices. The combination of the person and the available products allows for greater choice in society: "We are shaped by the arrangements that society sometimes allows, sometimes gives, sometimes enforces. What we decide, then is a mixture of choice and cultural formation.... No one sees quite the same thing, and there is no taste on which everyone will agree."[18] Think of the modern bars with dozens of new gins and whiskeys targeting specific consumers with particular tastes to be shared in public, or the popular, upscale wine shop and its many unique bottles, each attempting to stand out in a crowd. As societies and cultures change over time, new rules for how, where, and why someone talks about and chooses food changes. And as governments and political opinions change—either becoming more authoritarian or democratic—conversations about foodstuffs representing a particular location also change; the totalitarian and unsophisticated wines of the early Franco regime, for instance, have been replaced with the stylish and democratized wines of today's Spain.

Following the conversation about food and its purchase, the cooking and serving of food shows how the identities of these commodities shift over decades. Using gastronomic texts and cookbooks from Spain, Lara Anderson explores the creation of culinary nationalism in the nineteenth and twentieth centuries. The authors of these texts, motivated by national pride and in an attempt to distinguish themselves from foreign culinary traditions, aimed to unify and clarify national cuisine. "From the mid-nineteenth century onwards, however," Anderson writes, "increasing numbers of Spaniards realized the importance of gaining control of the images of their country that had been put into circulation by foreigners."[19] For those in power during the early twentieth century, "creating national culinary cohesion, re-vindicating Spanish cuisine in the face of French cuisine and turning Spanish cuisine into a profitable industry were seen as key ways to improve the image of Spain both nationally and internationally and to strengthen and modernize the country's economy."[20] Therefore, both individual food writers and the government could see the advantages in unifying and codifying Spanish food. In this way Spanish wine producers and the Spanish state both wanted to centralize wine production to produce good wine to sell for a profitable industry. At the same time, Spanish wine was constantly under the pressure of comparison to its northern rival, and Spain's producers needed to take back their identity.

The restaurant, in all its forms, influenced how food was identified and understood by the consumer and producer as well. As anthropologist Isabel González Turmo discusses in her study of restaurant culture in Seville from the mid-nineteenth to the late twentieth century, "In the mid-19th century there was a considerable range of places to eat in Seville: restaurants, inns, cafes, *cervecerías*, taverns and, depending on the case, also some casinos. Only a few decades later did food houses, fried food cafeterias, and tapas bars appear. What characterizes this whole period is the tremendous ambivalence in the denominations of these establishments."[21] All of these locations, González Turmo explains, served not only different types of food but also different types of customers from different classes and professions. Locations like hotels and casinos served the upper class, while *cervecerías* "democratized" locations offering food service to all neighborhoods.[22] In Seville during the lean times of the post–Civil War 1940s, "basic food was scarce, as in the rest of the country and the black market was in fashion. Forced by necessity, restaurants adopted popular, traditional Spanish cuisine, or whatever you might call it: in short, by requiring fewer ingredients, it was better adapted to the tastes of customers, and, why not, to the ideological guidelines of the times. What better dish for a proud Spanish inn that a *tortilla de patatas*, flamenco-style eggs, stew, or battered hake."[23] During an era of hunger and pain, these restaurants used local ingredients—which were still hard to find—to create something special. The restaurant thus became the location for defining what food meant to the community. The interactions between the diner and the restaurateur experimented with those products that became acceptable or demanded by the community.

While these locations created solidarity around food, the state did take a role, especially in the 1960s, as both national and international tourism grew in Spain, and more middle-class diners ate at Seville's local establishments. As González Turmo explains, the Francoist state allowed slightly greater freedom of expression during this period, which influenced restaurant culture. "Only from then on," she writes, "were habits required today that seem elementary but were not before, such as the existence of a price list, complaint books, menus of the day, translations of the menu into other languages and cleanliness in bathrooms and kitchens! To take care of the follow-up of these regulations, a body of inspectors was created; a task until then no one had done, among other reasons, because they had not known what to inspect."[24] The fact that customers could file complaints against a restaurant if they did not follow certain guidelines—for bugs in the food, unlisted prices, poor or rushed service—gave more power to the consumer.[25] With the slow liberalization of politics came a slow liberalization of food culture. As with Spanish wine, what one drank had meaning for one's identity, and, as times changed, the meaning of these products based on their reputations changed in turn.

As can be seen, many factors influence the meaning and understanding of food and its study. Consumers, producers, sellers, the state, and many others all had conversations about the idea of food and its identity in society. This project looks at a variety of these actors and their interactions and discussions. Spanish state agencies worked from above to try to create a meaning for Spanish wine in the hopes of selling more, both nationally and internationally, funding fairs, festivals, advertisements, and other events. Those with more personal connections to wine also contributed: some producers created new styles of wine, and consumers made the decision whether to buy them or not. This project explores both these top-down and bottom-up conversations that created a changing identity for Spanish wine. By using a wide variety of sources for this work, I aim to show how these various groups, each with their own goals, constructed the identity for Spanish wine from the mid-nineteenth century until today.

When discussing the meaning of a food item, especially wine, one must look to France as an archetype. France has been the most successful Western nation to develop its food identity, and it is necessary to understand what the Spanish would have been aware of across the Pyrenees. Whereas at various points in history Spanish wines were thought of as a substitute for French wines, the reverse was not the case: Spanish wine has often been defined as a cheaper product compared to lux French wines. Kolleen Guy explains that "by the turn of the [twentieth] century, innate, national taste and 'authentic' quality wines were so intertwined and 'rooted' in France that it was difficult to invoke one without eliciting the other. Although French luxury wines could serve as symbols of social stratification, the wines of France, more generally, and the unique *terroir* that produced them were encrusted with myths and national genius."[26] As symbols of French national achievements, agricultural goods, and wine in particular, were meant to be celebrated. "References to a particular regional wine," Guy writes, "might be used to signal social class, but references to French wine in both popular stories and national debates about issues ranging from public health to agricultural legislation were designed to evoke shared national character traits. In this way, wine became a complex symbol, used to delineate class boundaries and yet at the same time evoked as a unifying national patrimony."[27] Wine and agricultural goods were not just made in France, but they were part of what France meant. Drinking French wine was not a simple choice to Frenchmen, but an open declaration of one's Frenchness and, therefore, character. Spain did not have this strong agricultural character with its products, but this book will show how a variety of actors tried to create new identities for Spanish wine.

As Thomas Parker shows, "The tradition in France of linking the food each person consumes to his or her character dates back to theories on the humors popular throughout Europe in the Middle Ages. The practice became all the more common when Renaissance France began to construct a part of the country's cultural identity by evoking the casual power of land to create differences in food, language, and people."[28] The roots of an agricultural and a seemingly soil-based superiority notion, then, has a long tradition in France. For centuries it has been "Europe's most developed agricultural and wine-producing country, providing ample opportunity for terroir to expand in importance literally and metaphorically in the course of being evoked in everyday life."[29] Terroir and wine were not solely understood as products for wealthy consumers; ideas about them trickled down to all levels of French society, from farmer to restaurateur to consumer. This connection between land and product meant "that a food's taste may be determined and appreciated according to its origin is easy enough to understand, but historically the French took it further. They posited that terroir affects not only the cheese *but also* the cheesemaker, not only the produce but also the farmer."[30] France's relationship with its food commodities was seemingly the strongest in the Western world. Every aspect of French agriculture was tied to the land, which made France superior. This does not mean that Spanish goods were of lesser quality, or that the producers did not have as strong of a connection with their commodity or land, but that the French expressed this idea to their nation and to the international consumer more effectively. The Spanish hoped to reproduce this potent identity formation, and wine was a useful product, as demand was often strong, and prices were high . The problem for Spain was that the country was more reactionary than progressive. French farmers and producers established their identities and used them to their advantage over the course of centuries. French wine had meaning; to compete, Spanish wines needed to construct their own meanings. When plagues destroyed French vineyards in the nineteenth century, Spanish producers tried to take up the slack by offering a replacement product of equal quality, but, once French wines recovered, the replacement beverage was no longer in high demand. As French gastronomes redefined the meaning of wine and food in the mid-twentieth century, Spanish food and wine experts raced to copy those ideas. As this book will show, imitating the identity of another product may have success in the short term, but, without an obvious plan to clearly express quality and self-identity, Spanish wines would always be at the mercy of comparison.

This book will explore the idea of Spanish wine from the mid-nineteenth century until today. I chose to begin in the mid-nineteenth century because it was a period of upheaval and rupture for Spain and wine production. The contentious reign of Isabel II, combined with the loss of most of the American colonies, presented serious issues for the country's economic growth. The first major nineteenth-century wine plague, oidium, arrived in the 1850s and began a march across the continent, destroying vineyards. These political, economic, and agricultural challenges created a new moment for wine in Spain. I explore aspects of Spain's internal concerns, such as consumption levels, production goals and challenges, scientific conversations, marketing plans, and cultural meaning. Each of these issues changed and adapted as time progressed, and each of them changed the country's understanding of Spanish wine. Externally, I look at issues relating to exports, fears of competition, and the attempt to establish a clear identity of Spanish wine for foreign consumers. As global concerns and international trade shifted between the nineteenth and twentieth centuries, the idea of Spanish wine also changed. To understand what Spanish wine means today, we must investigate both national and international historical developments.

As this book deals with the extensive topic of Spanish wine, I think it is necessary to explain what this book is not looking to discuss. First, it is not about how to taste and describe wine; I will not be discussing all regional varietals and their flavor profiles, as might be found in a wine guide. I am similarly not interested in defining the best-tasting wines, as taste is completely subjective. While regional grapes will be mentioned, they will be used as examples of local productions. Second, this book will not discuss every wine region or wine producer. Clearly this would be impossible, as Spain has over eighty protected regions, with thousands of producers. For the sake of this work, some larger producers will be explored, as they were willing and able to provide information for the project. Similarly, the time periods under discussion were chosen because materials specifically related to wine could be accessed in archives. All this being said, surely books that focus directly on specific regional production or investigate other time periods would be much welcomed in the future and would complement this work.

Overall I argue that wine producers and the Spanish state understood the importance of wine to the economy and national identity, especially from the mid-nineteenth century onward. They wanted the product to achieve greatness, but problems stood in the way. Both producers and the state tried to create plans that allowed Spanish wine to adapt over the decades, but these strategies often came as a reaction to fresh concerns rather than as a preemptive action to take the lead in wine identity and economy. These entities knew they had to do something to succeed, but they relied too heavily on the interests of other states rather than creating a clear goal of their own. Often it appeared that Spain understood all of its wines as exactly the same, and producers worked to create homogeneity, seemingly ignoring the regional specializations of the country. In some instances Spain copied the actions of foreign wine producers, but these changes were often too late. In general Spain clearly understood the importance of its wine at many levels and the fact that the beverage was central to Spanish identity; however, expressing this importance to national and international consumers was the greatest challenge, and one that was never fully overcome.

In exploring the history of Spanish wine identity, this book is divided into seven chapters and in three sections. The first section begins in the mid-nineteenth century, as Spain's empire collapsed and northern European states industrialized at a faster rate, and explores concerns specific to that historical moment: the economy and science. Chapter 1 highlights the times when the Spanish state focused its attention on the economic importance of wine exports, especially to Europe. The century began with the power of sherry exports, but, after the

1870s, sherry was decimated, and state agencies needed to find replacements to fill this major void. A national census of wine production was needed to determine how much wine was being made and exported. Chapter 2 explores the growing role of science in wine production. Science and agronomy were not called upon because they were trendy, but because they were necessary. The three great wine plagues of the nineteenth century almost destroyed European wine production, resulting in the necessity of studying these plagues and developing treatments for them. At the same time, as unscrupulous producers tried to take advantage of high demands, low yields, and rising prices, producers and government agencies needed to find ways to guarantee the reliability of Spanish wine. Substandard wine cheated the consumers and ruined reputations.

The book's second section examines the transition of Spanish wine identity over time during the dictatorship of Francisco Franco (1939–75). These chapters show how members of the state apparatus and consumers discussed wine during this authoritarian period. Chapter 3 raises a question: How to drink wine? For centuries wine was viewed as a necessary food product, but at the end of the nineteenth century questions rose about the health benefits of alcohol. The chapter discusses the important change to the identity of wine consumption and its meaning to society and nutrition. With such a large production of wine, Spain needed to find a way to tell its people how to consume it responsibly. State agencies under the totalitarian Franco regime took an active role in trying to persuade its people to buy and drink local wine as a sign of patriotism. The state did not want dangerous drunken mobs in the streets, but it needed people to buy wine to support the economy. Therefore, consumers needed to learn wine-drinking best practices created by the regime, and state media was a perfect tool. Chapter 4 investigates the development of wine fairs—both locally and internationally—from the nineteenth century until the end of the Franco period. These events highlight the issues of production, sales, and consumption of wine. State intervention supported each of these events, and their development over time reveals the similarities and differences of wine festivals for Spain, each of which worked to showcase Spanish wines to locals and foreigners. Chapter 5 continues to take up the question of how to drink wine well at Franco-era wine festivals with a case study of the Exposición y Feria de la Viña y del Vino (Exposition and Fair of the Vineyard and Wine) in the Catalan city of Vilafranca de Penedès, an event hosted in 1943, 1953, and 1963 in the primary wine-growing region outside Barcelona. While it was meant to showcase Spanish wines, the festival atmosphere was also key in getting locals to understand how to better drink wine, according to the regime. Similarly, given the decade-long gaps between fairs, the periodicals generated around them show the changing attitudes toward wine production, consumption, and identity.

The final section, of two chapters, discusses the changing role of Spanish wine from the final years of the Franco regime until today. As Spain's dictator tried to open the country to new economic growth, new concerns arose for Spanish wine. Chapter 6 explores Spanish wine's interactions with its largest markets: France, Scandinavia, the United States, and Britain. In each situation changing markets and adjusting tastes in the post–World War II boom economies meant that Spanish wine needed to adapt. As more options became available to consumers in wealthy nations, and as new trade agreements were established to secure peace, producers of Spanish wines often found themselves in a constant battle to protect their products. Chapter 7 looks at the culmination of change for Spanish wines at the end of the twentieth and the beginning of the twenty-first centuries. Under democracy Spain entered the European Common Markets; therefore, Spanish wines could compete better with their European rivals. Most importantly, with more choices and easier travel, especially to Spain, wine could reinvent itself one more time. In this period Spanish wine was not a replacement, but a cool and trendy product that walked a fine line between tradition and experimentation.

The idea of wine is not stagnant: it began as a form for storing produce, became nutritional, adapted to medicine, defined class designation, turned into an economic commodity, and finally represented style. Spanish wine producers needed to deal with each of these concerns, just like producers from around the world. At times Spanish producers succeeded and gained large market shares; at other times Spanish wine sales collapsed. While some have viewed Spanish wine as cheap and low quality, others know it for its unique style and special grapes. A person's taste in wine is subjective: drink what you like, not what you are told is good. With that being said, there is a way to look objectively at Spanish wine's history and its goals to establish a unique identity and a cultural meaning of true Spanishness.

1

How to Sell Wine

EVALUATING NINETEENTH-CENTURY
SPANISH WINE ON THE MARKET

The Iberian Peninsula has produced wine for millennia, beginning under the Phoenicians and then under Roman control. Even during Islamic rule, Spanish farmers still produced grapes, using some for food and medicinal purposes, with others expressly fermented for wine production. Improved Arab agricultural and irrigation techniques allowed the region, especially Andalucía, to become a farming success story.[1] With this long regional history of wine production and consumption, along with a rich Catholic religious tradition following the Reconquista, it should not come as a surprise that, as Spain entered the nineteenth century—a period of major change—wine cultivation continued to be an important cultural and economic crop. The century began with Spain losing most of its American colonial territories, which ended its monopolistic control over imports to the region. As a result, Spain needed to find new markets for its exports, mainly in Europe. While Britain and France underwent rapid industrialization and developed a growing bourgeoisie with extra cash to spend, Spain continued to rely heavily on agricultural production for its economy.[2] Luckily for Spanish exporters, during the nineteenth century Britain and France purchased between 50 and 70 percent of all Spanish exports.[3] Even with this important avenue in place, changing tastes and fads, new empires, agricultural plagues, public health concerns, and political conflicts could derail export security at any time. Of the many Spanish agricultural exports in this period, wine often led the way. Between 1850 and 1873, the famous fortified wine from Jerez, sherry, accounted for between 10 and 20 percent of the value of all Spanish agricultural exports.[4] With such a reliance on these exports, clearly the country needed to protect this crop at all costs.

This chapter explores the crucial period of the mid-to-late nineteenth century when Spanish producers and government agencies realized the powerful influence of wine in the national economy and tried to find ways of guaranteeing its success. As this chapter will show, even with this awareness of wine's importance to the Spanish economy, success was not always guaranteed. State and regional agencies, along with local agricultural and oenological societies, used their authority to study the place of Spanish wine and its economic value in a series of markets, both nationally and internationally. These agencies wanted to judge the current state of their wines and find ways to improve the public perception of their wines to market them to European bourgeois consumers. First, I will discuss Spanish reactions to wines at the 1855 Universal Exposition in Paris, highlighting the perceived understanding of where Spanish wines fit in European markets due to their quality and price. Next, I will explore agronomists' conversations between 1859 and 1860 about producing better wines and standardizing their productions to protect exports. From this point in time, the rise and fall of sherry exports would become a central factor. Sherry had once been the shining star of agricultural exports, but a lack of adaptation dramatically reduced its export numbers. Finally, I will discuss the 1884 survey created by the Spanish Superior Council of Agriculture, Industry, and Commerce that identified numerous concerns related to wine production throughout the country, in an effort to inform the Spanish state exactly how much wine was produced and how much could be exported. In each situation Spanish agencies understood the importance of wine to the country's economy and identity, but a clear pathway forward to improving production could not always be identified.

RESULTS FROM PARIS, 1855

The Exposition Universelle des Produits de l'Agriculture, de l'Industrie et des Beaux-Arts de Paris 1855 (Universal Exhibition of Products of Agriculture, Industry, and Fine Arts in Paris) invited artists and agriculturists from around the world to show and display their wares and products to the French citizenry and foreign visitors. As France's southern neighbor, Spain sent a large delegation of agricultural goods. The following year organic chemist and agriculturalist Ramón de Manjarrés y de Bofarull reported on his findings. A large, international variety of agricultural producers welcomed the visitors, with fruits, vegetables, cotton, wool, wheat, legumes, sugar, olive oil, silk, and wine being major draws

for the crowd. Upon seeing the crops produced in Spain and elsewhere, Manjarrés y de Bofarull stated, "But few of them can sustain the comparison to ours."[5]
According to Manjarrés y de Bofarull, Spanish agricultural production was
second to none in the world; in the favorable Spanish climate, farmers developed
high-quality crops, mostly destined for export. However, with the expansion
of French imperialism, Manjarrés y de Bofarull noted that "the production
from Africa has many analogies with those from Spain and they are destined to
compete with ours in the foreign markets, supplied until now almost exclusively
by Spain and by some other privileged countries by their nature."[6] The growing
French presence in the Maghreb threatened Spanish agriculture, as both regions
shared a Mediterranean climate, allowing for long growing seasons. Increased
French imperial exports could endanger Spain's economy. With this new threat
to Spain, there was a growing need to shore up the identity of Spanish products
on the international export market.

Manjarrés y de Bofarull turned his attention to Spanish wines, specifically those
from Catalonia: "The 25 wine expositors presented by the Catalan Agricultural
Institute truly honored the exhibition, and together with 6 other Catalan expositors represented our provinces."[7] These wines, he touted, were clarified without
any chemicals or artificial agents, yet they appeared clear, putting them on par
with those from other states. Importantly, he noted, the wine-tasting jury was
impressed that these wines had such a low price "of 15, 10, as low as 7 *centime* a
liter."[8] Producers must have been proud of these attractive and reasonably priced
wines—their value being key to their competitiveness in the market. The most
significant moment of the exposition for wine producers was this jury tasting.
Manjarrés y de Bofarull saw some issues with the process, however; for, "despite
the impartiality and good wishes of the Jury," he wrote, "I do not know if their
opinion about the wines of Spain was then quite correct. The way of trying
them did not seem to me the most convenient, and I think it is impossible to
judge correctly from such a large collection of wines, trying them all in about 4
or 5 hours."[9] With so many wines to sample, and in such a condensed amount
of time, this complaint from the organic chemist appears to be reasonable. In
addition, there was no commentary about if the wines were spit out after each
tasting or if they were swallowed, leading to intoxicated jurors. He continued,
"What had to be expected happened and it was: that they concluded by rejecting
all dry wines, not appreciating them more than those that due to their sugary

flavor made a good impression on their already tired palate. On the other hand, said Jury was made up only of French and English, and perhaps the Spanish are not entirely in agreement with them regarding the merit of a wine."[10] As will be explained, sweet wines, such as sweet sherry, dominated exports to Britain in the 1850s; therefore, the jury's judgment does make sense. Spanish wines did not win any awards—a result about which Manjarrés y de Bofarull was skeptical. Most interestingly, he pointed out that the jury was made up solely of French and English tasters. Was there deceit on their part? Had their palates been ruined after five hours of drinking wine? Did the French fix the results to win in their own country? These questions cannot be answered, but the exposition did have an impact on Spanish and Catalan wines: while they were modestly priced, in 1855 they did not impress the jury. As the importance of Spanish wine to the national economy continued to grow in the ever-changing nineteenth century, defense of its wines internationally became more critical.

Even without receiving any wine awards at the event, Manjarrés y de Bofarull saw this fair as a success for Spanish agricultural and wine producers. "The wines of Spain figured in the first line in the Universal Exhibition," he reported, "and [our] agricultural products do not yield anything to the rich collection presented by Austria, and wine menus of France, Italy, Prussia, and the Germanic Confederation."[11] Spain, with its series of successful products, was respectfully represented. While Spanish wine producers encountered difficulty when it came to besting their competitors, overall, their actions met with success. Manjarrés y de Bofarull noted a unique problem: while countries like Austria and France developed sparkling and compound industrial wines, these products did not exist in serious quantity in Spain. For him Spanish wine was an "agricultural industry," unlike in these other states.[12] This raises two interesting points. First, Spain was still a few decades away from the creation of cava, or Spanish sparkling wine made with the *méthode champenoise* in Catalonia.[13] Without a sparkling wine industry, the Spanish could not compete in this field. Second, according to Manjarrés y de Bofarull, Spain neither produced large amounts of industrialized fabricated wine, which included hard alcohol, nondistilled alcohols and brandy made from wine, items that represented only small export percentages. As will be shown later in relation to sherry, this industrial alcohol and wine mixing actually created major problems for the identity of quality Spanish wines. Overall, however, Spain exhibited skill at producing still traditional wines in the 1850s, and its solid performance at the exhibition separated the wines of the country from the adulterated wines produced to the north.

At the end of his report, Manjarrés y de Bofarull wrote, "Here I have reviewed the Universal Exposition of 1855 in its part on agriculture. The outcomes of this exposition will be beneficial for the nations that have known how to take advantage of the circumstances; they would be almost nil for those who looked at it coldly."[14] This event allowed serious agricultural producers like Spain to showcase their products for a large European market, which was key for the country, as its losses in the Americas needed to be compensated. Manjarrés y de Bofarull concluded by stating, "France invited all nations; and although it is true that in imitation of what England had done years before, it was somewhat selfish in the distribution of the grounds, but for this reason it did not stop justifying the merit, and granted to the other nations all the importance they deserved. The large number of prizes awarded to our farmers is proof of what I have just said."[15] Interestingly, he noted that the French seemed to take all the best locations for themselves. Since they were the hosts—and a much more formidable world power in the nineteenth century than Spain—this would make sense. While Spanish wines did not win any awards at the exhibition, other agricultural products did—a significant accomplishment. However, the failure of Spanish wines to win any awards at the event meant that Spanish producers needed to take a serious look at their own products for future success.

MAKING BETTER WINE

A few years later, professor of agriculture Jaime Llansó wrote a thorough paper on the process of fermenting wine. His goal was to show that Spanish producers needed to be more consistent and use better methods when producing wine to gain respect internationally. "We are convinced that Spanish wines did not reach the credit that they deserved for its quality," he asserted, "but rather we are trying to give them the precision that corresponds for the good understanding of winemaking. And it is very prudent that other nations, less privileged than ours with good weather, France for example, have been able to get nominated wines, for the intelligence with which growers proceed in the art of producing them."[16] Spanish producers needed to follow logical guidelines in production. Countries without Spain's climatic advantages produced quality wines because they followed appropriate standards. Llansó explained that Spain's vineyards must continue to refine their process "if we want our wines to enjoy the reputation they deserve for goodness in the markets of the vine. And keep in mind that outside those years of calamity due to the powdery mildew that has attacked the vines, wine is one of the most important crops in the peninsula, due to the climate conditions of the largest number of its provinces."[17] Other wine-producing nations had clearer standards, and unless Spanish producers could adhere to some of these specifications, they would not be able to compete in the market. Critics like Llansó did not intend to be condescending, but, neverthe-less, "the wine industry, mainly, needs these special aids. Because it is impossible to obtain good quality wines if the operation is entrusted to spontaneity and is not directed by art."[18] While the creation of wine was not overly difficult, it was crucial to make sure that the wine was made well and at the highest standard.

In this report Llansó demonstrated interest specifically in the fermentation of wine to guarantee quality in a final product. If the practice of fermentation could be standardized and properly followed, then a better product could be ensured. The winemakers did not need to know all the chemical processes of fermentation, but they did need to know when it mattered. According to Llansó, "It can almost be said that the theory of grape fermentation cannot be explained satisfactorily without the auspices of chemistry, because only it allows us to appreciate the causes that retard or accelerate wine fermentation, and to examine with certainty the phenomena that operate and they follow one another while the vinification occurs."[19] Better fermentation practices had been studied, and producers needed to follow these guidelines. While some may seem simple, traditional wine practices surely would have varied greatly, especially for those smaller or less-educated producers. First and foremost, producers had to work in a clean environment, washing all grapes before crushing them and cleaning all tubs before they were filled.[20] If producers had cleaner materials to make the wine, then contamination of the end product would be less likely. Another basic principle, Llansó said, was consistency when filling wine tubs, being sure to do so during the daytime hours, in order to regularize the temperature. At the same time, these tubs needed to not be over- or underfilled but be all at the same level.[21] The more consistency in production, the better the final product.

In the case of fermentation, sugar is a key element. Llansó had an interesting suggestion: "We have indicated that sugar is one of the essential substances for grape fermentation; and as it happens that in rainy and low heat summers not enough [sugar] is made, obtaining then small mellow grapes, in this case we must add to the mass fermenting the amount of common sugar, proportionate to the amount that is lacking."[22] Some regions frowned on the addition of cane sugar to the must, but, for Llansó, as an agriculturalist and scientist, this addition was scientifically sound. He stated, "The owner will not find this practice advantageous except when it comes to wines of good quality and that are sold at a high price, because in the inferior ones it cannot be resolved to the waste caused by the purchase of sugar. But as an addition to this material sometimes damages the good qualities of the wine, especially distorting its precious fragrance, in these cases we will flavor the must with some buds of the pear, almond, or some handfuls of elderflowers."[23] Again, this suggestion of adding additional products to the wine must may come as a surprise, but the issue was not in making wine but in making wine that consistently tasted good. The addition of materials to make up for alcohol or flavor were seemingly harmless, but, as will be seen later, adulterating wine became a serious problem as unscrupulous producers looked to make quick cash.

Some winemakers used covered tubs while others allowed theirs to be exposed to the air during fermentation. For Llansó, not only did the grape and geography affect the wine's quality but also something as simple as controlling the tubs. "Winemaking methods," Llansó asserted, "should not and cannot always be the same; on the contrary, they vary according to the quality of the grapes, the nature of the land, and the particular state of the atmosphere during the duration of the operation and the fermentation. In this sense, modifications have been proposed that we will appreciate in their fair value, principally with regard to the advantages or disadvantages that open tanks offer."[24] With a covering, the must in these tubs would ferment quicker, which in the end would produce a better wine, as faster fermentation was preferred. Closed lids also allowed for greater consistency across production. If tubs were not exposed to the air, then other detritus could not fall into the wine and contaminate the product. With open vats anything could get into the must—a scary thought. A closed tub also decreased the risk of the must's putrefaction. If the juice were to spoil, then the entire batch could be ruined. In the end the advice was clear: a closed tub reduced the risks to the must and allowed for greater consistency.[25] Llansó's advice to wine makers was not groundbreaking in its scope, but the fact that this professor of agriculture wanted them to execute clear and consistent practices for fermentation meant that this practice had come into question. At the same time, if this practice could produce a better-tasting and more respectable drink, then higher demand and higher prices could lay in the future for Spanish wine.

FROM TERROIR TO TERRUÑO?

One of the most dominant concepts in contemporary wine culture is the idea of terroir, which "is used today worldwide to emphasize the unique character of wines with respect to the soil and climate under which grapes are cultivated in specific locales. It is commonly believed, therefore, that the taste of wine is specific to the soil and climate from which the grapes are harvested."[26] For some wine drinkers, terroir explains all the tastes, colors, and feelings associated with wine, while, for others, this concept signifies nothing more than regional identification. Robert C. Ulin explains that terroir is difficult to understand completely because, "somewhat paradoxically . . . although the concept of *terroir* assists our critical understanding of wine as a commodity through associating wine with a specific geographical domain and an imagined culture of production and consumption, it nevertheless contributes simultaneously to its enduring mystification."[27] Terroir is, in a way, something one either does or does not believe, as no scientific or quantitative method exists to measure the quality of every wine produced in every climate, or even microclimate. Most importantly, as we all know, taste is subjective. Ulin hypothesizes that "once the focus is on wine as a fetishized commodity and not the social and historical relations that give rise to wine, it is much easier to assert that the reputations of noteworthy wines are simply a consequence of their favorable climate and soil."[28] Therefore, while a wine might be good if its terroir is believed to be great, then some might assume that a particular wine from that location must be great as well; there lies the irony. As the movement of people and goods increased in the modern era, and as mass industrialization created a common culture, the idea of being special fell away. Ulin concludes, "The strong associations of wine to particular places, even micro-terrains, and their growers are from the part of consumers a reaction to generic commodities that even when well packaged and marketed add very little to imagined distinctions that have become such an important component of the pleasures and aesthetics of drinking wine."[29] Those places that manage to secure a defined terroir of quality will have goods with extra panache, gaining possible control over the market: think French wines.

While terroir is often associated with modern wines, the aspects of location and commodity are not new. As early as the seventeenth century, the French had contemplated the importance of location and food. According to Amy Trubek, "Soil and roots are at the heart of French cuisine as well. In [Oliver de Serres's] discourse, places make unique tastes, and in turn such flavor characteristics and combinations give those places gastronomic renown."[30] This idea of place and taste continued to develop in the French mind into the nineteenth century, creating unique identities for a variety of food products. As Amy Trubek explains, "By the late nineteenth century, everyday rural agricultural practices—a reliance on certain crops or livestock because they responded to the local climate and geography, harvesting and bounty of nearby rivers and seas—came to represent the building blocks of regional cuisines. A new connection emerged between how the French farmed, lived, and supped."[31] This idea of terroir did have implications for wine: "The 1855 Bordeaux wine classifications are considered the first attempt by those involved in wine production and sales to promote the quality of wines by their place of origin. They were developed internally by those involved in the Bordeaux wine industry, particularly wine brokers, to be used at the 1855 Exposition Universelle in Paris."[32] Trubek notes that these ideas were not protected officially by the French state, but would lay the groundwork for the twentieth-century's Appellations d'Origine Contrôlée (Designations of Controlled Origin). When they exhibited Spanish and Catalan wines at the 1855 Universal Exposition in Paris, Spanish producers and representatives must have been aware of the importance of this new concept in protecting wine and developing a classification associated with quality.

By August 1860 the Catalan Agricultural Institute of San Isidro had begun to publish a series of articles about the cultivation and creation of wine. Written by institute ranking member Miguel de Foxá, these articles do not use the term "terroir" or the Spanish word *terruño*, but, upon close reading, one can see notions about location and quality of wine being explained. As Foxá described, "A production, so remarkable in our soil, demands a very particular attention, especially if it is taken into account that a very active trade will soon be established between nations that, impossible to practice the cultivation of the vine.... We have therefore thought it appropriate to focus the attention of our growers on the most recommended practices that the cultivation of this precious plant supports and the most successful preparation of its highly conditioned alcoholic juice."[33] Thus, the goal was to help producers improve their grapes and produce a better product, especially when Spain needed to export more quality wine to Europe. The connection between nature (or the environment in which the grape is planted) and the end product was especially crucial. According to Foxá, "Spain, so favored by nature, can become the country that produces fortified and red wines with excellence. It is therefore important to improve our crops, improve winemaking."[34] Producers needed to pay attention to the environment and types of grapes used to create excellent wine.

To help wine growers, Foxá presented a series of issues of importance. The first issue he discussed was the soil, noting that the type used for planting would have major effects on the vine and fruit: "In short, we grow vines of the same variety in dry, fresh, and humid soils. The first grape will yield a lot of sugar and little acid, the second more free acid, albumin and mucilage in quantity and little sugar. It is therefore probable that such a difference should be attributed to the physical properties of the land, and that they are what cause the variety that exists in the products of the vine."[35] Therefore, the type of soil directly affected the sugar and other components of the same grape; grapes needed to be planted in the appropriate soil to obtain the proper juice. Different soils either retain or lose water at different rates, which will affect grape growth and sugar content. The general elevation of the vineyards also plays a role in production: grapes in lower and more humid locations will ripen at different rates than those in higher and drier climates.[36] If the type of soil, treatment of the grape, and location of a particular vineyard are taken into account, then a better juice can be made: "After having thus slightly indicated the causes that can modify the vine products and their varieties, the nature of the land, its physical properties, its fertility and atmospheric influences; we must consider the most recommended practices in planting, fertilizers, work, pruning and harvesting the fruit."[37] While not offering a full definition of terroir, Foxá—much like modern winemakers—does begin to acknowledge the impact of location on taste. Growers needed to pay attention to these factors. Even if a grower wanted to plant garnacha, unless the environment was correct, the choice would fail.

While terroir might seem like an art, the concept also takes a great deal of science into consideration. Foxá stated, "This operation is determined by the vine species that is cultivated and the climate. It is good to go back to the scientific principle so as not to make mistakes that have been generated by the diverse practices created by empirical ignorance."[38] As Jaime Llansó had addressed earlier, good science was necessary to create a good product. If a wine grower chose the wrong grape for the wrong soil in the wrong environment, they could still grow grapes and make wine, but that wine would be of poor quality. Poor quality wine would have low demand, not be sold at a decent price, and, therefore, endanger the image of other wines produced in the region. As Foxá noted, many decisions needed to be made: "The merit and quality of a wine emanates from the variety; the hallmark that distinguishes it is marked on each of the vine species. The terrain, the climate, the year, and the sun respectively, alter this symbol of the species, but do not destroy it, and thus it is always distinguished from the others. Art cannot change nature; so, to obtain good wine, good species must be chosen; be collected early and methodically; the rich clusters are separated from the medium ones, and especially from the bad ones."[39] Wine, then, involved more ingredients than grapes: the environment and the producer had just as much of an effect on the product.

While Llansó and Foxá do not specifically mention the 1855 Exposition Universelle, the fact that, at the event, Bordeaux wines attempted to establish the connection between location and quality must have been on the minds of Catalan wine producers and scholars. As wine exports were so important to the Spanish economy in the nineteenth century, every wine agronomist would want to work to produce a quality crop for sale. If winemakers produced a subpar crop, then demand and price would fall. Also, as with modern terroir, these scholars acknowledged that wine was not simply an art, but a practice that required a mixture of science and nature to make the best wine.

THE CURIOUS CASE OF SHERRY

The most iconic Spanish wine is sherry: a fortified wine produced only in the Jerez region of Andalucía, where it has a long history. Phoenicians were likely the first to import wine grapes to the region, and these successes of antiquity extended into the Roman era. Even during the Moorish invasion, wine continued to be produced in Jerez. Following the Reconquista wine production grew. Purportedly, Jerez wine exports made it to England as early as the twelfth century, and, by the fifteenth century, demand for these wines had grown across northern Europe. During the sixteenth century, demand for sherry increased in England, with more shipments made each year. To sustain this connection with England, foreign wine merchants invested in Jerez during the seventeenth and eighteenth centuries. With these connections secured, sherry became a mainstay in England, and, by the 1860s, close to 87 percent of all sherry exports went to Britain.[40] Sherry production, though, was not like that of other wines, as three groups controlled the market: the *cosecheros* (harvesters), *almacenistas* (producers), and *extractores* (shippers). With these groups controlling important parts of sherry production, many levels needed to be reached. If one of these levels had problems, then all levels could suffer.[41] Therefore, for Jerez and the Spanish economy, England was the key to success, and as long as drinkers there wanted sherry, things would be great. The problem, though, is that sometimes things are too good to be true, and poor decisions, combined with a lack of scruples by some producers and exporters, created a damaging result.

On the one hand, having such a strong link to the English market and the support of English investors in the seventeenth century greatly benefited the Spanish economy, but, on the other, having one primary market for the product meant that decisions made in England would have severe repercussions in Spain. The idea was that sherry had become less a Spanish product than an English drink. As British hispanophile Richard Ford wrote in 1840, "The people at large in Spain are of scarcely acquainted with the taste of Sherry wine, beyond the immediate vicinity in which it is made. . . . Sherry is a foreign wine, made and drunk by foreigners; nor do the generality of Spaniards like its strong flavour, and still less its high price."[42] Thus, decisions made about sherry production did not seem to be Spanish, but were based almost exclusively on the opinions of the British consumer. English tastes even affected what wines were made. At the start of the nineteenth century, the British preference was for sweet sherries, often drank after meals, but, by the middle of the century, tastes had changed to drier wine choices.[43] This shift in consumer interest meant that sherry makers decreased their production of sweet sherry and ramped up their production of the ultradry fino-style sherry, which, after their first export to England in 1858, became the leading wines drank there.[44] These British decisions of taste, class, style, and interest became the driving forces behind Jerez production.[45] Again, when the market was robust and the connection between Jerez and London strong, this constituted a simple change in production, but, if English drinkers had a serious change of opinion about sherry, the results could be disastrous.

The first half of the nineteenth century was one of success for sherry. With stable prices, increasing exports, and growing British demand, sherry harvesters, makers, and exporters would have all been happy. The 1860s started with better news, as prices went higher, and demand still rose.[46] This happy state of affairs, however, would not last long. Sherry's price increase did not occur simply due to demand, but due to a powdery mildew infestation that decreased overall grape production in Jerez. A dramatic increase in price and a drastic decrease in production levels produced a short-term boom, and, by 1863, prices began to drop. At the same time, the quality of sherry greatly decreased. Poor harvests led to poor sherry, leading to chaos for the sherry market.[47] With demand still high, producers looked for grapes outside of the Jerez region—which was generally not allowed—to meet the growing demand for juice. These grapes were not of the same quality as those grown in Jerez and were also much cheaper. The addition of this non-Jerez juice led to a reduction of the final product's price.[48] The attempt to meet English demand with any grapes available in the region was a short-term solution with long-term consequences.

At the end of the eighteenth century, many of Jerez's bodegas made a major change to their production styles. Previously, after the fermentation process had begun, producers placed the wine in individual barrels to be aged until ready, which meant that each year's vintage of sherry would be different. The initiation of the three-tiered solera system was meant to fix this problem. In it new wine was put in the barrels at the top level to begin the aging process, while wine from the bottom level would be removed as needed for shipping. Therefore, wine from the bottom barrel would be replaced with that from the second level, and wine from the second level would be replaced with wine from the top. This process had some important advantages for producers: storage costs could be reduced, as one barrel would not have to wait an extended period before it was ready due to the mixing of the sherry in the solera system, and wine could be tested to create consistency across the years.[49] As a result, wine sold each year would taste the same—a serious advantage for exports. The problem, however, was that this system was unlike that of any other major wine-producing region, which led to confusion. When purchasing sherry consumers could not rely on vintages, as, in theory, some portion of wine in the bottom level of the solera could technically be from the first time that barrel was ever used.[50] If vintage became a primary way to understand wines from other countries, for sherry this was going to be an issue.

The continued demand for sherry at the start of the 1860s and rising prices were originally a boon, but serious repercussions loomed on the horizon. As previously discussed, to meet this demand, producers used grapes of lesser quality to make sherry, which reduced its value. At the same time, the solera system itself involved the mixing of wine, which meant that unscrupulous producers could add other wines at any point in the process, adulterating the final product. Additionally, since the producer was often not the same as the exporter, it could not be ensured that the exported wine was the same as the original liquid, opening the door for possible wine fraud in many markets.[51] As prices were still high, there was no guarantee that the product being sent to London was actually sherry itself. Fake sherries from South Africa had begun to enter the market, along with, even more dangerously, a German knockoff called "Elbe" sherry, made with potato spirits, water, other wines, and capillaire syrup from ferns.[52] Why would anyone pay high prices for a beverage that may not even be authentic?

As questions about the quality of real sherry from Jerez became more urgent, and as these imposter sherries from South Africa and industrial sherry from Germany began to enter the British market, serious questions were raised about the beverage. With poorer quality being sold, all sherry, regardless of its origin, was now under serious suspicion. Dr. John Louis William Thudichum wrote a letter in 1873 to the *Times* condemning the beverage, claiming the use of gypsum in the crushing of grapes and sulfur for the fumigating of barrels, posed serious health risks for the consumer.[53] It would take twenty years for this article to be refuted, but by then the damage had been done. As James Simpson suggests, "Sherry producers and shippers did little to try and convince consumers that the drink was actually safe."[54] Sherry was no longer the drink that it had been—well trusted and high quality—but a cheap liquor without style, and now dangerous to consume. Exacerbating this problem was a reshaping of British tax laws on alcoholic imports. In the 1860s tariffs were reduced on lower-alcohol wines, which made those wines cheaper for the consumer.[55] Because sherry was fortified and had a higher alcohol content, its prices were not reduced. For the first time in generations, French wine consumption was on the rise at the expense of sherry. By the late 1880s, red wines from Tarragona represented 70 percent of Spanish exports to Britain; sherry had collapsed.[56] James Simpson concludes, "It seems apparent that the decline in sales of sherry from the early 1870s can be attributed to a decline in the confidence in the drink, encouraging consumers to turn to other wines which they believed were safer."[57]

The nineteenth century was a wild ride for sherry. At the start of the century, sherry exports to Britain rose year after year. This success, however, caused problems. Rising demand and rising prices were met with bad harvests in the 1860s, requiring the use of non-Jerez grapes. Other producers and exporters took advantage of this demand, and the importation of cheap knockoff sherries hurt the image of the drink. As Álvaro Girón Sierra suggests, there is no way to tell how much sherry was actually mixed with other things, and likely few producers used external alcohol to adulterate the wines, but the winemakers in the region still imported 3,221 butts of industrial alcohol from Germany between 1876 and 1881.[58] In all likelihood this industrial alcohol would have been used to increase the alcohol content of sherry produced in the region. Even the suggestion of such imports could have continued to damage the image of sherry in the export market. With these cheaper sherries also came fear as the consumers were met with health warnings: no one would want to purchase a drink that was deemed hazardous. At the same time, as tariff rules changed, wines with lower alcohol content became cheaper. This perfect storm came to a head in 1873, when the consumption of sherry collapsed in Britain. What had once been a central market for sherry now evaporated. As mentioned earlier, sherry had represented between 10 and 20 percent of total Spanish agricultural exports between 1850 and 1873—a figure now greatly reduced. What could Spain now do to expand its wine exports and recuperate this loss?

SELL MORE WINE!

Even with the collapse of the sherry market, wine still remained a vital export commodity for Spain in the nineteenth century. In 1850 Spanish wine exports totaled 621,834 hectoliters. From there wine exports mainly grew steadily, reaching 1,660,681 hl by 1857. In 1858 the market experienced a crash, likely due to the wine plague oidium (to be discussed in chapter 2). It would not be until 1868 that wine exports went above the precollapse level at 1,816,873 hl. In 1873, the final great year, total wine exports spiked to 2,643,917 hl, but for the next five years they did not grow much overall. Finally, in 1879 wine saw dramatic growth in exports to 3,870,085 hl, which coincided with the problematic plague of phylloxera (also covered in chapter 2). From there wine exports leapt to 6,220,870 hl in 1880; 7,032,600 hl in 1881; 7,671,108 hl in 1882; and 7,564,383 hl in 1883.[59] Even in the face of solid growth, by the mid-1880s exports seemed to have peaked and began to level off. Because sherry had been such an important export, and its collapse constituted a scary moment, the growth of other regions, assisted by wine plagues, must have seen the potential for their own success. If this substantial growth could be reproduced, it would be a serious boon for Spain. There was a question, though: How much more wine could be exported? With that in mind, the Spanish Superior Council of Agriculture, Industry, and Commerce initiated a substantial survey to investigate the wine production levels of each province.

The council's survey came with a memorandum dated May 1, 1884, which contained the rationale for the project. The goal of the survey was "to formulate the program of information to be opened to study the means of facilitating the export of our wines."[60] The council knew the importance of wine to the Spanish economy, and they understood that a complete survey of Spain's wine producers was needed to create a plan for the future. Before this there had been no formal and complete attempt to study this issue. The survey stated, "The statistics of our wine production have not reached the attention required for the primary wealth of our peninsula, and we have only been able to gather semi-official data and private news, which show such differences as the one we found among the 33 million hectoliters which are calculated in 1858, and the 30 million in 1877. But in any case, from any of these data that we start, it is in everyone's mind that the vineyard production of wines has increased since that date and is increasing every year more."[61] Even with a seeming decrease in total hectoliters of wine, production still represented a key for Spanish success. The council believed it would be helpful to understand the internal consumption level of wine in order to determine how much wine could be dedicated for export. "Once the domestic consumption is covered," they reported, "we have a surplus of production that we dedicate to export, to the manufacture of alcohols and vinegars and to the creation of fortified wines; but of all of them nothing should attract more attention, nor does it deserve further study, than that which refers to foreign trade."[62] In recent years Spanish exports had increased, but a recent slip resulted in financial losses: "In the year 1850, 621,000 hectoliters left Spain, increasing, with little discontinuation until 1873, when we exported 2,643,000 hectoliters; from here it went down until 1876, as if to gain strength for a prodigious rise, reaching in 1882 the figure of 7,671,000 hectoliters, valued at 333,200,000 pesetas; but already in 1883 it begins to drop at 106,720 hl, valued at 7,258,414 pesetas."[63] To better understand the reasons for these losses, the council believed a full census of the country's wine was necessary.

Importantly, the council understood that Spain had to protect its exports and continue to make improvements on them. Previous successes seemed to come by happenstance; now it was incumbent upon these producers to be deliberate in their actions. At the same time, other wine-producing countries saw their chance to earn greater share of the market:

> In this export branch, Spain needs to add, not subtract; and the loss suffered in 1883, together with the large number of vineyards that are being planted in Spain, the fact that the phylloxera plague is decreasing in France and the production of wines is increasing, that our rival Italy is making private and even official efforts to achieve greater exportation, since Portugal in the last year has increased the sale of its wines in England, reducing ours from Jerez, has just alarmed the Spanish winemakers and they fear with good reason, that if we do not get out of our lethargy and we understand a prompt and effective campaign, we are going to lament serious ills in the general wealth of Spain.[64]

A serious and official role was now required to help defend these exports on the global market, and the council wanted to take the lead: "For the Superior Council of Agriculture, Industry and Commerce, which does not forgive any of the means within its reach to place Spain at the forefront of agricultural progress, cannot be indifferent in the fight waged between wine producers from different nations, and it is proposed to help our company . . . to seek and use the means to improve the production of Spanish wines and increase their export."[65] This national survey would allow a connection between the state and the producers to help develop a plan, for "it is necessary to turn to the corporations, producers and merchants of the different provinces of Spain for help, and asking them for news, data, studies and deductions that will guide them correctly in the work they undertake, because of the great danger that closes in."[66] This joint study was critical, and "the news requested today must be exclusively for the practical study that the Council intends to carry out; In order that the export of Spanish wines does not decline, increasing it as much as we can, and that we do not allow other nations, which do not have the resources of ours, to advance in the career undertaken, establish their trade, accustom those palates to their wines and that ours are unrestrained."[67] By working at all levels of wine exportation, a serious plan could be developed that had not existed previously.

Even with the possible dire warnings that other states were working to undermine Spanish wine export numbers, the council did have hope. "Fortunately," they wrote, "in this fight we are ahead today; but we must not rest, because our rivals are powerful and put all their strength to get ahead of us; therefore, this Commission, echoing the unanimous interest of the Council, intends not to rest, going with equal effort to the Government, merchants and winemakers so that, together, we redouble our efforts, in order to give to our wines the conditions demanded by the consumer markets, increasing exports to open markets and looking for new locations to place the surplus of our production."[68] By working together, a solution could be found. "This thought, which the Council welcomes with so much interest today, will be tomorrow, with perseverance and work, a reality that must make wealth for the country and prosperity for the patrimony."[69] Wine was critical, and the council hoped that its survey would shed light onto a vital aspect of Spain's economic health.

By early 1885 regional wine authorities began to return their surveys to the council. They answered a series of questions about wine production, providing information such as the amount of land devoted to vineyards, the amount of wine produced overall, the style of wine produced, the region's annual wine consumption, the export numbers from the region, and any internationally known wines produced there. These materials would be useful for the council in determining which regions were exporting a sufficient amount of wine, and which regions could make adaptations to improve their levels to assist exports. For the sake of this project, I will concentrate on those regions with the most significant wine production and export numbers.

The Albacete region of Castilla–La Mancha had 28,409 hectares of land devoted to vineyards in 1885 and had produced an average of 114,900 hl of wine for the previous five years, with 97,100 hl produced in 1884. The region was best known for its red wines, but it also produced a small amount of white wine. Of the wine produced, about 36,121 hl were drunk in the province, 31,166 hl were sold throughout Spain, and 25,702 hl were exported, mainly in Europe. With no official factories to produce aguardiente, the majority of wine made was sold in its original form.[70]

The province of Ávila in Castilla y León had 20,042 hectares of vineyards, which produced 1,001,200 hl of wine in the previous five years, with 200,420 hl produced in 1884. This region produced mainly white wines, with about 101,900 hl consumed in the province, 60,520 hl sold in Spain, and 38,000 hl exported mainly to Europe. White wine, however, had much lower demand for exports. Ávila had 121 registered factories to produce distilled alcohol from wine.[71]

Badajoz in Extremadura contained 29,738 hectares of vineyards and produced 136,954 hl of wine in the previous year. The region produced both red and white wines, many of which with high levels of alcohol at 15 to 16 percent. The province consumed 126,916 hl and exported close to 62,782 hl of wine going mainly to France each year.[72] Exports to France were likely driven by the phylloxera plague, but, as that was decreasing, this could affect future exports.

The province of Barcelona was home to the powerhouse production area of Vilafranca de Penedès. The region had 160,000 hectares of vineyards and had produced a whopping 2,000,000 hl of wine on average for the previous five years. Like some other regions, Barcelona was beginning to suffer from the phylloxera plague (to be discussed in the next chapter). In the case of the large city of Barcelona, it should not come as a surprise that between 800,000 and 900,000 hl of wine were consumed annually in the province. For exports red wines were sent to both the Americas and France. With such a large amount of wine produced, Barcelona was clearly an asset to the Spanish wine industry.[73]

The Cáceres province in Extremadura had 12,376.88 hectares of land devoted to wine and produced 67,652.65 hl the previous year and 330,942.77 hl over the previous five years. The region produced mainly red wines, totaling 89.42 percent in 1877 and 92 percent in 1881. Cáceres also represented a problem for Spanish wine; even though the region produced a substantial amount of red wine, which was preferable for exportation, almost no wine was exported internationally. Only a small amount of wine was sold internally, mainly to Salamanca and Ávila. As no wine was exported, it could not assist the bottom line.[74] It was regions like Cáceres that needed work. How could this wine production increase to support exportation as in neighboring Badajoz?

In comparison the province of Cádiz in Andalucía contained the export powerhouse of Jerez. The region had 20,640 hectares of vineyards, with 7,850 being in the municipality of Jerez de la Frontera, the home of sherry. The region produced approximately 450,000 hl of white wine a year (mainly used for sherry) and 45,000 hl of red wine. Between 180,000 and 200,000 hl of wine were drank in the province each year, but not all was made there. Between 250,000 and 260,000 hl were exported each year, with three-quarters sent to Europe (mainly England) and the remaining to the Americas. These export numbers from Jerez, however, were much smaller than they had been decades earlier, indicating the region's weakness. The entire province had thirty-seven factories for aguardiente, with seven located in Jerez de la Frontera, likely to make brandy.[75]

Ciudad Real in Castilla–La Mancha had 66,320 hectares of vineyards and had produced an average of 3,000,000 hl of wine over the past five years, with 2,702,871 produced in 1884. Both red and white wines were grown in the region and commonly consumed in Castilla and Andalucía. The region did export wines to France, Italy, Cuba, and Puerto Rico, as needed, but a consistent export number could not be given.[76]

The Catalan province of Girona had problematic news in 1884. Even though the province had 20,000 hectares devoted to wine and had previously produced upward of 400,000 hl annually, due to the wine plagues of phylloxera and mildew the province had only made 20,000 hl of wine in 1884—a dramatic decline. This wine, which was mostly red, had been destined for an export market to France, but, due to this devastating ecological blow, the region was now a shell of its recent success. Other regions needed to produce more red wine to offset this predicament. Problems like this would be crucial for the council to note in its report.[77]

Part of the famous La Rioja region was contained in the province of Logroño, which had 31,684 hectares of vineyards and produced 316,041 hl of wine in 1883, increasing to 421,386 hl of wine in 1884. Many of these Riojan wineries were founded by foreigners, especially from Bordeaux, to offset failures in French production. The region's report expressed the fame of its wines and its many similarities to those made in Bordeaux. The region exported an average of 40,000 hl of wine annually, with most going to France.[78]

Málaga province in Andalucía had 112,312 hectares of land devoted to grapes. Even with this large number, the region was under attack by phylloxera, with 41,634 hectares recently destroyed. Before this attack the region had produced above 325,000 hl on average, with 64,000 hl drank in the province. The majority of the wine was red and either sold in Spain or sent to Cuba and Puerto Rico. Málaga, like Girona, was one of the first regions to be devastated by phylloxera.[79]

The Galician province of Orense had 19,793 hectares of vineyards and usually produced around 390,000 hl of wine, but, like other regions in Spain, phylloxera had begun to devastate the vineyards, and hardly any wine was produced in 1884. Previously the region had produced mainly red wines, of which the community drank 290,335 hl annually. About 100,000 hl left the region for other parts of Spain, with small exports going to Cuba and Buenos Aires. With the recent devastation, however, these exports had ceased.[80]

Palencia province in Castilla y León had 30,548 hectares of vineyards and produced 229,326 hl in 1882 and 263,984 hl of red wine in 1883. Interestingly, the survey stated that, as 18 hl of wine should be produced per hectare, the region's production should be as high as 549,864 hl. Therefore, there was room for production growth in this region. Three-quarters of the wine produced remained in the province, with the remainder being exported mainly to France and some to the Americas.[81]

By 1884 the Catalan province of Tarragona had become the leading wine producer and exporter for Spain. The region had 110,066 hectares of vineyards and produced 1,577,606 hl of wine and 80,897 hl of aguardiente in 1884. Most of this massive production was red wine, but white was still produced. About 400,000 hl were drank in province, with about 50,000 hl sold in Spain, and 1,049,648 hl exported. These wines were sent around the world: France, England, Germany, Holland, Scandinavia, Russia, Italy, the United States, Brazil, Argentina, Central America, and elsewhere. France demanded dry wines, while Britain, the United States, and Scandinavia wanted sweeter wines. With these impressive numbers, it was apparent that Tarragona had become the biggest success story for Spain, and its numerous international connections did wonders for the economy.[82]

Valencia housed 102,230 hectares of vineyard and produced 1,642,535 hl of wine in 1883. This wine was mainly red, and 272,000 hl were drunk in the province. Like Tarragona, Valencia had become a major wine-exporting region, with 276,000 hl shipped to Argentina and 900,000 hl sold to France. The province also had 147 factories that produced aguardiente.[83]

Overall the results of the survey were a mixed bag. Regions like Tarragona and Valencia carried Spanish exports with red wines mainly sent to France and, to a lesser extent, the Americas. Other regions produced much smaller amounts of wine, with large percentages consumed in the province or sold in Spain.

Important to note is the fact that some regions had begun to report major losses due to the mildew and phylloxera plagues that had previously struck France. With this information the council could now develop a clear picture as to which regions were succeeding and which were faltering. One would assume that the council would want to mimic the successful results throughout Spain to earn more money for the country, but, as the next chapter will show, the wine plagues of the nineteenth century became the central focus of all winemakers in Spain.

HOW TO PROVE WINE WAS IMPORTANT?

The value of wine to Spain's economy and culture is both simple and complicated. Wine existed in Spain for millennia and was a critical element in the local economy and diet. Many regions produced wine for local use throughout the nineteenth century. The complications arise with Spanish wine and exports. As most wine was made locally and likely cheaply, it was sufficient for local consumption, but not for discerning international tastes. By the late 1850s, Spanish agronomists were publishing texts for producers to improve their wines to gain international respect, as well as international sales. The state and regional authorities saw a role for top-down planning and research, and regional agricultural agencies saw benefits to vineyard-level improvements to make more wine. The desire to quickly produce more wine made sense, given the growing market created by a rising bourgeoisie in northern Europe and a decrease of wine produced in France due to plagues. The problem was that quantity for export replaced quality in goods. Sherry is the perfect example: the desire to take advantage of higher prices meant producing a lesser-quality good, tarnishing its image for almost a century. As sherry production collapsed, other regions increased production of red wines to fill the void. In the end, however, these red wines were made to fill a market vacuum. Instead of cultural commodities with an intrinsic identity and value, as in Bordeaux, Spanish wines were often created to substitute for a desired good when the first choice was not available. As will be seen throughout this book, the problem with being a replacement commodity is that once the primary good again becomes available, or when a cheaper product is created, the substitute can easily be dropped by the consumer, and new problems will arise.

2

El laboratorio del vino

WINE DISEASES AND SCIENCE IN
THE NINETEENTH CENTURY

In 1859 naturalist and professor Fernando Amor wrote about the growing threat of a new biological plague attacking Spain's vineyards: "Oidium, that prolific fungus that has seized the vine, worries us today with its disastrous influence and gets the attention of all the agricultural countries in which wine is an important branch of wealth."[1] This powdery fungal mold swept across Europe in the 1850s, with particularly devastating results in the continent's vineyards. New methods of production, oidium's attacks, and the invasions of other pests created a roller-coaster for Spain's wine producers in the second half of the nineteenth century. "The sad fame of such a maleficent plant," Amor continued, "has already made its effects known in the vineyards of Spain, which is why it is very important to study how much was done in the means of extinguishing it."[2] On the one hand, these plagues devastated Spanish wine production; on the other, scientific and agricultural organizations worked quickly to develop strategies to combat them. While presenting a major crisis for Spanish wine, wine plagues unleashed new research efforts to improve the quality and quantity of wine production. Along with this scientific interest, the economic importance of wine was the primary concern of the day.

This chapter explores the intersections between the wine plagues of the late nineteenth century and the agriculturist movements working to save Spanish wine from total destruction. Oidium and phylloxera were double-edged swords for Spain. At first these plagues attacked Spanish wine's greatest competitor, France, allowing Spanish vineyards to thrive by both principled and unscrupulous means. Once these plagues entered Iberia, Spanish producers raced to find cures to save their vineyards. The recovery of French production posed a danger for Spanish producers, and Spanish agriculturalists rushed to establish new rules and regulations to certify the high quality of their wines in order to compete against the reputations of French wines. Connoisseurs feared adulterated wines; therefore, Spain needed to fix its image. In this chapter I argue that Spain's need to protect its wine industry from fraud and plague pushed scientific elements in the country to modernize in order to improve wine quality; however, the employment of unscrupulous methods to increase production made a stain on Spanish wine that would last for decades. Due to the plagues, the notion of making wine had changed. As Jordi Farré Huguet writes, "From the mid-nineteenth century, however, the word 'art' is disappearing from the *vitivinícolas* publications and [it is] becoming increasingly scientific and technical."[3] With the assistance of technological improvements and the study of diseases like oidium, Spanish vineyards grew from 400,000 hectares in 1800 to 1,200,000 hectares in 1860, at the height of the oidium invasion.[4] Science and wine became inseparable, with both positive and negative outcomes.

This chapter looks at three major aspects of wine and science. First, I explore the oidium outbreak of the 1850s and its effects on wine production. While serious, the infestation did not impact all regions of Europe the same way, which gave Spain a subtle early advantage. Next, I survey the largest wine plague ever to hit Europe: phylloxera. This aphid virtually destroyed Europe's wine industry, causing serious shortages. During this period Spain became the go-to vendor in Europe for wine, but many producers took shortcuts to increase their output, which hurt the wine's quality and raised questions about its safety. Once French vineyards stabilized in the 1880s, French producers targeted Spanish wine as cheap, low quality, and, most devastatingly, dangerous. Last, I investigate attempts by Spanish agriculturalists who urgently needed to find ways to prove that Spanish wine was safe and potable—otherwise the entire industry would be ruined. While the image of Spanish wine needed a makeover, this would prove difficult.

ASHY WHITE FUNGUS

As the story goes, English gardener Edward Tucker was the first European to notice something strange on his property in Margate in 1845: grapes in the garden covered with a "white efflorescence" and a "powdered-covered appearance" that killed all the bunches.⁵ From there this oidium plague reached mainland Europe, entering France by 1848, Germany and Spain by 1851, and Italy and Switzerland by 1852.⁶ Oidium is white, moldy fungus that grows on the leaves and fruit of grapes; once the ambient temperature reaches 15°C, it leaves visible marks on the vine, but, as temperatures increase to 25 to 28°C in more humid grape-growing zones, it can weaken the grape skin, causing the fruit to crack and, therefore, spoiling the bunch.⁷ Grape leaves can also curl, preventing enough area for photosynthesis. As oidium likes a temperate, damp climate, those places closest to the sea or with higher humidity would be particularly susceptible to it. Because oidium ceases to grow after the temperature reaches 35°C, hotter areas such as the central plateaus of the Iberian Peninsula were practically protected from its spread.⁸

French vineyards, with their moist and temperate climates, saw some of the greatest effects of the oidium invasion. Between 1852 and 1861, "France cease[d] to supply major overseas markets such as the British and US markets but it actually had to import large amounts simply to cater for its own domestic consumption."⁹ Catalan, Valencian, and Riojan wineries took advantage of this situation and began to export large amounts of red wine, especially to France. Between 1854 and 1862, during the height of the French oidium crisis, the prices of Spanish red wine skyrocketed, and vintners saw success in planting new fields. As Piqueras Haba shows, from 1841 to 1850 (before oidium's arrival to France), Spanish wine exports were 250,000 hectoliters annually, but exports reached 1,297,000 hectoliters of red table wine by 1857.¹⁰ At the start of the 1860s, winegrowers in dryer and warmer regions, like Rioja and Navarra, extended their vineyards into areas previously devoted to cereal production to take advantage of increased prices.¹¹ Even with this early economic benefit, oidium soon found its way into Spain and began laying waste to vineyards there. By 1851 oidium had entered Spain at three points: the Río Minho of Galicia, the Catalan-French border, and the Valencian coastline.¹² Vintners hastily planted new vineyards in Spain's interior to support demand. In the late 1860s, the combination of sulfur sprays and new American rootstock slowed oidium's spread, but these foreign roots also introduced a new and even more destructive foreign environmental plague for Europe.

Thanks to developments in science, oidium was identified and combated during the late nineteenth century. During the middle of the eighteenth century, Jordi Farré Huguet notes, all wine diseases were classified as either "blight, discoloration, and phthisis. There were not only three diseases, simply there were three groups of similar diseases but there was no capacity to distinguish between them."[13] By the time oidium arrived, agriculturalists worked to uncover the mystery of the plague and find ways to combat it. By 1858 conversations about the signs and development of oidium appeared in the *Revista* of the Catalan Agricultural Institute of San Isidro. In 1860 Miguel de Foxá spoke of the identification and the Academy of Science of Paris's warnings about its spread in Europe, stating that the disease was a "fungus or plant tumor," and that it was "very difficult to avoid the bad consequences."[14] While agriculturalists knew of the basic requirements for oidium, such as temperature and humidity, it still remained puzzling as to why some areas were more affected than others. Foxá wrote, "The anomalies of oidium are many. Years have passed since it has appeared in some countries and disappeared from others: others that have sprouted and have been invaded by other strains . . . and finally, in many that have been so invasive and hurtful that has spoiled entire vineyards."[15]

In 1858 professor of agriculture Jaime Llansó wrote in *Revista* about the issues surrounding the spread of oidium. What, he asked, were the causes of this phenomenon? He responded: "The mysteries of life are so deep and the agents that put it into play are so little understood that all theories are an act of presumption that we do not want to fall into."[16] Llansó exhorted, "Do not make illusions: if you want to prevent the current disease of the vineyards, if we want to stop the ravages of the oidium, if we are to trust that our vineyards will return to the owner the source of wealth they were for so many years, let's hope that the causes that motivate it, and that are unknown to us, have a happy solution; or let's place the treatment of this disease in another area where we can try modifications that have been obtained with sulfur."[17] While oidium had been identified as a serious disease, debates still existed as to whether the mold itself was truly the malady or a symptom of a greater threat. Llansó explained, "The most sustainable opinion about the efficient cause of oidium is that of a vital disturbance of the vine, which is felt by the symptoms that we all know. For those who understand the value of physiology, for those who study the laws of life and of their action, it is still a problem if oidium is a cause or an effect."[18] With this being said, it was necessary that vineyards not use "home remedies" or untested processes to combat the disease, that the treatment should not be "a product of fantasy or good wishes" but should rely on science.[19]

In 1857 the *Revista* offered vintners advice to fight the spread of oidium in vineyards across the country developed from a national special commission. "The Ministry of Agriculture thought it desirable a few years ago to appoint a special commission to examine the trials that are practiced to counteract the disastrous calamity of the disease of the vine."[20] The special commission and the San Isidro Institute recommended one specific treatment: the use of sulfur. As early as 1856, fertilizer and pesticide companies like Cros in Catalonia began translating works on proper sulfur application in the fields for regional producers.[21] According to the article in the *Revista*, the previous reports and studies "found a remedy, but failed to find a way to implement it."[22] By 1857, however, there was a plan in place: "The operation to sulfur the vineyards, consists in dusting with the sublimated sulfur all the green parts of the vine, grapes, branches and leaves."[23] The article went on to outline a new, proper course for treating vines with sulfur powder. As oidium could affect any green portion of a vine, it was necessary for winegrowers to inspect their fields regularly, spray every portion of a plant, and repeat the process again if necessary, because, "in one word, all that can be green can be attacked by the disease."[24] The problem in some locations, however, was that sulfur spray was not applied soon enough; farmers tried less scientific solutions that they created on their own, allowing the ailment to spread.

In 1858 the *Revista* published a "practical section" by Jaime Llansó to discuss the use of sulfur and its effects on oidium. One of the core issues discussed was whether or not sulfur was in fact a "cure" for the fungus. To the question "Can one consider sulfur as a means to cure oidium?" Llansó responded, "Surely not."[25] He stated, "It is only a method to combat the disease," and "the sulfur does no more than cure the eruptions without preventing them."[26] Sulfur, therefore, was a useful tool to combat the plague's effects, but it could not protect those vines already infected by the disease. In concluding Llansó asserted that the exact cause of the oidium fungus was still uncertain, and that further study was needed, while there was a seemingly clear connection with moist cool climates and its spread.[27] It would make sense that, following the outbreaks of the fungus, Spanish producers would try to find warmer and drier locations for their vines, such as in La Rioja and Castilla.[28] Therefore, while this disease produced a great deal of concern in Spain, and attempts were made to combat it, winegrowers continued to plant more fields in hopes of cashing in on the increased international demand and prices available for red wine production.

In 1859 Fernando Amor published his article on sulfur treatment for oidium that offered proper advice on making the sulfur box:

> The box to sulfur the vines is quite simple construction: it consists of a can cylinder of 9 inches in height and 5 inches in diameter, with the bottom formed by metal cloth that serves as a sieve: in it fits another cylinder with the upper part closed and divided to the first third of its height by a horizontal partition with holes somewhat larger than those of the fabric and which have been opened in the direction of the lid: this apparatus is armed with a rope or handle to be able to use it with a hand.[29]

This simple construction allowed winegrowers to either build or purchase their own sulfur boxes, which simplified and reduced the cost for protecting fields. Amor gave an example from France, of a Mr. de la Vergne and the sulfuring process on his vineyard:

> Six women have sulphured in the vineyards of Mr. de la Vergne for the first time, and in a very few days, an extension of 18 fanegas [one fanega is approximately 1.6 acres in Castilla] of land; traveling on average two bushels per day in a vineyard, all the same and aged 16 to 20 years, producing an expense of 3 francs for the six wages, and 5 francs for 25.5 pounds of sulfur powder. The other two times do not need as much quantity, resulting in the most economical operation; so that it rarely exceeds 12 francs to sulfur three times each fanega, even assuming that it has 6,000 vines, which is the maximum for some varieties, since it is generally 3 or 4,000.[30]

The process of sulfuring an average-size vineyard could be completed over a few days with only minimal extra cost to the owner. Similarly, the process should be done at specific times: "This agronomist concludes by stating that in order to prevent the disease from happening, the operation will be done shortly before the bloom of the flower; the second sometime later, and the last when the fruit is unripe."[31] This systematic and scientific approach to fighting this plague could allow wineries to save their crop.

To conclude his report, Fernando Amor offered a series of considerations for winegrowers to protect themselves from the possibility of invasion and for preventing the disease. First it was important to make sure that vines were planted with care, and that no foreign plants were introduced to the fields that might contain diseases. He recommended: "It is better to practice sulfur too early than too late," as once the disease is seen, nothing can be done. Sulfur should also be applied at the time of flowering, because "this substance destroys the oidium at the time it exerts on the grapes the greatest damage." When using sulfur powder, one must apply it to all parts of the plant: "The sulfur powder should not be saved because it is a bad economy." Clearly, by saving a little money on the use of sulfur powder, a winegrower could lose a lot more in the end. If it rained shortly after the application of the sulfur, the farmer should wait until the fields dried and then reapply the powder, given that moisture contributes to oidium's growth. Windy fields might require slightly more sulfur usage to ensure appropriate coverage of the plants. Winegrowers needed to wait ten days to make sure that the sulfuring process worked in the vines. Sulfur was not a panacea: just because a winegrower sulfured his fields, it did not mean he could ignore the usual processes to make sure his fields were safe from other problems. Sulfuring too late, especially after mid-August, would not be beneficial to dark grapes; it should be completed by mid-June to offer "the harvest a protection from the disease."[32] Overall, Amor provided a plan for protecting fields from the threat of oidium with clear directions backed by evidence and examples.

By the mid-1860s, oidium began to stall in Spain and throughout Europe. Sulfur powder did offer a valuable tool to fight the mold. When oidium hit Spain, fear arose that it could destroy the entire national crop, but its arrival created two interesting outcomes. Places like Galicia, with its humidity and white grape varietals, were hit hard by oidium's attack. Other regions, however, that were warmer and dryer took advantage of the geographical shifts of wine, and the growing demands for red wine and price increase, and planted thousands of new vines.[33] Some regions of Spain saw success during this period, but France, too, survived this plague and once again began to produce wine. One idea to combat oidium was to import the heartier North American rootstock for grafting, but, in the end, this would unleash the greatest threat European vineyards would ever see.

THE GREATEST WINE PLAGUE THE WORLD HAD EVER SEEN

In 1863 a new invader came to Europe on American rootstock: phylloxera, an aphid with multiple dangerous forms. Agriculturists explored the use of these heartier roots to combat oidium, the first American plague, thinking they could be used for grafting to protect Europe's numerous varietals. This dangerous hitchhiker, a native of the eastern portions of North America, spread rapidly, feasting on grape plants at an alarming rate.[34] By 1868 phylloxera was ravaging the French vineyards that had just begun to stabilize. Phylloxera's spread was slower than oidium's; it did not get to Spain until 1878, via Girona, Málaga, and the Duero River Valley.[35] In fact the plague took close to four decades to reach central Spain. Phylloxera, like oidium, had two important effects on Spanish wine production. On the one hand, the sheer destruction of French wine production meant that once again Spanish vintners could produce and sell more exports and gain a larger international market share. On the other hand, regions in Spain needed to prepare for this invader and find ways to combat it should it arrive. Spanish producers took great advantage of French weaknesses, but, in a race to fill international glasses, the quality of their product slipped, weakening the image of their wines as France recovered.

Phylloxera is an extremely complicated insect, taking many forms and attacking in a variety of ways. Phylloxera eggs can appear on roots, from where the newly hatched "crawlers"—which molt up to four times—feed on either roots or leaves by draining sap. The wingless forms then emerge from the ground, molt, grow wings, disperse, and both females and males lay eggs asexually. These eggs may hatch, molt four times, and mate, and then a female will produce an egg that can survive the winter.[36] Phylloxera survives best between 22 and 26°C; at that temperature, eggs can hatch in six days, with close to 90 percent surviving, with strong humidity. The underground form of the insect exists for close to two weeks and then reaches full adulthood in a week. From there adult females will produce between two to ten eggs a day.[37] Other than via the winged form, phylloxera can spread by wind and can ride human clothing, shoes, and plows to travel from one field to another. The insect prefers soils with high levels of clay that can crack, exposing the underground nymph to the plant above. Very sandy soils do help prevent the life cycle, as water entering the ground can drown these younger forms.[38]

Phylloxera's insatiable appetite for sap creates serious damage for the vine. Jeffrey Granett, M. Andrew Walker, Laszlo Kocsis, and Amir Omer name three main possibilities in which phylloxera can weaken the vine, leading to death. First, "removal of photosynthates may cause loss of vine vigor" as the consumption of leaves prevents the vine from growing strong and feeding itself; second, "root mortality caused by secondary pathogens entering feeding wounds can cause water and nutrient stresses leading to eventual vine death" as other infections can enter the plant; and, third, "physiological disruption other than through direct removal of photosynthates or water stress can occur" as the insect's existence on the plant creates strain.[39] The combination of these problems damages roots, leaves, and other parts of the plant, possibly resulting in the death of the vine and destruction of the fields.

Even though phylloxera first hit France, it did not mean that the Spanish vintners were not getting ready for the inevitable invasion of the pest. The Spanish Cortes debated and later approved a project: the Law of Defense against Phylloxera, enacted in 1878. This law promised 500,000 pesetas to combat the spread of this plague and work on scientific treatments to defeat it.[40] It was soon discovered, as with oidium, that American rootstock, which was responsible for the importation of the plague, could be used to save Europe's wineries and rootstock could be imported and used for grafting; within weeks the Central Commission for the Defense against Phylloxera and the Spanish Ministry of Development began the process of importing it from North America. Ten kilos of roots were imported from September to October 1878 for a trial process.[41] On July 21, 1879, the Ministry of Development recommended that these American seedlings offered the "best results" for combating the disease.[42] From 1880 to 1881, the Ministry of Development spent 16,800 pesetas to purchase more North American rootstock for the country.[43] As it became clear that these roots were the only hope for preventing the spread of the disease, various regions in Spain, particularly Catalonia, opened nurseries to grow new plants to save the country's wineries.[44] In 1879 don Adolfo Parada y Barreto, chief engineer for Forestry, wrote: "This is the only way to conceive that an insect so small, barely perceptible, can bring disturbance and alarm to a country, setting in motion all its forces, as if it were an invading army."[45] Even with this more aggressive national and regional approach, the plague would not be fully defeated until the 1930s.

This moment in between the increased exportation of Spanish wines and the arrival of this disease highlights the scope and stakes of the fight the Spanish government and its wine producers saw developing. As don Parada y Barreto noted in 1879, it was necessary for all portions of Spain to work together to defeat this pest: "Go science with science; capital with capital; and the worker with arms, and all together, Intelligence, Capital and Work, Providence will do the rest, removing from our fertile soil the legions of the destructive insect."[46] In the end wine was simply not a small agricultural product, but a central commodity for the Spanish economy that offered "prosperidad para la patria."[47]

Interestingly, the initial arrival of phylloxera to Europe, particularly its attack on French vineyards, was a positive for Spanish producers. As French production collapsed, "wine frenzies" broke out across Spain as producers planted large new vineyards to compensate.[48] In 1850 Spain exported an estimated 621,000 hectoliters of wine, but by 1873 that number had increased to approximately 2,643,000 hectoliters.[49] The Catalan province of Lleida, hoping to take advantage of the French failures, doubled its number of vineyards, but their crops were soon destroyed by phylloxera's invasion.[50] By 1877 there were an estimated 240,000 hectares of vineyards in Catalonia, but by 1889, even with an almost total destruction of Girona's crop, Catalonia had 363,000 hectares.[51] Clearly these growers raced to produce more wine to fill the void left by France. With the need to plant more fields and produce more wine, the Catalan wine region of the Penedès saw a population boom reaching 105,312 people in 1887 as more labor was needed.[52] Central Spanish provinces also saw great success and increased production during the phylloxera years. Rioja became a greater producer for the French markets, and some French vintners even traveled to Rioja during this time to purchase land to grow French grapes.[53] One example is "BODEGAS FRANCO-ESPAÑOLAS ... founded in 1890 thanks to the golden age that Rioja experienced in the 19th Century, when the French, whose vineyards were agonizing under the attack of the phylloxera plague, came to the region in search of replacement vineyards. This marked the beginning of the development of 'fine Rioja wines.'"[54]

The wine plagues of the late nineteenth century also benefited science and technology. Juan Piqueras Haba suggests that these diseases "prompted such an overwhelming response from the scientific world" in their attempts not only to fight the disease, but also to support the economy.[55] Scientists had to develop new "pesticides and fertilizers" to protect their crops; winegrowers needed grape diversification, as those varietals that suffered the most needed to be replaced with heartier types; wine cooperatives were strengthened as producers worked together for the survival of their livelihoods; and the development of new wine-making processes would modernize Spanish production to keep up with the growing demand.[56] Engineers also worked to create new means of spreading pesticides to protect plants, created machinery to uproot dead or infected vines and quickly plant new ones, and introduced trains to regions like Rioja and the Penedès, which both saw the need to move their product more rapidly.[57]

The rush to produce more wine had negative repercussions for these regions as well. Phylloxera was going to enter almost every region of Spain and impact production, leading to an inevitable collapse; this would then be exacerbated by the fact that French producers would recover, undermining Spanish exports. The increase in vine planting throughout Spain also resulted in changes to Spain's "social character" and economics.[58] A region's historical connection to the growth of vines seems to have a direct relationship to the possible survival of the wine industry. Marc Badia-Miró, Enric Tello, Francesc Valls, and Ramón Garrabou argue that a region's traditional connection to wine production helped in the long run: "A *true* culture in these specialized rural areas that was tightly rooted in agrarian societies and cultural landscapes" enabled regions like Barcelona and Tarragona to survive the phylloxera outbreak, but regions like Lleida and Girona, which quickly planted grapes to take advantage of the wine frenzies, did not fare as well.[59] Specialization in wine production allowed for sounder planning and greater knowledge over the long term. Barcelona and Tarragona slowly increased their wine production from the seventeenth century onward, which meant that the product was not hastily planted and existed in "complex agrarian landscapes" with clearly defined locations for particular goods, thereby producing a variety of crops and grapes necessary for agricultural survival.[60]

With the increase in production, the attack of phylloxera in Spain, and the stabilization in France by the 1890s, a glut of overproduction in Spain quickly caused wine prices to drop. In 1892 France passed protectionist laws for its wine, reducing Spanish imports while increasing exports of wine from Algeria (a French colony).[61] During phylloxera-based shortages, some producers made lower-quality wines like piquettes (beverages made from dried grapes and often including distilled alcohols).[62] As Spain's grasp on Cuba began to weaken, Spanish farmers, fearing a shortage of sugar, began to cultivate large amounts of sugar beets, many of which were transformed to distilled alcohols, which pushed the production of wine-based alcohols out of favor. As the price of wine plummeted yet the availability of wine remained constant, wine producers could not use distillation, which had been a "safety valve for large harvests and low prices."[63] When demand was still high for wine, Spain imported large amounts of distilled alcohols, particularly from Germany, to fortify its wines (or simply to raise alcohol levels for exportation). During wine shortages many overlooked this adulteration, but once markets stabilized, questions arose about this process, earning Spanish wines a poor reputation.[64] While the rush to fill the void of French wine production had short-term gains for Spanish producers, questionable choices hurt the identity of Spanish wine in the long run.

As was the case with oidium, phylloxera's invasion of Europe had grave consequences for many places on the continent. While oidium needed specific environmental factors to spread, phylloxera could do so more thoroughly and reach more areas of the continent. Phylloxera almost destroyed European wine. With this dramatic decrease of wine production, particularly in France, the Spanish got ready for the invasion while exploiting their rival's failure, rapidly planting thousands of new hectares. Their early financial successes, however, would not last. Unwise planting choices and unskilled production led to lower-quality wines. When the demand was high, this problem was overlooked, but, once French producers stabilized, Spanish wines were viewed as inferior substitutes and replaced just as quickly. The tiny phylloxera aphid caused serious upheavals in European wine production and helped to establish new battle lines among humans for the nature of wine.

ADULTERATION AND WINE

With the uneven arrival of wine plagues to Europe and the fluctuating demand for wine sales, vintners tried to earn as much money as quickly as they could. As prices increased due to shortages, and winemakers hurried to increase quantity of production, quality fell by the wayside. Many winemakers "adulterated" wine: adding water, industrial alcohol, chemicals, or other items, dramatically affecting the quality of the drink and creating health hazards for consumers. As shortages decreased toward the end of the nineteenth century, French winegrowers targeted Spanish imports for their supposed poor quality and possible risks. The period of wine adulteration and shortages in relation to the European wine plagues established an identity of low-quality Spanish wine that would haunt the country's producers for decades.

The definition of wine was "unstable" for centuries. True, wine was created from "fermented grape juice," but, until the 1889 French Griffe Law, the specific or legally specified definition of wine was unclear.[65] Rod Phillips writes that it was not until the twentieth century that "consumers [could] be reasonably certain that the wine they thought they were buying was the wine they were actually buying."[66] Wine adulteration would be known historically as "sophistication," as a product of lesser-quality would be mixed with other products to allegedly elevate its status.[67] Water could be added to wine to reduce the alcohol level and therefore reduce the taxes paid wholesale.[68] Fabricated or distilled alcohols were added to wines to increase the proof and make them more stable for transportation over longer distances.[69] Juan Piqueras Haba explains that exporters of cheap table wines from Vallès and the Penedès increased the alcohol percentage of wines destined to the Río de la Plata to 18 to 20 percent, as tariffs were independent of alcohol level, and wines would be watered down to 12 to 13 percent before they were served.[70]

As France had been the global leader of wine production in the nineteenth century, all European producers needed to know their rules. As the following chapters will show, massive French imports of wine meant that Spanish producers must have been aware of French concerns. With Spanish government agencies pushing to export more wine, and with France as the main target, these producers and agencies needed to follow the new guidelines. In defining the true identity of wine, the French continued to lead in legislation. The 1889 Griffe Law defined wine as a product derived from grapes, but it did not fully prohibit dried grapes from being used.[71] The 1891 Brousse Law prohibited any additional adulteration to wines, restricted the use of plaster to two grams per liter, and required sellers to indicate if any adulteration had occurred.[72] Even with these new rules for the sales of wine in France, a loophole existed that allowed sellers to indicate if the wine had been watered down or fortified.[73] While the goal of these laws was to protect French wine producers from lower-quality imports, they and others allowed French consumers to know what was in their wine. Lower-income consumers could purchase cheaper, watered-down wines that were free of chemicals. For Spain the Wine Act of 1895 was the first law to give protections to natural wines, but, as Jordi Planas concludes, little was done to enforce it. Not until the 1926 Spanish Wine Act were policies strengthened in the Primo de Rivera Dictatorship to define wine and its production, and even then these policies were often vague.[74]

With the development of modern chemistry in the nineteenth century, the definition of wine became a battleground across Europe. Urbanization, industrialization, and new technical practices created a greater distance between consumers and producers, making the exact origins of a product more obscure.[75] Thanks to organic chemistry, wine could be produced from dried grapes or other chemicals that ran counter to the historical understanding of the beverage.[76] Because wines could be industrially produced or watered down, other products were added to protect them for shipment; Spanish wines were infamous for the addition of plaster to prevent spoilage for long trips. In 1891 the French government prohibited the importation of plastered wines, drastically decreasing Spanish wine sales in France.[77] Industrial or watered-down wines also lost their vibrant red color, which consumers demanded. To combat the loss of color, gypsum, fuchsine (rosaniline hydrochloride), and even arsenic were added to give wines a redder hue.[78] With all of these possible additions and fabrications, it would be virtually impossible for any consumer of cheaper wines to know what they were drinking, or if it was actually wine.

Adulterating wines makes it exceedingly difficult to determine if the beverage had been changed by the producer or the exporter. The technological advancements of the late nineteenth century meant that new chemicals could be added, the effects of which were often not fully understood by producers or consumers.[79] Even for the modern wine specialist, it is virtually impossible to detect wine fraud "through smell and taste alone."[80] As Jordi Planas notes, the Spanish government was slow to act on concerns about overproduction and therefore to develop any policies regarding testing of wine. Spanish winegrowers were much weaker than their French counterparts, less quick to respond as these crises developed, and much more suspicious of national-level intervention, and they did not have the necessary attention of the state.[81] Spanish producers seemed to enjoy the possibility of greater exportation of wine at better prices, but this overall lack of cohesion among producers created many weaknesses in Spain once foreign production levels stabilized.

The growth of the late nineteenth-century hygienist movement also raised concerns for wine producers in France and Spain. The hygienists worried that people were drinking too much, and they wanted to restrict their alcohol consumption. For quality French wine producers, the hygienists represented a threat, as they could work to reduce the common person's alcohol intake. These high-quality producers, however, used the movement to fight against adulteration and counterfeit wines that ruined reputations.[82] Hygienists said "no" to drinking dangerously, but drinking "well" was fine. Fine wine producers in Champagne and Bordeaux looked to create the French Appellation d'Origine Contrôlée (Controlled Designation of Origin) to protect the identity and image of their wines not only from foreign adulterations but also internal French cheats who looked to take advantage of lax standards.[83]

Even with these manipulations, some in the industry defended these practices. For Spain the overproduction crisis was not caused by the manipulation of wines, but the fact that Spaniards did not drink enough nationally produced wine and therefore needed to find export markets, which in turn made their products cheaper for overseas buyers.[84] If more Spaniards drank national wine, then producers would not have needed to tamper with their wines to undercut foreign pricing. Similarly, the production of these artificial or industrial wines created a cheaper product, allowing lower-income individuals to purchase a similar product and "raise the standard of living for the lower classes," who could mimic the experiences enjoyed by the bourgeois class.[85] If high-quality and reputable wines were too expensive for the average consumer, adulterated wines allowed members of the lower middle class to "compromise between their need for social status and their relatively limited incomes."[86] It was also believed that "there was no tavern or roadside hostelry that did not sell artificial or adulterated wine."[87] Therefore, for Europe's emerging middle classes at the end of the nineteenth century, social status seemed to be just as powerful a concern as health.

By 1879 Spanish wine commissions and agronomists had begun to suggest ways to produce wine without the use of chemical or external adulterations to protect quality. The Commission on Wines outlined a series of concerns that producers needed to acknowledge to protect their crop—for instance, creating wines with the appropriate amount of acidity or sweetness without adding foreign agents to change the taste. All of the grapes' natural fermentation processes needed to be consistent and stable. Wine clarification had to occur naturally, with the use of something like egg whites, not chemicals. Procedures must guarantee a stable alcohol level without the addition of industrial alcohol or water. Producers were obliged to pay attention to the types of grapes being used and to be clear about which varietals appeared in each bottle. Winemakers also had to be aware of the amount of plaster that was put in their wines, especially as debates grew over the use of plastering for exports, as well as the process of coloring for wines.[88] By paying close attention to the production of their wines, they could then certify that their products followed higher guidelines and, hopefully, alleviate exportation fears. The problem, however, would be that all producers would have to follow these guidelines—and this would prove to be impossible.

Debates ensued about how to test for and prevent the overusage of fuchsine in wines. This manmade red chemical could be used to make lower-quality wines look redder and, therefore, serve as an agent for fraud. In discussing the threat represented by fuchsine, Catalan chemist and industrialist don Ramón de Manjarrés y de Bofarull explained how producers and sellers could test for it: for instance, by placing some strands of white wool or silk into the wine for ten minutes and then washing them with clean water and pressing them. According to Manjarrés y de Bofarull, if fuchsine was present in the wine, the strands would maintain a pink color, but, for an unadulterated wine, they would wash clean or have a light gray hue to them.[89] Manjarrés y de Bofarull claimed that "the minimum amount of fuchsine that can be used for the fraudulent coloring of a wine is perfectly discoverable by this method, and if the pale coloration obtained on silk or wool makes one doubt its nature, it would suffice to resort to remove any doubt" by either testing again, or trying other methods.[90] A mixture of water and hydrochloric acid, water and ammonia, or chemical reactions from endocrine papers could be used as follow-up tests to determine if the wine had been tainted. Manjarrés y de Bofarull believed, however, that the identification of fuchsine in wine did not always mean intentional adulteration. In some cases only a small amount was added to already red wines to intensify the color; at other times, Manjarrés y de Bofarull thought that a false positive could result from the breakdown of other chemicals in the fermentation process related to tannins. "It is to be believed," he wrote, "that the cases in which indications of fuchsine have been found in the wines do not indicate an immediate criminal action, but that their origin must look for purely accidental causes."[91] The problem was that, if fuchsine was identified in the wine, it was difficult to determine its origin. Nevertheless, Manjarrés y de Bofarull did recognize that some unscrupulous producers did use it: "The addition of Fuchsina to the wines as a fraud is an absurdity and this makes us hope that this bad habit will not take root."[92] In the same year, the San Isidro Agricultural Institute sent a letter to the Ministry of Development warning of the use of fuchsine in winemaking, suggesting that because foreign consumers wanted a wine "loaded with color," producers were adding the chemical.[93] Therefore, continued foreign demand for wine that looked high quality was a driving factor in the use of this chemical.

By 1886 France had grown concerned about the Spanish wine industry. As the French wine industry stabilized following the phylloxera crisis, French wine producers worked to defend their crops against the cheaper Spanish imports in the face of adulteration concerns. The Spanish Laboratorio para el Analisís de Vinos en Paisajes (Laboratory for the Analysis of Wines in the Countryside) highlighted the growing tensions between the two countries and the changing French regulations that could affect Spain. The laboratory explained, "The great interests of Spanish wine exports have gone through an acute crisis in the first half of this year."[94] The French government outlawed the importation of wines with more than 15 percent alcohol by volume—a level much lower than produced in Spanish warm weather reds. Similarly, potassium sulfite and plaster were further restricted to no more than two grams per liter. The French state, with the support of its national producers, was looking to impede damaging imports. The concern with these new regulations for the laboratory was strong, as previous treaties between France and Spain had allowed for wine to contain over 15 percent alcohol by volume; these agreements also had lax standards concerning the proportion of plaster allowed in wine.[95] In response to these new threats from the French state, the Spanish wine industry and government needed to act quickly to confirm the export quality of Spanish wine to protect the product. The laboratory explained, "The Spanish Administration in turn seems committed to inspect with great care the class and composition of the exported wines, with the double and laudable purpose of avoiding losses to the exporter in good faith, and to impede the discreditation of this national product in the foreign markets."[96] Without an increase of testing by the Spanish, close to one-tenth of Spanish exports to France could be prevented within a few months, deeply hurting the economy.[97] Seemingly, it was not that the Spanish producers took the initiative to check their own wines, but the increased threat by the French to stop Spanish imports that unleashed this new concern.

The addition of industrial alcohol, or alcohol fermented from cereals or other goods, was not only a serious problem for exportation but also a serious health risk to consumers in Spain. In 1884 Spain imported 657,000 hectoliters of industrial alcohol, 948,000 in 1885, and a whopping 1,086,000 in 1886.[98] The majority was mixed with low-quality wines, particularly from those regions most affected by the spread of yet another plague, mildew, which was first spotted in France in 1878 and spread quickly throughout the country, finally reaching Spain in 1883. Luckily, mildew could be treated in a similar manner to oidium, but the rapid spread affected many humid regions in Spain between 1884 and 1887, greatly reducing the grape crop.[99] While industrial alcohol was a cheap and easily accessible product that could increase alcohol content in wine, it corrupted the product.

On May 23, 1887, a group of Spanish vintners and medical professionals sent a letter to the Sociedad Española Vinícola y Enológica (Spanish Society for Wine and Winemaking) to express their worries about the corrupting and dangerous factors of industrial alcohol and to call upon this wine society to push for a prohibition of the mixing process. The signatories of the letter asked the organization to prohibit the mixing of alcohol distilled from potatoes in particular, as that drink "causes in the human organism taking it as a drink, an infinity of illnesses of stomach, of the brain, the spine, the trunk, and others."[100] Potato alcohol not only resulted in physical illness but also psychological infirmities; "the men of science are confident in that the criminality, the suicides, the machinations, or such inabilities have increased" among those individuals who drank industrial alcohol.[101] The letter ended by explaining that it was industrial alcohol that led to the creation of alcoholics, not the consumption of normal wine. Industrial alcohol not made from grapes was foreign, dangerous, and detrimental to Spain's economic survival because "wealth is the wine."[102]

Eloy Lecanda, the founder of Bodega Vega Sicilia in the Ribera del Duero, and Marcial Prieto, agronomist and Secretary of Agriculture, Industry, and Commerce for Burgos in 1872, sent a letter to the Ministry of Development on June 6, 1887, regarding the effects of industrial alcohol on Spain's economy and health. The letter stated: "Considering that the first duty of every Government is to ensure public health, and it has been proved that the ingestion of industrial alcohol into the animal agronomy is highly harmful, to the point of representing its effects in this sense ten or fifteen times greater than that produced by an equal amount of wine alcohol" it would be necessary for the government to prohibit the increase of this beverage.[103] The invasion of this industrial alcohol could change the identity of Spanish wine as local distillation came from grape products and not cereals, which could ruin traditional practices and represent "a danger to our national way of being." This joint letter suggested that the Spanish viewed the consumption of cereal-based alcohol as "the type of drunk [who is] disgusting, the virtue of temperance that we care to preserve for being one of the most outstanding characters of our race."[104] Drinking wine, for these men, was not the same as drinking industrial alcohol. In a way, wine was still considered a "natural" product, but, as the name states, "industrial alcohol" was not viewed as the completion of a natural process. Economically, the addition of industrial alcohol to Spanish wine tainted the image of the product and endangered its international success. "Considering how harmful such cheap alcohols have powerfully contributed to the discrediting of our wines in foreign markets," the letter continued, "and the case of being confiscated large consignments of [table wines] in French Customs, part of which have been thrown into the water."[105] Overall, industrial alcohol did nothing more than damage Spain and its people.

The Conde of Roche in Murcia, Enrique Forter, also wrote to the Ministry of Development in 1887 to offer his opinions about the problems of industrial alcohol. For Forter the arrival of industrial alcohol to Spain was just as great a threat as phylloxera. "The so-called industrial alcohol," he wrote, "imperfectly rendered, becomes the cause of the decline of wines . . . causing at the same time serious disturbances in the health of the consumers and ruinous competition to the harvesters."[106] Forter complained that "said alcohol, with some natural coloring substances and a little wine are made in enormous quantities [and] is sent abroad with the name of wine from Spain, which after contribute to lower the price of natural wine" and harming the chances for finding new markets.[107] Action needed to be taken to stop this practice and save Spain's wealth: "Therefore, it is essential that effective measures be taken so that wines with industrial alcohols cannot . . . contain substances harmful to the health, and that the production of alcohol of good quality is favored, so that the substances of wine that are exported do not discredit the excellent products of our vineyards."[108] Like Lecanda and Prieto, the Conde understood that the falsification of Spanish wines and the use of industrial alcohol did not only create health risks for consumers, but could also have long-lasting negative consequences for the country. The Conde did not simply blame the producers, "because the shopkeepers and sellers find great advantages in the adulterations and thus the wine is sold, within the towns, at a price much lower than its cut in the warehouse."[109] This crime, therefore, did not occur only in the vineyard, but in stores as well. The Spanish state, Forter believed, needed to take a stronger role in the policing of Spanish wine production and sales to save the product from possible disaster.

Lecanda and Prieto had some ideas as to how to protect Spain's wines from adulteration and industrial alcohol usage. They believed it was necessary that consumers be made aware of what was in their wines. They wrote: "All wines or liquors manufactured or traced with industrial alcohols are declared to be harmful to health, understood as those coming from the distillation of pulps of cereal or potatoes and in general all those containing amyl alcohol, whatever its origin."[110] They also suggested that "all wines artificially colored with extraneous materials to the grape and all those containing any drug, which alter their composition, constitute a harmful falsification of the natural product, are declared harmful to health."[111] Even as some winemakers and experts spoke out against the dangers of industrial alcohol, chemical coloration, and other additives that could harm the consumer and Spain's reputation, the practice was difficult to halt; therefore, the image of Spanish wine continued to deteriorate.

The Spanish government created a Royal Order in 1880 to push for the creation of Oenological Stations in Spain to check for quality, but this process stalled.[112] The Conde of Roche reiterated the need for these stations in 1887. Their purpose was to test wines rigorously, analyze the wines for export, design new laws to fight adulteration, put limits on artificial wines, reduce the use of industrial alcohol, and work to modify the taxation systems for wine.[113] By having a scientific and governmentally funded location to test Spain's wines, the government and the producers could guarantee the quality and value of their products. The first station opened in Haro in 1892, with others in Vilafranca de Penedès in 1902, Reus in 1905, and others in the following years.[114]

THE GOOD AND BAD OF PLAGUES

The arrival of the major wine plagues to Europe in the nineteenth century had profound outcomes for the identity of Spanish wine and the use of science and technology in the nation's agricultural sector. At first, when oidium and phylloxera arrived in Europe, scientists and winegrowers did not fully understand these mysterious diseases. The plagues spread unevenly, with some regions quickly succumbing while others did not see the negative repercussions for years. For Spain these diseases produced interesting outcomes. As oidium began to ravage

France's fields, Spanish producers quickly jumped on the red wine shortages and increased output to fill the void. Spanish producers saw a serious advantage in France's devastation, but the disease would soon cross the Pyrenees. With the help of scientific studies that identified the fungus and created techniques to combat it, Europe's wineries were able to stabilize within a few years. The problem, however, was that one technique to combat oidium was to import North American rootstock and testing its resilience to the disease: these new roots brought with them phylloxera, and the greatest devastation European vineyards had ever seen. As with oidium phylloxera's attacks on France gave Spanish producers a leg up, and they were able to export more wine. Spanish winegrowers ripped up other products quickly to plant grapes to take advantage. Once scientists discovered that the key to combatting phylloxera was to import more North American rootstock (*Vitis rupestris*, *Vitis riparia*, and *Vitis berlandieri*) for grafting.[115] Tens of thousands of hectares were torn up and new vines planted. The recovery of the French wine industry, combined with the increase of Spanish production, weakened the market and initiated economic problems for Spain.

When diseases reduced wine production, growers in France, Spain, and other countries adulterated their wines to capitalize on the increased demand and prices. Winegrowers added water to their wines to stretch the amounts, industrial alcohol to increase the alcohol percentage, chemicals to color the wines, and other chemicals to help them ship better. In each of these cases, the quality of wine dropped. As phylloxera's destruction slowed, and producers stabilized, the amount of available wine increased, and prices dropped. French producers, worried that their market share would be slow to recover, pushed their government to pass legislation to prevent the importation of adulterated wines. Hygienists and scientists spoke out against these adulteration practices as well, hoping consumers would purchase better-quality (meaning French) wines. In the end the French condemned Spanish producers, their questionable practices, and their lack of any national standards for wine; French wines would once again be the quality good, and Spanish wines suspicious. Spanish wine came to be identified as a replacement for French wine, with uncertain qualities and ingredients, and it would take decades for this stigma to fade.

3

Saber beber

MEDIA, SCIENCE, AND DRINKING WELL
IN EARLY FRANCOIST SPAIN

In October 1952 the Spanish magazine *Fotos* published an article entitled "A Wine
for Each Hour and an Hour for Each Wine" that outlined some simple rules
for the reader on how to choose the appropriate wine at the appropriate time.[1]
Over the decades following the Spanish Civil War, the Spanish media produced
a number of newspaper and magazine articles about the country's drinking habits and wine industry. While critics discussed problems associated with alcohol
consumption, a greater number of commentaries offered suggestions on drinking
the proper wine and showing national pride in choosing Spanish vintners. By the
1960s agencies like the Spanish Sindicato Nacional de la Vid (National Syndicate
of the Vine) and the Ministerio de la Información y Turismo (Ministry of Information and Tourism) actively worked to disseminate propaganda about wine,
its consumption, its production, and its importance to the national economy.

This chapter explores the way the Spanish media and the Spanish state portrayed the changing identity of wine and its consumption in the country. The
identity of the wine consumer and the culture associated with wine consumption
have changed substantially at various points in the early modern and modern
periods. Similarly, Spanish state apparatuses placed great emphasis on the production of wine as part of the national economy and national patrimony. During this
period Spain was not the only country exploring the relevance of its wine industry;
its greatest production rivals, France and Italy, also started similar conversations.
Questions raged in Europe concerning appropriate alcohol consumption and its
effects on the state and public health. Spanish producers, however, appeared to be
most interested in increasing consumption and quality inside the country.

In this chapter I argue that the state and its media made a conscious effort to transform the drinking habits of the Spanish citizenry by showing them how to drink wine properly and how to understand what wine meant to the country. The idea of "patriotic eating" in Spain had its roots in the Primo de Rivera dictatorship (1923–30), when a weakened Spain tried to reestablish some national pride.[2] These articles and press releases worked to remove the old idea of the *vino de la mesa* (table wine) and create a new standard of quality for Spanish agriculture. Proper alcohol consumption—in this case, of wine—was necessary to create a positive identity for the Spanish state in this period of rapid global transition. If Spaniards could learn to drink wine well, this could help to improve their image and gain them international respect. The rules and reasons to drink wine were numerous, but their changes over time highlight what societies viewed as important concerning this drink.

This chapter will focus on three primary issues related to the consumption of wine in Spain and Europe. In order to trace the changing attitudes toward wine consumption, it is important to understand how wine changed from a nutritional food to a tool of culture, politics, and economics. First, the chapter will look at a conversation about wine consumption in the Renaissance and early modern period, during which ideas associated with the drinking of wines spoke overwhelmingly of issues concerning health and nutritional value, with only slight attention paid to the risks of overconsumption. Second, this chapter will explore issues relating to the end of the nineteenth and early twentieth centuries, when new questions about the health and social impacts of alcohol consumption grew due to new modern complications. Spain's greatest wine-producing rival, France, debated numerous questions about alcohol abuse. In both France and Spain, discussion ensued about avoiding the negative aspects of alcohol while promoting appropriate drinking behavior. Lastly, this chapter will investigate the plans developed in Spain to develop a positive and culturally significant identity for its wine and its consumption. In each of these sections, my goal is to highlight the reasons why people drank wine and show the changing ways in which people thought they should and did consume the beverage.

THE OLD WAY TO DRINK

In a contemporary mindset, people choose wine based upon factors like season, food-pairing, and terroir. With modern gastronomy's increased influence, today's wine-drinkers have many choices, and connoisseurs are well aware of the rules when choosing a glass. This style of drinking, however, is very modern. During the Renaissance and early modern period, wine consumption was not dominated by taste or style, but directed primarily by questions of nutrition and the body's humors. It is necessary to take note of these earlier views of wine consumption to understand how the rules concerning wine changed in the twentieth century.

For the overwhelming majority of wine's existence, its consumption was governed by the studies of Galen and his theories of humorism. These classical rules dictated the hows and whys of drinking wine as late as the eighteenth century. One primary reason to drink wine, according to Galen, was for its nutritional value.[3] Because red wine was so similar to human blood in appearance, it was assumed that it entered a person's system quickly, delivering them the nutrients they needed.[4] By the fourteenth century, the concept of wine as an important nutrient in the human diet was the dominant opinion in Southern Europe. Numerous treatises and reports were written justifying this opinion, and "the dietary notions . . . ended up being repeated and circulated so often that they finally constituted a body of knowledge whose guidelines were adopted well beyond the inner circles of the medical profession."[5] By the fifteenth century, the ideas concerning the nutritional value of wine had become so ubiquitous that it was not uncommon for nondoctors to write about its health benefits.[6] Allen J. Grieco notes that "the massive and capillary circulation of medical knowledge deeply influenced the way in which consumers behaved," and that these ideas "actually percolated down to the lower reaches of society, where they ended up being lodged in an oral tradition that has survived more or less to the present."[7] One might think of the Spanish axiom "Con pan y vino se anda el camino," which literally translates to "With bread and wine one goes on" but proverbially means "Things never seem so bad after a good meal."[8] The two primary ingredients for a filling and successful meal, therefore, were bread and wine.

Medieval and early modern doctors viewed wine as a tool to control the humors of the body and affect their four qualities: hot or cold, dry or wet. These supposed effects of wine directed the choice of consumption. As Grieco describes, during the summer, drinkers should choose "cold" wines to make themselves more comfortable, while the "colder" elderly should consume "hot" wines for their health.[9] Early modern scholars created a spectrum for wines to help the drinker choose, with sweet wines being considered strong and more acidic wines considered weaker. Due to this spectrum, it was recommended that sweet wines only be drank in moderation, while the more acidic wines could be drunk more regularly, as they were considered healthier.[10]

By combining Galen's opinions with the spectrums associated with wine varieties, scholars established a (sometimes contradictory) set of rules for determining what type of wine should be drank. To keep one's humors in check, drinkers should think about four issues: the constitution of the person, the food accompanying the wine, the time of year, and the location where the wine was to be consumed. Younger people were considered "hotter" and therefore should not consume too much wine, as it, too, was a hot substance, yet, conversely, as the elderly were "colder" in nature, the consumption of wine gave them the benefit of warmth. When it came to food choice, the goal was not a "function of matching tastes in a pleasurable way but rather was meant to oppose hot and cold elements as to produce an ideal equilibrium" that established "compensatory drinking."[11] Interestingly, this second rule of choice primarily acts in direct opposition to many rules of modern gastronomy. In the early modern period, cold foods like fruits and vegetables were served with a strong wine, something not often recommended today, unless one pairs spicy foods (considerably hot foods) with colder and higher-acid wines. The time of year played an important role in what wine should be chosen: cold wines in the summer and hot wines in the winter, to compensate the humors. The fourth rule was that people in warm areas should drink colder wines and vice versa.[12] These two final guidelines made their way into modern wine culture, as white and rosé wines have become commonplace in the summer and in warm locations, while red wine best embodies wintertime consumption. Therefore, while Galen and early modern rules for wine do not completely correspond to modern and contemporary drinking, some rules have been adapted into this conversation.

Even with the perceived nutritional and health benefits associated with wine, questions began to arise in the sixteenth century about health and societal problems associated with its consumption. The Protestant Reformation and the Catholic Counterreformation emphasized "public decorum and morality," which influenced the drinking of wine.[13] A conversation started about how people should drink wine: one should consume enough wine to obtain the benefits from the drink, but not drink so much as to become drunk. One debate revolved around sleep and wine, the assumption being that wine created "cloudy vapors" during digestion that would move to the brain and allow one to sleep, but when too much wine was consumed it led only to drunkenness and, hence, to poor sleep.[14]

In discussing the writings of Guliemo Grataroli, a Protestant who fled his native Italian community outside Verona and moved to Basel in the mid-sixteenth century, Ken Albala explains that "Grataroli's major concern [was] to lash out against drunkenness." Grataroli concluded that the health benefits associated with wine consumption were only moderate, and that wine "cools the body by suffocating the natural heat and leads to apoplexy, paralysis, tremors, stupor, convulsions, vertigo, lethargy, phrenitis, etc. It perturbs the senses, ruins the memory, makes men libidinous and 'fetid drunkenness makes men into irrational beasts.'"[15] His works were intended to "frighten people into drinking less" and assert the claim that wine was "inappropriate for children and especially women."[16] Wine, therefore, by this time was no longer viewed as a panacea and nutritional godsend, but—at least in Protestant circles—as an illness. By the seventeenth century, commentary about the negative impacts of wine had made their ways into Protestant vernacular: "Early to wine, early corrupted; Early a drunkard, early death."[17] Even with these graphic and prophetical warnings about wine consumption, these attitudes did not become the primary belief of all Europeans, in particular those living in Catholic Europe, and especially in Spain.

Although the belief in the supposed medicinal and nutritional values associated with wine continued to linger, the negative impacts of alcohol abuse, particularly by wine, became an issue for twentieth-century Spain. In "Defensa del Borracho" (Defense of the drunk) in the December 1945 issue of *Fotos*, Alfredo Marquerie explored the issues surrounding the behavior and actions of the typical street alcoholic in the city. "Yes, we already know that drunkenness is something horrible," he wrote, "that being habitually so is a modifying circumstance of criminal responsibility to the detriment of the accused and that alcoholism is considered just one of the plagues of Humanity."[18] The history of this drunkenness, according to Marquerie, was not new, as "we also know that Noah, although the Scripture does not say that he was the inventor of wine, planted a vineyard and drank excess juice from his winepresses and unwittingly got drunk."[19] The behavior of the drunk, therefore, was not a modern phenomenon, but had existed for as long as fermentation, and its consequences have not always been good, even for biblical personalities.

In his article Marquerie described the activities of a typical drunk. "We know all those things and many more about the damage of either history or the legend of wine and drunkenness," he wrote, "but today we do not want to talk about that; we want to tell something more trivial and simple; our meeting in the urban night of Saturday with a drunk man."[20] He provided a sketch of this familiar character:

> What was this man like? He had, as in the case of all drunks, his reddened nose and glazed eyes, in the imitation of the gaze in the ecstasy of love or of the crystalline, cold and turbid look of death. His body and arms swayed like those of sailors on the unstable deck of his ships on a stormy day, because drunkenness is always a difficult and stormy journey and, in the end, has the same consequences of dizziness! The man could not take his feet off the ground. If he did, he would feel the sensation of lifting with his large soles weighted of lead, of plucking and unraveling a deep root that had unexpectedly attached him to the earth. And also fall on the hard pebbles of the stream, because all—sidewalks, houses, lights, doors, windows—in balance flip continuously, in mad, in a carrousel shot and speed, would insist on making you lose balance.[21]

The drunk stumbles in the streets, frequently falling, and talking to no one and everyone alike about art, literature, and poetry as he passes them by. After a long evening of drinking whisky, wine, and champagne,

> at that point, the drunk's voice broke into a hiccup of sobs. He said terrible things about pain, injustice, ingratitude, the fickleness of inconstancy. And proclaimed again the brotherhood of Saturday's drunks with the cursed poets, discovered and betrayed without . . . the blind impulse of despair that had pushed him towards the vessels of the raging spirit and towards that terrible whirlpool, towards that whirling and whirling slide of houses and unstable ideas. . . .
>
> And there we left him, lonely and vociferous, embraced to the barbeque of the . . . middle of the street of the night, while we calm and bored, we went to sleep our bourgeois dreams, deaf and blind to the mysterious . . . of demented, of madness or of misery, from the drunkard on Saturday.[22]

In this description the drunk appears as a pitiful creature, reflective of the social and medical ills spoken of centuries earlier by Guliemo Grataroli. As for the bourgeois author and likely bourgeois readers of this article, he serves as a warning against the overconsumption of alcohol. The reader of this article may feel sorry for the drunk, but, more importantly, likely thinks, "Better him than me."

Only a few pages after offering this solemn view of the drunk, in the same edition of *Fotos* appears the article "The Fish of Colors: Since We Got into Revelry," which takes a light-hearted view of alcohol consumption. It jokes: "Wine has more classes than those smart kids who do all the Baccalaureate courses."[23] Wine and its consumption, in this piece, was not presented as something to be feared, but something to celebrate; the effects of wine on the borracho are more humorous than pathetic. "We all know—and we will not disguise . . . that drunkenness is a temporary embarrassment of the powers produced by the abuse of wine and other liquors. Some interpretations produce very tranquil effects. But what many ignore is that our language, richer than a sun, has a great variety of words to mention drunkenness, according to the class of those who enjoy it."[24] The article uses playful terms to describe drunkenness: *carniceros* (butchers) who drink too much are said to be *tajada* (slang for "legless"). Men who work in the fishing business are *merluza*, literally the fish "hake" but, in this case, meaning "sozzled." Musicians who drink too much are *melopea* (sloshed, or like monotonous singing). Construction workers who imbibe too much are *tablón*, literally "plank" or "beam," but in this case signifying "plastered."[25] "And there still remain in this situation," the article continues, "*jumera* [stinky drunk], *cogorzas*[smashed], *beodez* [drunken], *vinolencia* [wine-drunk], *temulencia* [temulence], *dipsomanía* [dipsomania], *pítima* [plastered] and *baba* [slobbery]."[26] Drinking too much had a special name for each time and place based upon the drinker. This language, while not complementary, does not condemn the actions of drinkers, but provides them with cute, apropos nicknames based on their behavior.

For the overwhelming part of two millennia, scholars saw wine as a nutritional, medically safe liquid that was part of a healthy diet. Only at certain points before the eighteenth century did any intellectual suggest any negative ramifications of consuming the beverage overall. True, wine could make one drunk and unruly, but, if simple rules were followed, this could be avoided. Even in 1945 Spain, the threat of the borracho was more of a warning than a real attack against drinking culture, and colorful names were given to the man who imbibed too much. In the late nineteenth century, medicine and society began to look more closely at alcohol and its effects on culture, and these issues would slowly make their way into Spanish discourse.

FROM DRINKING POORLY TO DRINKING WELL

In the mid-nineteenth century, conversations about alcohol and wine began to move away from their perceived health benefits to the negative consequences associated with excess. Increased alcohol consumption in Europe led to increased social ills and bad behavior. Governments, particularly the French, had a difficult line to walk: how to decrease negative aspects of alcohol consumption while protecting their local alcohol industries—namely, wine. French drinking had skyrocketed from 27,292 million hectoliters drank annually in the 1850s to 56,112 million in the 1870s, along with dramatic increases in beer and spirits.[27] These coincided with "a declining birth rate, a spike in prostitution, legalization of divorce followed by a rising divorce rate, young men disqualified from military service, an increase of work-related accidents, a growing number of mentally ill, and increase in juvenile delinquency."[28] These conversations in France were difficult ones, as wine was responsible for problems, but was also a part of the country's patrimony. Spain, too, had questions about social ills relating to alcohol, but, in a struggling economy, the conversation came to focus on how to help Spaniards drink their country's wine responsibly.

To deal with these newly identified medical and social ills, British physician Francis Edmund Antsie (1833–1874) began to work on the idea of "moderation" in drinking alcohol. Antsie "was convinced that alcohol was not simply a poison, food or medicine in itself, and that its effects depended on the dose administered."[29] Alcohol did have benefits for the body, but beyond that it had "obvious narcotic and harmful effects (the drinker became drunk and the body began to suffer the consequences of drinking)."[30] From his research Antsie established his "limit" in 1870, stating that 1–1½ ounces of absolute alcohol was the maximum amount one should drink daily. Sedentary types, like children and the elderly, should drink less, but the majority of "middle- and upper-class drinkers" were consuming much more than this.[31] Antsie was worried because "few people knew very much about what he called the 'comparative alcohol potency' of different drinks, and this was compounded by variations in glass sizes, which he thought were getting bigger, as well as by the vagueness in patients' descriptions of their consumption."[32] Antsie's limit, therefore, would allow drinkers to receive the health benefits of alcohol without its negative effects, but even the doctor had to admit that a variety of other topics prevented full implementation of his ideas.

In France medical concerns grew over alcohol consumption and its destruction of the social fabric. By the 1890s an anti-alcohol crusade had developed in France, as doctors spoke out against too much consumption. The irony, however, lay in the fact that France was a leader in wine production; therefore, an attack on drinking wine would harm the state's economy. French doctors declared wine a *boisson hygiénique* (healthy drink) and other alcohols to be the real problem. For these doctors wine was safe to drink, even though it still contained alcohol. It was not science that drove this argument, but French identity. French wine was viewed as a patriotic beverage, and societal and cultural health would be protected by its continued consumption. Because quality French wine represented the drinking of the middle class, consuming it would be viewed as healthy.[33] Spain would also begin to address questions about wine consumption and teaching its citizens how to drink Spanish wine well.

Wine remained a vital part of Spanish culture at the start of the twentieth century. The saying "Dime lo qué bebes y te diré quién eres" (Tell me what you drink, and I will tell you who you are) provides a good starting point to understand why some Spaniards were drinking and to show the importance placed on drinking and identity.[34] The type of alcohol chosen can determine many characteristics about the drinker. At the same time, trying to change the type of alcohol a person drinks, or the reasons why someone would drink, could possibly change the identity of a person or a population.

In his 1945 article "El vino corriente: Bebida de moda" in *Fotos*, F. Hernández Castanedo explored the drinking culture in Madrid, having interviewed bar owners and bartenders in Madrid to gauge the current climate for wine consumption and tastes in the city, with some very telling conclusions. Barman Fernando Gaviria told him: "Yes, we are selling much more wine and in establishments like mine, more sherry." When asked why he thought this was so, Gaviria replied, "To a state of nerves provoked by the war. The people want to be happy . . . and they look to wine."[35] The stresses of the Spanish Civil War (1936–39), the constant global problem of World War II, and the economic problems in Spain put heavy pressure on the lives of its citizenry. Due to this they drank. Even Antsie claimed that moderate alcohol consumption could have positive effects; in this case, wine helped to calm people's nerves.

Hernández Castanedo also spoke to Máximo and Demetrio Hernán Gómez, husband and wife owners of a bar near the Palace of Justice, about drinking habits in the city. He asked them, "Are the people drinking much more wine now than before?" Máximo replied, "Much more." When Hernández asked what led to this increase, Máximo responded, "To the war. During it, the people accustomed themselves to drinking wine. Alcohol, as they say, always suits." Demetrio added, "Also it's a motive of style. There has been effective propaganda in making Spanish wines." When asked if the drinkers request any specific wines, she stated, "Certainly, no. What is served is the common wine. Much more white [wine] than red."[36] This brief exchange offers some important insights into the drinking culture of the city and its bars in 1945. Again, the conclusion is drawn that the wars created tensions in the city that led to increased alcohol consumption. State propaganda pushed for the consumption of Spanish wines as global conflicts reduced exports. Importantly, drinkers did not order anything specific; just the wine that was currently available. However, if given a choice, drinkers preferred white wine. When asked why, Máximo responded, "A fundamental reason is based on the domestic economy. The housewives, in these moments struggle with soap, they prefer white wine. This does not stain the tablecloths."[37] Access to wine remained important, drinking was still a popular activity both at bars and at home, and the quality of a wine seemingly did not matter. Hernández reported that about 320,000 liters of wine—1,920,000 glasses—were served in Madrid each day.[38] Conservatively, that would mean that each person in Madrid, including its children, would have almost a glass and quarter of wine a day, each day of the year.

With so much wine being indiscriminately drank in Madrid, what type of propaganda could work to get locals to choose Spanish wines, or wines of better quality? A few pages later in the same issue of *Fotos*, head of the Spanish Syndicate of Wine, Beer, and Beverages discussed the importance of wine to the Spanish state. The article opened with information about Spanish wine and this syndicate:

The cultivation of the vine, ancient in Spain, has in our country extraordinary importance as, the evidence being, in normal circumstances, [Spain is] the third [largest] producer in the world, immediately after France and Italy. The vine is essentially a colonizing plant, growing throughout Spain, because, if it disappeared, [Spain] could not be sustained by any other crop, apart of course, to lose the great richness that is. Its importance, an annual harvest making 2,100,000,000 liters, has led the foremost media to a constant concern for the protection of this crop and to defend its products and byproducts through the establishment of the corresponding corporative entities collected first (in 1932) by the National Wine Institute, now integrated, since 1941, into the National Syndicate of Wine, Beer, and Beverages.

The Syndicate oversees the production of wine growers in Spain, one thousand four hundred liquor makers, some wine alcohol manufacturers and their remnants, one thousand low-grade impure alcohol producers, about one hundred thousand winemakers and five hundred houses or export companies.[39]

Wine production, therefore, was an integral part of the Spanish agricultural and national economy, and this new syndicate had been created to protect the many workers associated with the production of wine. Readers of this segment would likely feel a great deal of pride and understand the duty to choose Spanish wines. When asked to identify the greatest threats to this industry, don Fernando Comenge, head of the syndicate, answered:

There are two main problems that we fear. The improvement of the quality, both of the grape and wine, and the best management of it, that is to say, promotion of its consumption, both in the domestic market and abroad, and greater use of all by-products derived. For the improvement of the quality it is necessary to divulge the teaching of the perfect elaboration and this is addressed by the Syndicate by means of specialization courses. And they have celebrated those of viticulture and enology, being in preparation of other grafts, form to fight the plagues, etc., all of which will be given in the corresponding times to combine always the theory with practice, to achieve the best results.[40]

The Spanish wine industry thus needed to work on producing quality grapes and wines and protecting the industry at all costs. Readers of this interview could see the attempts of this syndicate to improve the quality of Spanish wine. As Máximo and Demetrio had claimed, people did not choose a specific wine, but whatever was available. Now an official government agency existed to improve wine production and to hopefully create a better and more quality identity for Spanish wine.

Another article in the same issue featured Fernando Castan Palomar's interviews with a variety of Spanish celebrities who spent time outside the country. When asked to name their favorite Spanish wines, these cultural icons had important things to say. In discussing the quality of the country's wine, Spanish painter Sanchis Yago stated, "A typical wine here is an extraordinary wine overseas."[41] Catalan philosopher and essayist Eugenio d'Ors explained, "For me, the wines most looked for have always been from Vilafranca ... during my residency in France, I would drink with singular preference the wines of Spain ... finding in them a special flavor."[42] Interestingly, this Catalan author in Francoist Spain chose wine from the viticulture capital of Catalonia. "For me," said singer and actress Lola Flores, "I prefer the Andalucian wines, in them I see the proclamation of my land that goes to all parts of the world. And, so fused with the song and with the dance, that there is no way to talk about this wine without a song coming to our lips: 'I love your laughter a little bit like I drink, girl for what I like, my wine.'"[43] Bullfighter Pepe Bienvenida told him, "I am an enthusiast of Sherry. I believe they are always good. And their flavor is appropriate for whatever hour of the day or night."[44] Each celebrity mentioned a particular region, each well known for the production of wine. One could argue that having celebrities suggest their favorite Spanish wines was one way to get readers of the magazine to try their suggestions. In effect these celebrities offered free advertising for Spanish wines, just as the Syndicate for Wine, Beer, and Beverages would have appreciated, lending Spanish wines the panache they needed.

Spain, like France, wanted its population to continue drinking wine, as it represented an important part of the country's culture. While people were drinking a lot of wine in both countries, questions developed as to how much and what type of alcohol was being consumed. In the case of Spain, the national wine syndicate wanted Spaniards to see their national crop as something more than simple table wine, but something of quality.

HOW TO CHOOSE GOOD WINE

In the years following World War II, the medical establishment continued to raise questions about drinking alcohol, with more doctors identifying problems associated with alcoholism. Wine-producing states, like France and Spain, continued to struggle with concerns about people drinking too much at the same time as they tried to defend the national importance of their wine industries. To protect the Spanish wine industry and the Spanish people from overconsumption, Spain needed to teach its population how to drink wine well, like the French.

Post–World War II French markets continued to be flooded with cheap wine from the Midi and Algeria, much of which came from vines planted during the nineteenth-century phylloxera crisis. Doctors and nutritionists condemned this cheap industrial wine, which they linked to alcohol abuse.[45] The statistics relating to wine production and consumption in France were shocking. In 1932 the average Spaniard drank 55 liters of wine a year, compared to 105 in Italy and 139 in France; by 1954 this was 140 liters in France![46] At the same time, small French vintners pushed for the expansion of the appellation system to protect both their products from cheaper industrial wines and their national patrimony.[47]

Spain, too, had serious problems associated with alcoholism in the years following World War II. In a study of the dramatic increase of alcoholism in Spain between 1945 and 1975, Francisco Alonso Fernandez contends that 9 percent of Spain's population, or close to 1.5 million Spaniards, would be considered alcoholics during that time.[48] The ratio of female to male alcoholism in Spain went from 1:9 in 1954 to 1:4 in 1976. The highest rates of alcoholism could be found in northern Spain, with one out of seven adults drinking too much. Alcohol morbidity in Spain also increased from a low of 5 percent of deaths to a maximum of 20 percent.[49] Alonso Fernandez writes: "Alcoholism in Spain is classless and ubiquitous, occurs independent of normal living standards or economic well-being. The enormous increase is due to changes induced by a technological revolution that has over-reached itself and can cause disruptions of a psychocultural and psychological nature."[50] According to Alonso Fernandez, the majority of these alcoholics could be described as "psychologically addicted drinkers [who are] assailed by the unbearable feelings of loneliness and despair," who wish to "escape from [their] feelings into this world, which requires a certain state of drunkenness."[51] One important aspect to blame was the changing technological environment of the post–World War II era. New technology meant individuals moved to new locations for work, creating upheaval in the Spanish family, severing its multigenerational connections.[52] Large numbers of rural peasants relocated to the unplanned suburbs of major cities like Madrid, losing their previously secure familial connections.[53] In concluding Alonso Fernandez makes the interesting suggestion that the Spanish media and television create an "'alcoholic environment' . . . encouraging that which is the motivation of the alcoholic as an exciting stimulant and presenting it as 'the right way to live,' which can only be regarded as hidden propaganda."[54] As will be discussed, this propaganda in the 1960s was not actually hidden, but overt, in an effort to encourage Spaniards to drink more wine. Spain and France both had serious alcohol issues, but their solutions did not always solve the perceived societal problems.

The French appellation system worked to establish quality over quantity for French production. Health professionals and technocrats viewed higher-quality wine as helpful to public health and the economy. The goal was to prevent lower-quality wines from harming the image of quality regional wines, which in the long run would produce a stronger image for French wines while increasing their prices.[55] This system would additionally remove wine varietals seen as toxic to society. By creating better wine with clearer labels and rules, the French consumer could purchase a healthier product that supported the French economy. Medical professionals and advocates of the appellation system helped to establish the identity of quality for French goods both inside and outside of France. Joseph Bohling explains, "A touch of snobbery would go a long way in helping sober up the population."[56] Spanish wine producers, clearly aware of the conversations concerning French viticulture, would make some similar attempts to improve the quality of their wines.

Over the same period, the Spanish wine industry aimed to secure its internal and external market. The three primary concerns for Spain's producers were to increase the *calidad* (quality) of wine, increase internal consumption, and fight against the growing consumption of beer.[57] In the early twentieth century, only the wines from Jerez (sherry) and from Rioja enjoyed any prestige on the global market. The wine industry wanted to promote the idea that wine had an important social role in Spain, but it also had to combat the fact that a great deal of Spanish wine was grown in poor conditions, resulting in a subpar product. Between 1941 and 1957, the Franco regime created new Consejos Reguladores (regulatory commissions like the French appellations) to develop proper rules for producing regional wines. The 1970 Spanish Wine Statute introduced a restriction on the planting of new vineyards and put new guidelines in place for its production to align the industry with the European Economic Community.[58] While this same statute ordered all Spanish restaurants to serve wine, the success of this plan could not be judged. During the 1960s concerns had been growing as wine consumption continued to fall and beer and soda drinking increased. In 1968 the Comisión de Compras de Excedentes de Vinos (Wine Surplus Purchase Commission) conducted a survey of Spanish wine drinking habits that delivered terrible news about decreasing consumption: Spanish producers must combat wine fraud and increase the quality of the beverage or they would not survive.[59] As with the French, Spanish wine producers needed to connect the agriculture of wine to the country's patrimony and show that the beverage was truly important to Spanish identity.[60] If Spain could "evoke an agricultural past [it could] exalt the importance of current wine."[61] If producers could make wine a positive symbol of Spanish identity, improve its quality, and teach its populace its benefits (and the drawbacks of other alcohols), then the Spanish wine industry could sustain itself in a new internal market.

Moreover, it was necessary to teach the Spanish population how to drink well. The idea of "how" to drink wine properly became a popular conversation in the period following 1945. Scholars of wine offered their advice on choosing and consuming the beverage, which helped to establish a connection between Spanish identity with its wine. The simple rules of gastronomy, along with the association of wine with Spain's patrimony, became a common talking point in magazines, on radio, and eventually on television. The Primo de Rivera regime had successfully taught its population to eat oranges to save national pride; therefore, drinking wine could also act as a protection for the national patrimony.[62] The Franco regime wanted to show its people that eating Spanish goods were patriotic while persuading them that these locally produced products kept them healthy, even when they did not.[63]

Choosing the correct wine was important, and *Fotos* offered some counsel to its readers in 1948: "Today we speak a little to shopkeepers, merchants and grocers, and, before the next Christmas Parties, we offer you an assortment of wines to have [or] drink for the entire month. Remembering the well-known phrase of 'in variety is the taste,' we wish that none of our wines go to your head."[64] The two-page spread offers little quips about a variety of wine, mostly Spanish, such as moscatel, rioja, amontillado, manzanilla, fino, oloroso, offering the reader a little written description of the wine, encouraging them to try it.

The magazine *Mundo Hispánico* offered readers two articles in 1951 to discuss the proper ways of drinking wine. Rafael García Serrano wrote: "There are two things that I have already advocated more than once: the teaching of good drinking and the teaching of mus." For his classes on wine, "it would be explained in the courses everything related to the different ways of drinking, from the *porrón* to the boot, passing through the game and the complicated and wonderful protocol of sherry wine, which is well organized so they have the knowledge of wines and hours, brands and types, courtesies and toasts."[65] Like mus (an Iberian-Basque card game) there were rules to the proper drinking of wine, from the style of serving (in the regional ways like the porrón, a glass wine pitcher with a long spout) to the type of wine to drink at the proper time. Castillo Puche advised readers how to drink different types of wine from various styles of glasses or implements; "ideally," he advises, "go slowly, racking the wine in short drinks, going from one to another without noticing that you are drinking but savoring with perfect calm what the wine has of mystery beyond the juice and aromas." But, no matter how you drink, Castillo reminded the reader, "wine makes the heart of man happy, says the Bible."[66]

In the same issue noted historian and gastronome Joaquin de Entrambasaguas presented a historical and cultural look at wines from La Rioja, which he lauded: "La Rioja integrates the glory of having created and raised [these wines] in the Paradise of its land these so-called table wines, so called because they are the only ones that can ally themselves with a good meal."[67] Not all these grapes of Rioja were native to Spain—he noted their eighteenth-century arrival from France—but, as time went by, the grapes became integrated into the identity and gastronomic culture of their adopted homeland.[68] Even though some of these vines were imported from France, Entrambasaguas made it very clear that, after many centuries, they had become truly Spanish: "Since then they are Spaniards, they have blood of Spain, juice on their soil, the warmth of its sun accompany the wines, with perfect harmony, the most exquisite delicacies in all the good tables of our country: the wines of La Rioja, with their Latin and Iberian phonetics, with their universal renown, which find the most passionate praise on the lips of all the cuisines of the world and come from that primitive wine."[69] The wines of Rioja had the spirit of Spain in their juice. Readers of this article could feel patriotism about this wine; they could feel the history of their nation in the drink.

The 1953 Exposición y Feria Oficial de la Viña y del Vino (Exposition and Official Fair of the Vineyard and Wine) in Vilafranca de Penedès in Catalonia printed a daily newsletter about the events of the fair. In the October 9, 1953, newsletter, an article entitled "Saber beber" (Know how to drink) offered its readers information about drinking wine correctly. It stated: "An art, with many easy secrets, but forgotten. The glasses, the temperature and the moment of serving the wines, form a subtle science of refined pleasures."[70] The article gave advice to the average wine drinker about how to enjoy their wine at the festival and at home:

> Knowing how to drink wines within the best libertarian orthodoxy is a small art with easy secrets, usually ignored or forgotten. A good drinker is not that vulgar being—vulgarity of ways—put daily in the tavern to rake glasses of wine without order or method and without seeking another pleasure than in the action of libations enter places that, as qualities, distinguish the perfect taster.
>
> A good taster, to be one, must be someone more than a regular entrant to the tavern: he must possess a sensitivity capable of making him know the taster's delight, which is what turns into art the simple but difficult fact of drinking.
>
> Actually, it is such a simple thing, and without complicating our existence, should be done with a little bit of care, not mixed with water or sweets, nor alternate drinking with cigarettes, so common among tavern drinkers. Ideally to define oneself as an excellent drinker is to purify the mouth first with a little bread, which will leave it in better condition to enjoy.[71]

The article aimed to demonstrate that drinking wine was not something vulgar to be done to get drunk, but an art that could be easily learned and that would likely raise one's personal standards. The article went on to discuss choosing the proper glass, serving wine at the appropriate temperature, selecting wine from the best regions, and pairing with the correct foods; in so doing, it helped to establish the rules for gastronomy and drinking wine. Other articles discussed these simple rules about tasting and serving wine to make a more informed drinker. In 1956 *Fotos* published an interview with wine taster José Carlos de Luna entitled, "Drink Wine with a 'Palate.'" In the article Luna stated: "The palate knows good wine. You must drink it in small sips . . . you have to smell it, even if you use the tongue instead of the nose."[72] The article also contained advice about serving the appropriate wine with the correct food. In 1966 the magazine *Destino* published "Adaptation of Wine with Plates," offering guidance about what wines to serve with what types of food. Clear points are made about drinking white wine with fish, red wine with meat, sweet wines with dessert, and avoiding wine with dishes heavy in vinegar.[73] While these rules were important to gastronomy, they also created drinkers who knew how to drink. The hope was that, if wine drinkers could see the art in their consumption, this could lead to a reduction of alcohol abuse and an increase in the purchase of good wines.

The National Syndicate for Wine, Beer, and Beverages, along with the Ministry for Information and Tourism, worked to develop a plan in June 1966 to educate the national population about wine and increase wine sales in the country. Both groups negotiated free television "spots" on TVE (Televisión Española) to promote their agenda. These spots would comment on "the characteristics of the wine [with] special mentions being made to the qualities and properties of the wine."[74] Other material shown on the program *Conoce Ud. España* (Do You Know Spain) highlighted the "Spanish vinicultural wealth from different regions."[75] This material, which contained images of the wine harvest throughout Spain, would be sent to cinemas across the country to be shown in the newsreels. Radio Nacional de España aired short clips to be played on the show *Alimentación* at 10:05 a.m. containing "a series of articles and comments on wine that the National Secretary of the Syndicate prepares and sends; this emission is directed principally to the housewives pretending to interest them in the purchase and consumption of *vinos de la mesa*."[76] The syndicate secretary also produced a series of brochures that would highlight the "qualities of wine [and] their tastes."[77] By using the Spanish media, these two government agencies could sell the benefits of drinking Spanish wine to the populace, especially the women who were in charge of purchasing food.

Both groups established other plans to increase consumption and formulate a positive identity for wine. The national secretary of the syndicate contacted the Fraud Repression Service in the Ministry of Agriculture to convey the request "with the greatest possible urgency... to avoid the excessive price that in some restaurants charged for wines consumed in them."[78] According to this agency, charging different prices for the same wine was a problem, as it might prevent consumers from ordering. The syndicate also announced a national poll to survey "the opinion on the consumption of wine, preferences, wine acquisitions, tastes, etc." of the Spanish wine drinker.[79] Finding out the tastes and preferences of the population would assist the syndicate in knowing what types of wines were popular. Lastly, the national secretary suggested that "a list of periodicals and magazines" be made to determine which ones would be willing to publish articles and notes friendly to the wine industry.[80] In all the wine industry tried to make more aggressive efforts to find out the interests of the consumers, while presenting them with propaganda cajoling them to purchase more wine.

A follow-up memorandum about the actions of the syndicate outlines the problems and hopeful solutions needed to increase wine consumption in the country. The file opens with concerns about "a related question about the low rate of consumption of wine in Spain. It was unanimous the opinion to promote increasing the consumption of wine by all means and actions."[81] In meetings of the syndicate in 1964 and 1965, it was determined that "the great problem that vitiviniculture was presented with is this decrease in consumption and that demanded the adoption of urgent measures, in order to ensure [the end of] low consumption levels observed in Spain."[82] One of the first problems associated with getting people to drink wine was that "it is known to all that there is an opinion contrary to the fact about drinking wine, no doubt due to ignorance of its real qualities and because some confuse use with abuse."[83] This internal memo mentions that people who do not drink wine do so out of a form of ignorance about the beverage—an interesting opinion to hold about possible new customers. Here one sees a mention of the questions about the abuse of wine, but to solve this the syndicate wanted to "publicize the properties and benefits derived from wine consumption."[84] Much like in the medieval and early modern periods and the nineteenth century, wine was not regarded simply as a drink, but as a beverage with true health benefits that maybe overrode concerns about overconsumption.

To get homes to purchase more wine, as mentioned in the early syndicate plan, it was important to get the primary shopper in the home to buy wine:

> A very important indicator, to which we dedicate preferential attention, is the one that can develop in the intimate circle of the home; we understand, that one of the main purposes of propaganda should be, to encourage the housewives who, it is so convenient to purchase a bottle of wine, such as bread, fruit or milk. Therefore, insisting on this aspect, using those magazines

or radio broadcasts that are read or heard by housewives, which we will involve a small contest on recipes that familiarize them to the use of wine in their daily condiments. And all this, always, under a form of concealed publicity in which commercial profit is not seen.[85]

As housewives were the main purchasers of foodstuffs, they needed to make buying a bottle of wine part of their daily shopping routine. This report clearly mentions the implied propaganda for the women in the form of articles, radio shows, and recipe contests that involve wine. If women would purchase wine each day, then consumption would clearly increase. As the Primo de Rivera regime had successfully changed the identity of orange consumption, making it a healthy food option, supplying housewives with recipes, and suggesting that desserts of native oranges saved time for the cook, perhaps the image and identity of wine could also be transformed for the housewife.[86]

The panache of wine had been lost over the previous decades, so the syndicate needed to restore its glamour—a feat that was going to be difficult:

> There is also a large mass of the public that must be won for wine. Unfortunately, it is a frequent opinion that wine is drunk by the lower classes, there are many cases in which we have seen modern establishments with the sign "wine is not served"; we have also been able to appreciate requesting a glass of wine in public, in more than one occasion, causing blushing or your request is met with an ironic smile. It is therefore necessary to start a campaign of public relations, in which through social events such as those already carried out and which are detailed below, we try to attract wine to the masses that today request exotic drinks, most of the time by "snobs." And this is not achieved by a massive propaganda in Television or Press, but by conviction that can be reached by more persuasive indirect means, if it is possible to expose, without apparent publicity, the damages of such errors.[87]

The fact that some restaurants in Spain stopped serving wine is a shocking detail for the third largest wine producer in the world. Wine was in a fight against the cocktail, and, to win, wine needed to change its identity from a low-class beverage to something with more style. At the same time, as tastemakers must have known, one cannot simply advertise wine and expect that people will drink it; wine needed to be made trendy, and the best way to do this was covertly. In a way Francisco Alonso Fernandez was correct in this study of Spanish alcoholism: clandestine propaganda in Spain associated alcohol, and in this case wine, with "'the right way to live,' which can only be regarded as hidden propaganda."[88]

Both the French and Spanish wine industries had important concerns in the twentieth century. French consumers were drinking too much wine, and at alarming rates, but the industry could not support teetotaling, as this would put hundreds of thousands of its citizens out of work. France needed to construct a new identity for wine, and the appellation system seemed to help. Wine was no longer a cheap and easily available industrial commodity that presented serious health risks but a quality and fancy beverage that, if consumed correctly, protected the national patrimony. Spanish wine producers had their own problems. National wine consumption was not as high as it should have been, and wine was viewed as a low-class beverage that was often abused rather than appreciated. Wine producers and the national syndicate needed to teach its population how to enjoy wine. There were many options available, and efforts were made to make connoisseurs rather than drunks. In the end it does appear that wine consumption increased thanks to the official government-supported propaganda, but the concept of a purely quality-based drinking system had yet to be established.

THE LESSONS OF WINE

From the medieval era until the early nineteenth century, wine was regarded not merely as a drink, but as a nutritional and medicinal beverage that helped the drinker. With the advent of better modern medicine, doctors began to question the health benefits of alcohol. At the same time, with the growth of an urban poor, many of whom drank too much and were uncontrollable, government agencies considered restricting the consumption of alcohol to keep these people under control. In both France and Spain, however, this plan posed a serious problem: both states' economies relied heavily on wine production, and reducing the sale of wine would be devastating. Therefore, a more nuanced plan needed to be developed to protect the national public health and sustain the wine industry.

For France the plan was the appellation system, which was put in place to create better drinkers who would appreciate the connection between their beverage and their culture. While the Spanish, too, wanted to improve the quality of their wine to earn more respect, their largest issue was trying to expand internal wine sales. Propaganda, either obvious or covert, worked to get Spaniards to think about wine differently. No longer would there just be red or white, but wines from regions like La Rioja and specialty wines like sherry received more attention in the media, highlighting their distinct characters and showing their important place in Spanish society. It was also considered necessary to teach the Spanish populace the rules of tasting and pairing. If drinking wine could be a skill or an art, then wine consumption could transcend the arena of the lower classes and take on a new bourgeois Spanish identity. By making Spanish wine convenient, quality, and classy, Spanish wine producers and the national syndicate gave Spaniards a new plan for how to drink wine and established a new meaning for the wine industry in Spain.

4

Wine Goes to the Fair

SPANISH WINE AT FESTIVALS AND CELEBRATIONS
FROM THE MONARCHY TO FRANCO

In his many books, eminent food scholar Sidney Mintz highlights the importance of food history. In a 2002 article he considers a variety of conundrums about how humans choose the foods they consume. "I used to argue that it would be easier to make a radical change in a country's politics than to change its fundamental diet," he writes, but "people can change their diets radically and quickly: a simultaneous conservatism, even obduracy, wedded to an odd lability or mimicry, this contrast lends mystery to food behavior—and the mystery is unsolved."[1] He continues: "I think that the significance of the difference between conservatism and trendiness in food can be made to yield analytically only by considering the backdrop of customary eating against which new foods or food novelties are tried."[2] As Mintz shows, while food is necessary for survival, choices of what food to eat are based upon long-standing cultural practices and trends, as well as trial and error. A key point for Mintz, however, is that national and regional cuisines "are brought into being by the political reality of the central state," suggesting that political will can influence what food or beverages are to be consumed to support national unity.[3] In the case of state-sponsored or state-funded festivals, the actions of those in power can manipulate or showcase certain understandings of food identity.

While the state does have a great deal of power, there are, of course, other actors who influence how the populace interacts with food. As mentioned in the introduction to this book, Montserrat Miller, Lara Anderson, Priscilla Parkhurst Ferguson, and Isabel González Turmo consider how interactions at the personal level—whether at a market, store, or restaurant—shape regional and national understandings of food. Therefore, while the central state may want to make changes to the perceptions of certain foods, the people purchasing and eating this food are also key factors in this development. Although wine is not necessary for human survival, people continue to drink it, try new types, or remain faithful to a particular type; it remains vital to the cultural identity of both the producer and the consumer. The success of Spanish wine producers was central to the survival of the national agricultural sector from the nineteenth century onward, when it became necessary to get more people to try Spanish wine, enjoy Spanish wine, and continue to drink Spanish wine. Consumers needed to see, sample, and incorporate it into their daily diets to protect the market. The wine festival acts as the intersection between the state, producers and sellers, and consumers.

This chapter explores a series of events sponsored by the Spanish government from the late nineteenth century through the Franco regime, its agricultural agencies, and its producers to showcase the country's wine industry. Fairs and festivals strove to develop a positive image of Spanish wines and introduced them to new consumers. Some events made wine their primary focus while in others it was one of many agricultural or cultural goods celebrated, but, in each case, planners gave special attention to the importance of wine to Spain's national identity. I argue from the late nineteenth century the Spanish government considered wine the perfect product to highlight the perceived improvements in the Spanish state, even when the rest of the country experienced numerous difficulties. These fairs and festivals presented Spanish wine in a positive light to consumers nationally and globally.

Food and drink have value to the producer and the consumer, and it is understandable that nations would be interested in displaying their most valued products. The history of consuming foodstuffs is based on "historical events [that] have a significant impact on the identifiable characteristics through the introduction of additional ingredients, cooking techniques, traditional methods of viticulture and winemaking methods to a region."[4] Therefore, food interests can change over time, as food is a "plastic commodity that operates in different ways all the time."[5] As shown previously with sherry, once popular styles lose market share, newer types may develop as interests change. As the image of food can change, outside forces can help to make certain commodities more desirable to the consumer. According to Melissa Johnson Morgan, "Food is a mechanism allowing people to make social distinctions and establish social linkages through the sharing of food and the expression of emotions towards others."[6] Therefore, "food and wine habits are derived by a variety of cultural norms and events that occur over time."[7] The wine prized today is not the same as it was in 1900; many events and issues have manipulated interests. Some of these events may be happenstance, such as environmental factors or accidental discoveries, but more deliberate issues can affect food choice as well.

This chapter examines how thoughtful choices can affect decisions made by consumers. Melissa Johnson Morgan makes the important point that "food should be recognized as a collection of contextual and evolving social practices where it no longer merely serves as sustenance but also a way to relate to other people in social, cultural, and political terms."[8] These choices have serious, yet possibly veiled, ramifications for their personal or national identities. This being said, these identities can be actively changed over time through government actions, innovation, or marketing. As Robert Harrington explains, "Historical events and governmental policies have a substantial impact on agricultural products. Taxation structures, inheritance customs and land tenure systems all affect how much food a farmer might keep for consumption or sell to the market and how much might be diverted to the ruling body."[9] If states support a particular industry, then governmental actions can help increase the sales of a particular commodity. As will be seen later, state-sponsored agricultural festivals can support one product and enhance the image of that good in the marketplace. Harrington explains that innovations in "food service operations can quickly take advantage of emerging trends and seasonal ingredients to satisfy the increasing desire for variety by consumers."[10] In the same vein, one could argue that producers of a commodity who make wise innovations at the point of production can capture more of the market. If a producer can get more of their product to market or survive a particular economic or environmental disaster, then their commodities can become more popular, such as the success of Codorníu cava following the phylloxera outbreak of the late nineteenth century. A third impact on food identity has been known to come from successful marketing, even before the establishment of the professional field. As Johnson Morgan argues, "Human desires obey various imperatives—tastes, fashion, status, culture and so on, and these desires shift as individuals absorb various social attachments. This means that desires and tastes are not static, that there is no fixed order or precedence in their satisfaction and actualization." One way to change these desires and tastes is to note "consumer demand for specific food items can be clearly aligned with trends in marketing."[11] If a government, regional agency, or producer can create a quality image of their product through wise marketing, advertising, or word-of-mouth, as the National Syndicate of Wine, Beer, and Beverages worked to do at the 1968 Casa de Campo International Fair in Madrid, then that product could hopefully gain new consumers in new markets.

A useful way to comprehend Francoist Spain's understanding of the importance of government actions, innovation, and marketing is to look at the bilingual booklet *España en forma* (*Spain Re-Shaped*), published in 1964 as a companion to Spain's appearance at the New York World's Fair. It opens with a letter from Franco ally and filmmaker-propagandist Gumersindo Montes Agudo, who states: "We present our publication with the sincere desire to serve the Spanish nation, with a spirit of perseverance and in recognition of the important collaborators we have been able to bring together. They lend prestige to our intention, they determine the documental key and the noble style of pages that are being opened on the marvelous opportunity that the New York World's Fair has offered our country."[12] This global event, centered in the cultural capital of the United States, would give Spain the opportunity to show off its progress and, hopefully, earn friends, especially during a time when trade compacts in Europe were becoming stronger. Montes Agudo continues, "Before the future integration of Spain in the European Economic Community—in which inappropriate jealousies and prejudices are still maintained—we present a sincere industrial balance, a panorama of our cultural, technical and economic situation, and a systematical review of our desires, achievements, and possibilities of a country unanimously moving towards the enterprise of national development."[13] This World's Fair would be a chance for Spain to market itself as a modernizing country on par with its European allies and rivals. Montes Agudo did realize, however, that Spanish development was not complete; he concludes, "We ourselves, aware of our limitations, shall prepare a new volume which will continue the realistic exposition begun in this one."[14] With governmental support Spain could display its innovations and promote itself, but there was more to do in the future.

España en forma also discusses the role and importance of festivals and fairs and their changes over time. From the earliest fairs, these events offered producers a chance to reach a larger number of consumers. *España en forma* explains, "Old-fashioned fairs were gatherings of buyers and foreign sellers, where the buyers stocked up on articles that were not produced in their region, where they oriented their production to the needs and tastes of the consumers, at the same time fixing and leveling their prices. But when economic life became rather intensive and capable of sustaining an active reciprocal current between supply and demand, the traditional fairs began to lose their old mercantile character. But then the modern Exposition came, renewing a long-interrupted mercantile tradition."[15] Modern fairs, while still offering producers and consumers a marketplace to trade, did have to adapt to changes in technology and increasing globalization, as the Spanish World's Fair commission understood. *España en forma* continues: "The dynamics of today's commercial movement demands a rapid, precise, and widest possible orientation on the products that pertain to each specialty and which will necessarily contribute to the success of the business. The buyers seek able producers and high-quality articles. The producers, a broad market able to absorb their production. Every merchant seeks, in our always smaller world, economic and commercial points of attraction which would be able to offer a concentrated, precise and the widest possible picture about the situation of his fields of interest in the world of trade."[16] Fairs stand at an important crossroads, especially for countries trying to change their global identity, as Spain had done numerous times. "The function of the fairs," according to *España en forma*, "is to give, receive, and mediate on the international commercial campgrounds. From them, one can gather a vivid impression of the market of the country in which the fair is being celebrated, with great efficiency and commercial capability in the field or line of manufacture which each fair serves."[17] These fairs allow other states to understand the demands of consumers at a larger scale. At the same time, they offer the participants various innovations: "Fairs and international expositions are the barometer of technical progress and of standard of living. They offer in the important fields of property, equipment, and consumption represented there an overall view of the presented products and a broad orientation of the international supply. As a market, information center, and meeting place, the fairs also encourage exportation of the participating countries."[18] Whether it was a medieval village fair or the 1964 World's Fair, participants understood the benefits to regional and national economies and the importance of participating and offering quality items. In this case the

Spanish government clearly understood that importance. This chapter will examine the role of government action, innovations, and marketing in a series of festivities meant to showcase Spain's vibrant wine industry and create new consumers for a vital economic product.

THE 1893 WORLD'S COLUMBIAN EXPOSITION, CHICAGO

In 1893 the Spanish Ministry of Agriculture, Industry, and Commerce planned to showcase Spanish wines at the Columbian Exposition in Chicago. At the end of the nineteenth century, as Spain's last vestiges of empire fell apart, the Spanish state-initiated policies of "economic protectionism"; in this context, actively wooing new markets made sense.[19] It was also necessary to ensure that the wine being sent was of a high quality and reasonably priced. This mattered because "the value of many regional products is based on more direct and immediate trust: the producer stands by and guarantees the product. . . . The consumer is promised quality."[20] In this case the Spanish Ministry needed to guarantee that a quality product would leave Spain and arrive in Chicago. Therefore, the ministry set forth a series of rules for those wine producers wishing to participate in the event.

First, it must be understood why the Spanish Ministry was so interested in participating in this exposition. Spain had only recently begun to recover from the large-scale phylloxera attack, and by 1892 exports to French markets had begun to slow down. With the changing global market dynamics, Spanish wine producers needed "to search for new markets, study the tastes and demands of these, to work out the elaboration taking into account these same circumstances, and, finally, to undertake an active, constant and intelligent propaganda to make wines and wines known everywhere, make them reach the consumer in all countries as directly as possible, in order to get in price, quality and purity, the greatest advantages in the rough competition with similar wines from other nations."[21] To get new consumers to purchase and later demand these Spanish wines, producers had to maintain a level of quality to compete with more established wine exporters, and the Spanish Ministry believed national quality had already been established. The ministry believed that Spanish wines "are already known and obtain great esteem and price in many consumer markets, competing with foreign classes already very old and distinguished."[22] As previous chapters have shown, however, it was still debatable as to whether or not Spanish wines had reached this level of prestige.

To succeed in this project, the government had to involve themselves in the production process:

> This General Directory, eager to contribute to this reviving project and to encourage it by all means within its reach, could not help but worry about opening up new horizons to our wine production and making the export path of this very important branch everywhere of our wealth. To this end and taking advantage of the happy circumstance of the great international festivities that will be held in the United States of America, this Center has agreed to organize in that country a great manifestation of our viniculture production, a manifestation that will consist of a collective exhibition of wines, spirits, and liquors, and that by the exceptional conditions in which it is carried out, it can make known at a single stroke, and by brilliant way, the expressed products in those very important markets, and be the opening of an active propaganda that assures and extends the consumption of our wines in those countries.[23]

This was a major opportunity for Spanish vintners, and it was necessary that it went well. Thus, this ministry wanted to check all aspects of the goods being sent. The memorandum continues: "In order for the success of this thought and to respond to the wishes of this Management Center and at the same time satisfy the needs of our viniculture production, competent and expert people were sent to North America in these matters, who, in addition to taking advantage of the circumstances of the Exhibition in favor of trade in Spanish wines, to study the conditions of that market and establish a wine production station, which permanently promotes and ensures our wine exports in that region." By sending experts the Spanish government hoped to strengthen the image of their products. Most importantly, this exposition would represent a display of government action, the presentation of innovation, and the marketing of wine:

> The General Directorate of Agriculture, Industry and Commerce has the decisive cooperation of the Spanish growers, who surely convinced of the benefits of this project will support the wishes of this Direction and will

contribute to the Exhibition of Spanish Wines held in Chicago within the great international exhibition is an accurate and faithful reflection of our vinicultural production and demonstrates to the view of the whole world there, and mainly of the North American people, unknowledgeable today of our wines, that these, for their quality, for their inexpensiveness, for such a rich variety of classes, can sustain victorious in competition with those of all the other wine nations.[24]

This unification between the government and local producers would be key for success, as both sides would benefit from increased sales in the Americas.

To create a positive image of these Spanish wines at the Columbian Exhibition, the ministry established professional guidelines for them. The more professional the packaging of the products, the more successful the ministry and producers would be in selling them. The ministry was "very satisfied if in this way it can maintain, in which it appears many Spanish producers want to go under the prescribed basis. The Agriculture Ministry will meet the expenses incurred for transport from Madrid, the exhibition, custody and preservation of the exhibited items."[25] Strict rules were required to participate in the event. To guarantee a professional appearance, "the liquids that will be exhibited will be sent in new bottles, provided with labels, indicating the class of liquid, its origin and the name of the exhibitor. Same label, with the same indications, must be in the other containers in which other articles are sent." To assure cleanliness of the product, "the bottles should be washed twice, at least, with water, and, finally, with a small amount of the same liquid that they contain." The product must be protected: "All bottles must be capped or sealed, so that there is no loss or alteration of the liquid contained therein. Efforts will be made to send these bottles in wooden boxes and covered with straw covers or wrapped in hay, to prevent the breakage of those." To guarantee sufficient product, "for common red and white wines, three dozen bottles of each type of wine, contained in a single box." To highlight the professionalism of the wineries, "on the outside of each box, a label or inscription with the name of the sender and class and origin of the product will be posted." The ministry also set clear dates for product registration (December 15) and for shipments of the wine to Madrid (December 25), rules for registration forms, and guidelines for commercial shipping manifests.[26] In each the Spanish government set forth clear rules and regulations for the producers. If they followed these rules to secure consistency and quality in the shipment, then they could participate.

Concerning the 1893 Columbian Exposition, both the Spanish state and Spanish wine producers saw great potential in this event. New consumers needed to be found, and establishing a quality image for their wines in the Americas would be a great help for these vintners. Government action could be utilized to create a new identity for this product and showcase its successes and innovations in a new market. By establishing clear guidelines for the production of quality wine, then consumers in the New World markets could appreciate the best of Spain.

SHERRY IN BORDEAUX

In 1895 sherry producers from Jerez de la Frontera sent their wines to France to be tried at the Exposition Universelle de Bordeaux. This was an important period for Spanish wine producers, as the French market for Spanish wines was reducing, but sherry had not yet gained traction in France as it had in Britain. This event would give sherry producers a chance to educate French wine drinkers about their products. The end of the nineteenth century was also an important moment in the discussion of rules, connoisseurship, and health issues surrounding the consumption of wine and alcohol. The 1890s were a period of concern in France as anti-alcohol advocates gained ground.[27] Even with the growth of anti-alcohol crusaders, the idea of wine representing an important part of French culture remained.[28] The idea was: drink better quality wine, and live a wonderful life. Hard alcohol, especially absinthe, was the true enemy of the French people; medical groups like the Academy of Medicine suggested drinking less, but "endorsed the increase in wine consumption."[29] Wine was considered different; it was part of French national identity. The consumption of quality French wine also expressed certain values key to an improving society, as "a visible sign of rank and class membership for the aspiring elite in public spaces."[30] Therefore, if one wanted to maintain elite status, or appear higher-class, they must drink quality wine as a public expression of this identity. To make sure one was drinking the correct wine, one had to know what good wine was. As Kolleen Guy explains, "Connoisseurship, however, depends also on 'intuitive judgment' or good taste. . . . Taste can be improved with proper education."[31] One could learn to drink good wine and consume wine well and thereby elevate themselves in class status. If sherry could present itself as a quality wine with a unique taste that could not be replicated and establish a trendy identity, then this wine could grow in the French market.

As France aimed to get its population to drink wine well (without overindulging) and learn about the product, producers from Jerez de la Frontera wanted to showcase their unique sherry wine in France. When the nineteenth-century oidium and phylloxera crises devastated the French wine industry, Spanish red wine producers took advantage of this fact, but Jerez wines did not see this boom in France. The sherry catalog for the 1895 Exposition Universelle de Bordeaux states: "The wine trade with France has taken a great expansion and increased the wealth of many Spanish provinces, but its beneficial influence has not been felt on the market of Jerez. This is because our territories do not produce red wines."[32] As sherry was not the wine of choice for the French, producers now had to market their product in France as a quality-based and special alternative. One key move was to educate the French about the location, innovation, and patrimony of this unique region and its wines: "The Committee of Xérès [Jerez de la Frontera] brings together several cities of Andalucía. In the first place, it is Jerez de la Frontera, then Sanlúcar de Barrameda, Chiclana, Chipiona and Rota. These five cities constitute the most important wine center of Andalucía. Jerez de la Frontera has an important agricultural school and it can be said that it is this city—in which, from all antiquity, the vineyard has been in honor—which has been, from the point of view of viticulture and wine, the educator of all over the region."[33] The producers boasted, "We have seen with pleasure to appear in this great wine festivity of Bordeaux 1895 the most complete collection that has ever been presented in an Exhibition, of our true Jerez: Amontillados, Olorosos, Pedro Ximénez, Moscatel, Manzanilla, Tintilla de Rota, which are without rivals."[34] The sherry producers were greatly satisfied to see "how much these wines have been appreciated not only by the Jury members, but also by the public," and to notice "that in all the official grand banquets given on the occasion of the Bordeaux Exhibition, Jerez wine was served after the soup course, appearing next to the great wines of the Gironde."[35] This event proved to be an excellent opportunity for sherry to receive attention in Bordeaux.

There was a serious obstacle, however, to sherry entering the French market in the nineteenth century. First, sherry is a unique fortified wine with an increased alcohol percentage, which presented problems exporting the drink to certain markets. For the French, though, the main problem concerning sales dealt with the process of making sherry and the activity of plastering: a process of adding gypsum, potash, or calcium sulphate to clarify wines, such as sherry. This was a major issue, as producers acknowledged: "But as far as France is concerned, it is well known that one of the main causes of these difficulties is the question of plastering. We have already indicated that, following a very old practice, our best wines show three or four grams of sulphate of potash per liter, whereas the recent French law tolerates only two grams," as France prohibited the plastering of wine and "prohibit[ed] their importation, raising formidable obstacles."[36] French plastering laws made the importation and consumption of sherry difficult if not illegal. Sherry producers, however, had a strong response to this issue; they tried to restrict plastering, but it affected the quality of the beverage. The producers asserted, "We have argued a hundred times, we will not reproduce them here, because they remain undisputed; but we must insist on the perfect innocence of our fine wines and liqueur wines, great even though they would have four or five grams of sulphate of potash, since their daily consumption is limited to very small quantities." They claimed that the "eminent professors, physicians, and the most distinguished hygienists" supported the fact that these wines were safe.[37] Interestingly, the sherry producers contended that since only a small amount of sherry was consumed each day, the plastering process did not outweigh the health benefits of the drink. This fit into the larger argument in France about alcohol consumption during this period. At the end of their catalog, the producers expressed their hope that the restrictions on the importation of plastered wines would not remain an issue, and that more sherry would be allowed to enter France.[38]

The sherry producers of Jerez de la Frontera used the Bordeaux exhibition to their advantage. Not only were they able to showcase their wines to the wine tasting juries at the event, but they were also able to have their wines tasted by locals. These producers wanted to communicate certain messages about their drink: that it was unique among any other beverage that could be purchased; that it came from a specialized region in Spain in a similar manner to French agricultural regionalism; that it had had health benefits that doctors of the time supposedly acknowledged; and that the supposed harms of plastering could be overlooked if consumers knew that they only needed to drink a small amount of sherry each day. Showcasing sherry introduced the French wine connoisseur to an innovative product that could become a new luxury item. However, even with this positive message, as future chapters will show, sherry never gained a strong foothold in France.

THE KING OF SPAIN AND THE KING OF CAVA

On April 17, 1904, King Alfonso XIII visited the small Catalan city of Sant Sadurní d'Anoia, the capital of cava, or Spanish sparkling wine. During this one-day trip, the king met with regional agricultural leaders from Catalonia and the Balearic Islands in Codorníu. The meeting and subsequent banquet were meant to discuss the regional agricultural successes, but of all the locations to be chosen, the celebration occurred on the property of the country's largest cava producer. Regional agriculture was the central issue, but, as reports from the event show, wine took the central stage. This section will explore a series of newspaper reports and communications from the grand meeting to highlight the power of Codorníu and other wine producers when discussing regional issues and highlight the grandeur associated with this meeting on both sides.

The choice of Bodegas Codorníu as the main location for this visitation is significant. The Codorníu family has a long history of wine production in the region, dating as far back as the sixteenth century.[39] What finally separated Codorníu from other producers was the development of cava, Spain's version of sparkling wine, first created by Josep Raventós Fatjó in 1872.[40] In 1879 Codorníu distributed seventy-two cases of cava in Barcelona, creating a frenzy among local restauranteurs.[41] In 1885 Manuel Raventós took over leadership of Codorníu, traveling to France to study the *méthode champenoise* to improve cava production and spearheading the development of new machinery in Sant Sadurní to increase production.[42] Cava uses different grapes than French champagne, relying on the local Catalan grapes of macabeo, xarel·lo, and parellada, but the process of its creation follows the same rules from France (to be discussed in chapter 7). Most importantly, Manuel Raventós was a scientific innovator in the region, using new methods to fight mildew attacks and phylloxera outbreaks in 1887. The newspaper of the San Isidro Agricultural Institute of Catalonia reported that Bodegas Codorníu stood "out as a green meadow in the middle of a desert wilderness" during the years of the wine plagues.[43] In a 1909 book, Sant Sadurní city clerk Pelegrí Torelló suggested that he was one of the "Seven Sages of Greece" who saved the region's agricultural industry.[44] Codorníu's cavas also got a boost in 1897 when Queen Regent María Cristina of Austria visited the bodega and made Codorníu the official provider of cavas for the Spanish Royal Palace and the Royal Army.[45] With all these successes and innovations, cava became inexorably tied with Manuel Raventós and Bodegas Codorníu. Therefore, it should come as no surprise that when King Alfonso XIII traveled to the region in 1904 to discuss agriculture, this was the estate he visited.

The king's visit to Codorníu was such a special occasion that the bodega collected all the newspaper articles they could find to commemorate the event. On April 25, *El Nervión* (Bilbao) explained a central reason for the king's visit to this bodega: "One of the most successful Catalan producing centers that has most impressed the Monarch, has undoubtedly been the industrial colony that don Manuel Raventós has established in San Sadurní d'Anoia, and whose growing aggrandizement is intimately linked to the celebrity that he enjoys, inside and outside of Spain, the Codorníu champagne, which is made there."[46] The festivities for the king would be lustrous, as Codorníu wanted to celebrate his visit with much aplomb: "Our dear chief don Manuel Raventós, president of the Catalan-Balearic Agricultural Federation, was honored by His Majesty King Alfonso XIII with a visit to the Codorníu Caves. To correspond with dignity, Mr. Raventós organized, in honor of His Majesty, a luncheon with the assistance of almost all the presidents of agricultural and economic societies of Catalonia and the Balearic Islands, resulting in a great celebration of our agriculture."[47] *El Noticiero Universal* reported on April 17 that "the entrance of the bodega was adorned with bows, flowers, and shields," and *La Dinastía* wrote on April 18, "On a white canvas with the red letters read, 'Today you work with permission of the ecclesiastical authority'" as Manuel Raventós made an agreement with the church to allow the monarch to see the production on a Sunday.[48] According to *El Diluvio*, on April 18, the city and this bodega were a wonderful sight with its five kilometers of caves, two million bottles of cava, large workforce, capital investment, and shining example of the successes of regional agriculture.[49] *La Dinastía* stated that, while visiting the bodega, "the King saw, one by one, those operations that go from the elaboration or composition of the champagne to the bottling, capping and labeling, being greeted by the passing of people who, enthusiastic about his presence, given incessantly by the workers, some of them expressing themselves in Catalan, with spontaneity that satisfied the Monarch."[50] The workers of the bodega had given the king a wonderful tour that allowed him to see the process of making this famous drink.

Following the tour of the buildings, the king and approximately two hundred guests joined Manuel Raventós for an elaborate luncheon located in the cellars. *La Dinastía* wrote:

> The grandiose central room of the cellars had been arranged in three tables capable of the two hundred guests, presided over by the Monarch, for whom the party occurred. The central table, occupied by don Alfonso, sitting on a sumptuous throne and having to his right the lords Raventós and General Linares, and to the left the lord Duke of Sotomayor and generals Polavieja and Pacheco.... For the restaurant *Maison Dorée*, in Barcelona, served a delicate and splendid menu, in which, and for times, included the Champagnes Codorníu *Extra Seco* and *Non plus ultra*, which were justified by their exquisite palate, that equals those of the best foreign brands.[51]

About the dining room, *Diario de Comercio* wrote on April 18, "The improvised dining room produced a beautiful effect. In the center, among ornaments of flowers, were the shields of Spain, Barcelona and Sant Sadurní, the figure of the monarch and a large poster in which the words of don Alfonso read 'I want to be the first farmer of Spain.'"[52] On April 20 *La Época* reported on the menu:

LUNCH IN HONOR OF HIS ROYAL MAJESTY, DON
ALFONSO XIII GIVEN BY THE HOUSE OF CODORNÍU:

González Byass Sherry: Broth and hors d'oeuvres.
Torre de Remey (white): Riojan Salmon
Codorníu *Extra Seco*: Beef Filet Real
Marques de Riscal: Galantine of Turkey, sweet ham and asparagus
Non plus ultra Codorníu: Roasted Capon
Marques de Camps: Biscuit Gelato
Fruit Salad—Sweets
Coffee—Cognac Domecq—Cinnamon calisaya

As one can see, all the wines are Spanish.[53]

Along with the illustrious meal came a short speech by Manuel Raventós, as reported by *El Noticiero Universal*:

"Welcome, sir, to this house where more than 70 societies of the Catalan Balearic Agricultural Federation are represented.

"All of us gathered in the visit to thank you, as admirers of the virtues of your mother; and hoping before your declaration of which you are the first farmer of Spain, evokes the famous phrases of Napoleon, that said 'The farmer who makes grow two ears in the land where it did not produce before more than one, double the territory of the State.'

"We, the Catalan farmers, want to double this part of our kingdom, but we stumble upon the instigation of the laws, with ever increasing taxes, with taxes and consumptions that indirectly foment artificial wine."

He made some references to the economic concert, adding that the direct administration is ruinous for Catalonia and for the Treasury.

"With this," he added, "it would be possible to double production, now contained within narrow limits, the effect of which existing laws annul particular initiatives."

"Here," he finally said, "you will find Your Majesty loyalty and desire to work, and with the help of God, without wasting time in sterile political struggles, we will give this region such greatness, that your greatest pride will be to govern us."[54]

Wine and cava, Manuel Raventós explained, were vital to the national economy. As Robert Harrington and Melissa Johnson Morgan have shown, government assistance, innovation, and marketing were key to the success and strong market share of an agricultural good. In this case Spain's most famous cava producer publicly told the king that the government needed to end practices that harmed vintners and prevented innovation. As Raventós makes abundantly clear, wine was an important component of the national economy, and these producers wanted to do as much as they could to help.

A strong agricultural sector in Catalonia would be necessary for the success of the Spanish state, as the king's visit was intended to highlight this fact. *El Nervión* wrote, "In the visit of King Alfonso XIII to Barcelona and other towns of the industrious Catalonia, demonstrative facts have been verified that this trip can be extremely fruitful for the great national interests, for those supreme interests that have their indestructible base and their powerful impulse in the intelligence and in the constant laboriousness of those who dedicate themselves to increase and perfect the production and industries of Spain."[55] On April 28, *La Gaceta del Norte* reported: "The analyses read and delivered to the King in his visit to the various regions and agricultural centers of Catalonia manifest the needs that must be met so that the agricultural industry, flourishing today in Spain, can operate with full force and give us all the fruit and the riches that we have the right to expect from it."[56] The growth of agriculture was not just economically important; as "lovers of everything that can contribute to the aggrandizement of the homeland, we gladly cooperate to propagate these manifestations of the national culture."[57] Wine and cava were patriotic drinks that needed to be assisted and protected by the state.

The visit of King Alfonso XIII to Bodegas Codorníu underscores the importance of wine production to both the national economy and national identity for Spain at the start of the twentieth century. Manuel Raventós innovated his product and its production to create a strong niche market for his beverages. While this event was not solely for wine producers, it was cava that received the most attention by the king and the press. By showcasing the successes of this bodega, regional vintners emphasized the central and vital identity of Spanish wine.

SHOWCASING THE SHERRY HARVEST

The Fiesta de Vendimia (Harvest Festival) begins the first weekend of September each year in Jerez de la Frontera to honor the sherry grape harvest and lasts approximately one month. Started in 1948, during the Franco regime, the event highlights the importance of the harvest and its connections to the local economy and culture. Today it includes a Catholic ceremony at the city's cathedral, a celebration of local *toreros*, motorcycle races, art exhibits, local performances of flamenco, tours of bodegas, tastings, and the crowning of the Vendimia queen.[58] This section looks at a sample of articles about the festival to explore the way these events foreground the local Andalusian culture while emphasizing the economic importance of the unique wine produced in Jerez. Although travelers—most of whom in the years following the Civil War were Spanish—visited this small city because of the wine, once there, they were exposed to other aspects of local culture that helped to define the region.

Local agricultural festivals can benefit the economy and enhance a local identity. As Abel Duarte Alonso argues, "Festivals constitute expressions of culture of the local territory, and their goals include promotion, dissemination, and the preservation of cultural heritage."[59] Especially in contemporary society, these food festivals help a region "brand" its location and local products while attempting to expand its market.[60] Food and festivals also increase local tourism, as many outsiders come to the location to attend the events and support local development. According to Bodil Stilling Blichfeldt and Henrik Halkier, "Specifically, food festivals have come to play an important role in many rural development and branding strategies that revolve around the commodification of local cultural resources."[61] The celebration of this wine supports a regional identity and a regional economy: come for the wine, stay for the culture, and spend money.

Harvest festivals take place in a variety of regions, often developed from smaller celebrations that formerly occurred on farms.[62] Many of these festivals share events in an effort to create a specific local identity as concepts cross borders. Grape harvest festivals in Switzerland, with their floats and religious symbols, inspired similar events in northern Italy.[63] While these festivals could occur under any type of government, totalitarian regimes did see a specific benefit in highlighting a specific crop that represented a country's national identity. As Lara Anderson shows, the totalitarian Franco regime was very interested in indoctrinating its people through food.[64] Italy celebrated its "National Day of the Grape Harvest Festival" in 1930 under Benito Mussolini as "an effective way to boost grape and wine sales nationwide through an extensive schedule of festivals centered on grapes and wine."[65] Fascist Italy considered these themed celebrations "to be effective tools to re-launch tourism and the local economy."[66] Specifically, these Italian wine harvest festivals were meant to "revive the wine growing and producing sector that had suffered. . . . These festivals had to be organized by local committees and had to conform to certain criteria: provide a contest for 'the best offer of grape sales' and set up a parade with people dressed up as traditional peasants and decorated harvest festival floats."[67] French wine producers in Burgundy created their own events to celebrate wine, going so far as to pay local journalists to write positive commentary about the beverage.[68] In 1934 a group of Burgundian wine producers created the brotherhood Confrérie des Chevaliers du Tastevin to construct a tradition of historical wine production in the region—a type of group that had never existed before. At many of their meetings, the brotherhood invited members of the community and food journalists to visit to try the local food and wine. Journalists wrote about "a gastronomic 'tradition' they themselves had helped to construct, and they expressed their great pleasure at having the opportunity to see it materialized by Burgundian vineyard owners."[69] In both democratic and fascist regimes, wine and the celebrations associated with it could be used to construct an identity for a region and its culture. The sherry harvest events in Jerez could rely upon government support and a sympathetic press to create a perceived identity for the region.

The magazine *Fotos* offered many pages to the discussion of the Jerez Vendimia Festivals of the 1950s. A sympathetic media paying a great deal of attention to the grandeur of this event surely contributed to their success. About the 1956 event J. F. Avellaneda Lucas writes, "We wanted the people of Jerez to be more purely rooted and enthusiastic about everything that represents praise in the name of Jerez that goes to the stage of honor . . . in which this beautiful and wonderful city also celebrates with national resonance festivals that it has extolled" for its wine and "for the prestige of our country in the world."[70] This celebration was not just for wine, but for the whole city. Of the Jerez city hall, don Francisco Paz Género explained, "More than 40,000 electric bulbs are installed, in addition to four entrance porticos of great showiness. They also place a multitude of garlands and thousands of pots that give it a fantastic look." The city supported an "amusement park [that] is considered one of the best in Spain. Imagine, that all the existing ones in the Fairs of Seville and localities of our surroundings come here" to see the park.[71]

About the 1959 festival, *Fotos* included the closing comments from the mayor of Jerez, Tomás García Figueras, to visitors: "Jerez de la Frontera has just celebrated with joy, beauty, and splendor its XI Festival of the Vendimia. It exalts in the city the annual birth of its famous wines, the origin of a creative and fruitful activity that directly or indirectly reaches all sectors of the city."[72] The festival was also meant to open the city to the world, as each year a foreign country was chosen to be honored; "this year has been Ireland, to participate in its happiness; Jerez, splendidly rich in external values: song, dance; in artistic and historical manifestations; in underlined aspects of its wealth, horses, brave bulls, coordinates each year these factors to the service of making singular the

Feast of its Vendimia."[73] By using its wines, Jerez invited new visitors to the region to assist the local economy.

This harvest celebration also provided an opportunity to highlight the role of sherry in the country's cultural identity. Right-wing poet and dramatist from Cádiz José María Pemán y Pemartín spoke of the importance of sherry and this festival in 1957. When asked what he thought about sherry, he replied, "I believe that wine has a cosmic entity.... All the wines have had literature."[74] There was a need, therefore, to create a new literature and language for the wine of this era. Pemán used the phrase "Wine is the only industry without a chimney" to indicate that its production could reach an industrial level, but that the factories did not look like those that are made of steel or machines.[75] When asked if he got something out of these festivals, he replied, "Undoubtedly. On the one hand, the literary contests that are being celebrated are a great success.... Last year many quotes from the Jerez wine were collected, motivated by the homage to Shakespeare."[76] When asked why Shakespeare wrote so much about sherry, Pemán stated, "England does not have wine. At the time when Franco-English relations were difficult, much Sherry wine was sold. Shakespeare, who captured and was receptive of English life, then took care of our wines, citing them on numerous occasions, and from then on, the export was on the increase."[77] Sherry was not only a drink but also a symbol in literature, and this festival was a place where the literary arts could also be celebrated.

That same year *Fotos* discussed the art of the *venenciador*, or man (*venenciadora* for a woman) who uses a long stick to remove sherry from its barrels to taste: "According to the dictionary, '*Venencia* (f) is an instrument composed of a cylindrical container of corrugated silver or other matter, of reduced capacity, and of a rod, usually of whalebone, of about 80 centimeters of length, ending in a hook. Used in Jerez de la Frontera to obtain small amounts of must contained in a boot. From *venencia*, then, comes to *venenciar*, to make use of it, and *venenciador*, the one that uses or manages it."[78] The art is "so graceful of its silhouette, [it] can be a symbol of elegance or subtlety."[79] While this action is used to taste the wine to check its quality during the aging process, it has also become a show for the tourists:

According to this *venenciador* [Pepe Ortega Garcia] and consummate teacher, the art of *venenciar* consists of a lot of pulse, precision, elegance, and in knowing, pouring the wine into the cup at the minimum height of one meter. "On some occasions, when visitors come in considerable numbers, I have many glasses." I was surprised by Ortega with sixteen glasses in his left hand ... *venencia* in hand, does not stop taking wine from his boots, under the gaze of the curious. "Not everyone, including those who live among the soleras of rich wines, knows how to use *venencia* and fill up even a glass." Ortega's mastery has been captured infinitely by film cameras, and those who know him know his agility, dexterity, and art.[80]

The act of serving sherry from the boot or barrel had become an art to be displayed to those visiting the city. Everything associated with sherry, it seems, had a practice and cultural meaning that could be celebrated at the Fiesta de Vendimia.

With the help of government support and a regional product, the Franco regime and its local allies boosted the public profile of this beverage. The product needed to be promoted correctly to gain more markets. Jerez de la Frontera had successfully branded itself as the capital of sherry, and this festival allowed consumers to get a firsthand view of the product. At the same time, the articles written about this festival allowed readers across Spain to experience the celebration and uniqueness of this place.

SHOWCASING WINE

Visitors could attend festivals to see the results of wine making, but the construction of cultural museums for wine also allowed tourists to understand the complete process of wine, from history and soil to processing and tasting. In 1968 the Spanish National Syndicate for Wine, Beer, and Beverages planned the installation of the temporary Museo Nacional del Vino (National Museum of Wine) in Madrid for that year's Casa de Campo (Cottage) International Festival. The museum would not only focus on the harvest but would also take the visitors through a series of rooms to trace the path of wine and highlight its cultural importance to Spanish patrimony. The syndicate wanted the visitors to understand clearly the cultural significance of wine to the country and to Western civilization.

While the museum for wine was intended to show the changing innovation in the wine industry over the centuries, it also needed to highlight the importance of the role of wine for national folklore. As Gilles Laferté writes, "The two perceptions of the countryside are directed at different and complementary contemporary markets: on one side, we have the modernist, technical perception . . . on the other side, we find the perception of the traditional village and the aesthetic and recreational use of land for the needs of tourism and luxury produce."[81] If the countryside could occupy both the roles of modern agriculture and traditional identity, then museums that displayed agricultural products needed to highlight these two concerns. The modern view of wine making could not discredit the historical past or folklore associated with its production, or it might diminish the message of what wine means to a nation and a consumer. Highlighting tradition and folklore in this museum could make a society feel proud about itself. As Laferté notes, "Folklore, therefore, was above all a cultural activity rooted in the dominant national ideology, with both a learned side—a search for would-be regional, national, popular, and ancestral origins, an unchanging civilization disappearing under the impact of industrialization and modernity."[82] The construction of this museum could establish this dominant national ideology, one in which wine was central to the country's history and identity. Laferté explains these folkloric events—or, in this case, location—for the public were "meant to revive those traditions among the people by trying to disseminate these localized practices among local elites."[83] Showing visitors, both elite and nonelite, the identity and folklore of the countryside could help construct a better connection between the rural and urban—something that would be quite useful for a modernizing Spain in 1968.

A March 13, 1968, memorandum from the syndicate highlighted the main points in the planned temporary museum and explained the goals for the displays. A visit to the Museum began in sector 1: "Mythology and Wine." In this section visitors would see writing about Dionysus, read portions of Homer's works on wine, and view copies of Greek and Roman amphoras provided by the National Archaeological Museum.[84] Sector 2, "Sayings and Wine," offered reproductions of scenes from *Don Quixote* that highlighted imagery from the sixteenth century, including glasses, books, and mosaics showing wine drinking.[85] Visitors then passed into sector 3, "Wine and the Bible," which contained installations that made reference to the drinking of wine in the Bible, displayed copies of chalices and drinking devices from the era, and showed scenes with biblical heroes like Noah.[86] The fourth sector of the museum, "Wine and Art," featured reproductions of artworks that highlighted wine drinking, such as

Goya's *El dios Baco*, Velázquez's *Los borrachos*, and Ruben's *The Harvest*. These first four sections worked to make concrete connections between wine and cultural identity, underscoring the religious importance of wine for Catholics while demonstrating that the casual consumption of wine had even reached high art.

From there visitors explored the technical aspects of wine making, storage, and service. Sector 5, "Ancient Techniques" displayed harvesting tables, pressing tables, and vertical presses used by older societies to produce wine.[87] Sector 6, "The History of Bottling Wine," featured ancient amphoras and modern bottles used to contain and ship wine.[88] Sector 7, "Glasses and Wine," exhibited a variety of containers used to serve wine, from fancy crystal glasses to the porrón.[89] "Man Has Always Wanted to Take Wine with Him" was the theme of sector 8, where a variety of barrels and other shipping and carrying devises were shown.[90] Following these educational sectors, visitors could pass to the reception center, where they could view a large mural showing the chronology of wine, pass through a bar, and sit in a relaxation area.[91] While not large, the museum did attempt to tell visitors a story about the importance of wine for the Spanish state. Visitors could see the history of wine and explore its production without having to leave Madrid. The rural was portrayed in the heart of Spain's largest city. By foregrounding the rural and the religious elements of wine production, this syndicate could make folkloric connections to the beverage and possibly increase consumption levels.

The National Syndicate for Wine, Beer, and Beverages also used this museum as a tool for foreign visitors interested in purchasing Spanish wine. Pío Miguel Irurzun made note of a visit of representatives from the United States to Spain to attend the II Gala del Vino y la Moda on May 6 whom he wanted brought to the museum. He wrote, "We will have the pleasure of receiving them in our Museum-Exposition of Wine at the *Casa de Campo*, the evening of that day they will receive an ample vision and reference to our general wine production in maps and graphics that are prepared, with a tasting of wines." The following day the visitors were to attend the Second Gala of Wine and Fashion.[92] Over those two days, these American visitors could gain insight into the history of wine in Spain and its place in contemporary Spanish culture.

Showcasing wine was like a performance. Events that celebrated wine, its production, and consumption displayed the successes of Spain's agricultural industry. While each event had its own goals and techniques for emphasizing the beverage, in each case organizers focused on wine. Organizers needed to get participants to be interested in their styles of wine, whether it was sherry in France or quality wines in Madrid. Governmental support helped offer gravitas and financial backing, making the proceedings possible. Each event emphasized the traditional value of wine to the patrimony and national economy and demonstrated innovations in techniques and styles to draw more visitors to Spain and, hence, more consumers of Spanish wines. Finally, each of these well-planned events relied upon marketing strategies to garner interest. The combination of these factors helped consumers to understand the vital role that wine played in Spanish society and why the commodity needed to be protected and celebrated.

1. Area seen by tourists at Bodegas González Byass, Jerez de la Frontera. Used by permission of La Fundación González Byass.

2. Vintage sherry bottles, Jerez de la Frontera. Used by permission of La Fundación González Byass.

3. Solera system for sherry at Bodegas El Maestro Sierra, Jerez de la Frontera. Used by permission of Bodegas El Maestro Sierra.

4. Early twentieth-century harvest at Codorníu, Sant Sadurní d'Anoia. Used by permission of Raventós i Blanc, ©raventosiblanc.

5. Bodegas González Byass near Jerez Cathedral, Jerez de la Frontera. Used by permission of La Fundación González Byass.

6. Solera system for sherry in bodega at Bodegas El Maestro Sierra, Jerez de la Frontera. Used by permission of Bodegas El Maestro Sierra.

7. Brandy Cardenal Mendoza solera at Bodegas Sánchez Romate, Jerez de la Frontera. Used by permission of Sánchez Romate.

8. Calle Ciegos in Bodegas González Byass, Jerez de la Frontera, which is part of the tour. Used by permission of La Fundación González Byass.

9. Cooperage for Cardenal Mendoza brandy, Jerez de la Frontera. Used by permission of Sánchez Romate.

10. *Pupitres* storing cava to have yeast settle, Caves Blancher, Sant Sadurní d'Anoia. Used by permission of Caves Blancher.

11. Vineyards Bodegas González Byass with their chalk-white albariza soil, Jerez de la Frontera. Used by permission of La Fundación González Byass.

12. Albariza chalk soil, Jerez de la Frontera. Used by permission of La Fundación González Byass.

13. Pupitres storing cava, Caves Blancher, Sant Sadurní d'Anoia. Used by permission of Caves Blancher.

14. Vineyards Caves Blancher, Sant Sadurní d'Anoia. Used by permission of Caves Blancher.

15. Modern grape collection, Caves Blancher, Sant Sadurní d'Anoia. Used by permission of Caves Blancher.

16. Vineyards Raventós i Blanc, Sant Sadurní d'Anoia. Used by permission of Raventós i Blanc, ©raventosiblanc.

17. Vineyards Bodegas González Byass, Jerez de la Frontera. Used by permission of La Fundación González Byass.

18. Mid-twentieth-century cava delivery truck. Used by permission of Caves Blancher.

19. Cardenal Mendoza Bodega, Jerez de la Frontera. Used by permission of Sánchez Romate.

20. Entrance to bodega storage, Jerez de la Frontera. Used by permission of Sánchez Romate.

21. Grapes entering storage, early twentieth century, Sant Sadurní d'Anoia. Used by permission of Caves Blancher.

22. *Venenciador* tests sherry at Bodegas Sánchez Romate, Jerez de la Frontera. Used by permission of Sánchez Romate.

23. Early twentieth-century harvest, Sant Sadurní d'Anoia. Used by permission of Raventós i Blanc, ©raventosiblanc.

24. Pruning of vines, Sant Sadurní d'Anoia. Used by permission of Caves Blancher.

25. Sherry glasses, Jerez de la Frontera. Used by permission of Sánchez Romate.

26. Pupitres storing cava, Caves Blancher, Sant Sadurní d'Anoia. Used by permission of Caves Blancher.

5

Exposició i Fira Oficial de la Vina i del Vi

A CATALAN WINE FESTIVAL IN FRANCO'S SPAIN

Vilafranca de Penedès, a small city located outside Barcelona in Catalonia, celebrated the third and final Exposición y Feria de la Viña y del Vino (Exposition and Fair for the Vineyard and Wine) in 1963. Vilafranca remains the center of the Penedès wine region, an important agricultural location for Catalonia and for Spain. The local *Diario* covered the celebrations, reporting on the wine festival and its participants. At this final festival, the *Diario* gave each of the three events a specific theme: 1943 "could be called the Fair of Confidence [*Confianza*], because it took place at a time of difficulties, not only in our country, but also in the whole world that was consumed by a terrible war; while in the Penedès the work of its men was exalted in the vineyard and in the field."[1] Only four years after the end of the Spanish Civil War and during the height of World War II, the Penedès hoped to establish some confidence in its local production. As Catalonia suffered serious damage during the Civil War, and the postwar period saw widespread economic destitution, "with declining living standards and serious falls in all major socio-economic indicators," it was hoped that a celebration of the region's wines could spark economic growth and regional relief.[2] The second festival, celebrated in 1953, was, according to the paper, "the Fair of the Opening [*Apertura*]." Finishing the blockade that Spain had to endure ". . . there was hope, the world opened to Spain and in this opening was present the men of the field, the vineyard, the men of the Penedès."[3] With the fall of fascism in Germany and Italy following World War II, Spain seemed politically and economically isolated, but the threats of the Cold War allowed Spain to act as a bulwark against the perils of European communism. By 1953

Spain could slowly open itself to globalization in the West and try to improve its still faltering economy. The *Diario* called the 1963 festival "the Friendship [*Amistad*] Fair, because in the world there is a wave that wants to retaliate against the inequities, the dislikes, the uncertainties, to a wave of brotherhood, of Friendship. Pope John XXIII with his encyclical *Pacem in terris* extolled Friendship, the effort of men of good will, which is a demand of the world and equal in Spain."[4] By the final festival, the organizers pushed for the idea of global friendship in the hopes of improving Spain's international interactions and economic connections. By 1963 the Spanish Planes de Desarrollo (Development Plans) were in full effect, hoping to create sustained economic and social success for a transitioning Francoist state.

This chapter explores these three exhibitions in Vilafranca and their coverage in the *Diario*, created to highlight the successes of the events. These newsletters offer commentary about the celebrations, report on events, and supply interviews with food and wine scholars about the reputation of wine in the Penedès region while providing readers with critical information about wine and its economic importance to Spain at three distinct moments in time. Overall, this chapter argues that wine production remained a vital part of the Spanish and regional economies, and wine fairs constructed and presented the identities of this beverage for national and international markets. Wine shifted from a local crop that supported a regional economy to a key ingredient that could help Spain establish an international economic identity. Through its coverage of these fairs, which served as showcases for the wines of the Penedès, the *Diario* wanted to help create positive identities for the region and the country.

FAIRS, FESTIVALS, AND REGIONAL IDENTITIES

The Penedès region is located in Spain's Catalonia, between the cities of Barcelona and Tarragona, encircled by the Llobregat River to the north, Gaià River to the south, mountains to the west, and the Mediterranean Sea to the east.[5] It is home to some unique Spanish grapes that have been used to make its distinct wines over the centuries: cariñenya, a grape needed for blending and rarely used to produce grand wines on its own; macabeo, a white grape that flowers late, helping it survive a possible late frost; parellada, a low-alcohol white grape; and xarel·lo, the star of cava (and this author's favorite grape of the province).[6] The region has a long-standing tradition of wine production.

In 1865 railways reached the city of Vilafranca and connected the region with Barcelona, allowing for greater shipments of wine.[7] In the 1870s the region developed Spain's version of sparkling wine, later named *cava*. In the late 1880s, the plague phylloxera arrived, devastating the wine sector and leading to a long recovery period.[8] Afterward the region made primarily red wines for export, but, following the Spanish Civil War, the region began to produce more white wines, especially cava.[9] In 1889 (as the phylloxera plague approached) the region had 42,131 hectares of vineyards; 41,030 hectares in 1920; approximately 17,149 hectares around 1945 (difficult to calculate precisely due to the end of the Civil War); and rebounding to around 20,923 hectares in 1975.[10] Even with the shift to white wines, the region primarily exported warehouse wine after the Civil War; Franco's pariah-like status after World War II also hurt the regional wine exporters.[11] It would not be until the 1960s that cava producers of the Penedès "finally consolidated their hegemony" over the product.[12] The first year that the value of bottled wines surpassed bulk-wine exports was 1968.[13] The Penedès, therefore, has a long history in the production of wine, but the region underwent serious adaptations and changes in the era following the Spanish Civil War and struggled to recover under the dictatorship of Franco.

To explore these festivals in Vilafranca, it is necessary to review a collection of studies on territorial identity and the importance of food and wine festivals in a variety of areas. As globalization has grown following World War II, territorial identity has become an important marker for the development of specialized agricultural goods. As Angelo Bonfanti, Paola Castellani, and Chiara Rossato explain in their paper on Italian companies, "territorial identity is an elusive concept that can be defined as the qualities that make a place capable of being specified or singled-out, as well as unique and separate from other places . . . uniqueness, singularity, specificity, and authenticity."[14] These four main characteristics are often times "defined in relation to its flow and network with other places, both near and far."[15] First, these identities are not static; they are capable of shifting, due to "a continuous interaction between a specific community and its relational space."[16] Therefore, both internal and external attempts to affect identity of a territory have power. In the case of this chapter, it is important to note both the internal attempts of the Penedès and the external attempts of the dictatorship for developing this regional identity. Second, these identities constitute "a process because there is no singular identity of a territory but a succession of identities."[17] For the Penedès the identities of these festivals shifted over time: confidence, opening, and friendship. Third, these territorial identities developed through a sense of unity or belonging that created a collective self. The festivals did not take place in a free society, however, so, in their case, the collective sense of unity was influenced by the state. Finally, these territorial identities are multidimensional, having "social, cultural, political, physical, biological, historical, and psychological dimensions."[18] This event was not just for the connoisseur, but was meant to include many different types of visitors. By combining these aspects, a territory can construct an identity—or a series of shifting identities over time, due to a combination of internal or external pressures.

Regional or territorial identity is not solely useful for creating a distinctive product; it can also be used to add value to that good. As Bradley Christensen, Martin Kenney, and Donald Patton argue, "Regional identity creation is being recognized for its economic benefits and as a strategic resource for production communities. A regional identity is not a brand; it is built through a complicated process of developing cohesion and sharing in the industry community and communicating outside the industry community to opinion-makers and consumers."[19] Regional identity, however, needs "legitimacy," which "accrues in a two side process; the identity creation and maintenance by the industry community which is the internal side of the process; and validation of the identity by key intermediaries and critics, and eventually consumers on the external side."[20] Therefore, those brands within a particular region that work to construct a positive identity need the support of external forces to justify their efforts. These festivals, therefore, could combine these internal and external identities in three distinct periods. As Gilles Laferté writes with respect to Burgundian wine, a dichotomy exists between the "modernist, technical perception [of] the production-oriented use of the land for mass consumption" and the "perception of the traditional village and the aesthetic and recreational use of the land for the needs of tourism and luxury produce."[21] Therefore, issues surrounding economic needs for a region and specialized local identity can exist simultaneously, but they can also be in conflict, depending on the needs at a particular time. These studies about regional identity and its importance focus on recent attempts, but the researchers' underlying messages also illuminate events such as the exposiciones in the Penedès.

When discussing territorial identity and wine, France and its vitiviniculture come immediately to mind. In her discussion of the development of French champagne as it represented a national identity, Kolleen M. Guy notes that drinking champagne represented a connection with a particular social, cultural, or economic group.[22] At the turn of the twentieth century, as sparkling wine was becoming popular in a variety of regions, both in production and consumption, and as tensions across Europe began to grow, the French state needed to protect what made it truly "French."[23] Champagne, therefore, had to represent what it meant to be French and to be protected by the state. Joseph Bohling explains the French also improved their ideals of connoisseurship along with their product, establishing new laws to protect the French wine industry by defending smaller producers while ending protections and subsidies for large-scale industrial wine. In this way "consumers increasingly put a premium on provenance and price. Quality came to equate with wine's origins, its rarity, and its high price. . . . Wine was becoming a symbol of economic status, a luxury and not merely a food."[24] In less than a century, the French had managed to change the way people viewed the consumption, production, and sale of their wines. Clearly aware of these protectionary measures in France, Spanish producers would look to support similar actions in Spain to protect the quality and identity of their wines.

In contemporary conversation it is understood that food and wine festivals create numerous advantages economically for their host locations.[25] Seohee Chang writes that "many small cities have developed festivals using their cultural and historical resources as a drawing power to attract visitors."[26] Festivals bring in tourists from wide geographical regions who can greatly help the local economy. But what brings these contemporary attempts to establish wine tourism into a historical perspective is the question of authenticity—of both products and their meaning to the geographical area. In their work on Italian wine festivals, Alessio Cavicchi, Cristina Santini, and Eleonora Belletti note that, "although the importance of typical food and wine events is recognized worldwide, research shows a lack in defining the linkages between the degree of authenticity in event experience and authenticity in the products that are served for on prem-ise consumption during food and wine festivals."[27] It is important, therefore, that these events deliver an authentic experience. "The role of perceptions in authenticity is extremely important," they write. "First of all, perceptions trans-form authenticity into a dynamic concept that changes according to visitors' personal settings and perception patterns; secondly, perception can influence food and beverage price expectations as consumers would expect a premium price charged; thirdly, there is a strong relationship between authenticity and the whole event and the perception of the authenticity of food and beverage."[28] Travelers to Vilafranca needed to perceive the authenticity of these events for those events to be successful. With this question of authenticity, the most important factor would be that of quality: "The competitive advantage of local wine and food events relies on the inner quality of local products, on the traits of the uniqueness and typicality that the one territory provides to products, and on the authenticity of the consumption experience."[29] Therefore, when a food or wine festival first launches, it would be logical to establish the identity of a quality product to entice visitors. Specifically, for wine, "tourism is a growing industry in the regional economic development of rural areas, and its success depends on viticulture, the wine tourism product (wineries, wine routes and festivals), the reciprocal linkage to regional development and the importance of tourist attractions."[30] These three Vilafranca fairs tried to connect these issues, premised on the belief that quality wine could create a positive perception of Vilafranca and Spanish wines.

The exposición in Vilafranca represents an important example for this identity construction, as the Penedès, Catalonia, and the Francoist State each worked to present a quality agricultural good and experience to expanding markets to develop economic growth during troubling times for Spain. Similarly, the recent growth in Spain of "gastronomy" tourism has opened a new view into the regional identities of the state. The development of this "experience based" tourism is believed to help visitors better understand the location they visit as travelers can taste those items identified with the specific zone.[31] "Tradition, innovation, [and] quality" are the contemporary buzz words used to discuss this new experience.[32] The discussion of products specifically related to a particular region in Spain has a long tradition. Similarly, as food and wine tourism does not merely assist the gastronomy of a region, "this type of tourism also includes a lifestyle experience, linkages to art, wine and food, and at the same time, it enhances the cultural values of a region."[33] Thus, these festivals do not simply act as a venue where visitors can taste food and wine, but create a location where outsiders can sample the goods of a region and while experiencing a multitude of events that define that region's identity.

While most of these studies look at the role of wine and festival tourism in an overwhelmingly contemporary framework, many of the concerns they discuss were expressed during the three incarnations of the Vilafranca event. These festivals worked to establish brand identity, create an image of quality, showcase aspects of regional culture, and find ways to increase economic growth in wine and other products. The following sections will explore the main issues discussed at each fair in 1943, 1953, and 1963, highlighting the themes expressed in each while examining how the decade-long periods between the events created new topics for festival organizers to explore.

1943: CONFIDENCE

The first Exposición y Feria de la Viña y del Vino opened in Vilafranca de Penedès on October 10, 1943. The *Diario* celebrated the event's inauguration, highlighting the importance of the festival for the region and acknowledging the support of the ruling national coalition of the FE y de las JONS.[34] The true star of the first festival was the dictator Francisco Franco, even though he did not attend. The opening editorial of the *Diario* celebrated "the Head of State, Generalissimo Franco, forger of a new era of prosperity and peace, who, accepted the Presence of Honor, has given the maximum enrichment to our first and only Exhibition and Official Fair of Vine and Wine. Vilafranca takes this opportunity to pay tribute to our Caudillo the act of gratitude and unwavering devotion."[35] Catalonia overwhelmingly sided against Franco and his Nationalists during the Civil War (1936–39), yet now, in the center of the Catalan wine region, he was being lauded as a hero and savior for all of Spain. A state-sponsored publication, the *Diario* would clearly have acted in propagandistic terms, but some Catalans reading about this event opening would have been appalled. During the inaugural event, regional governor don Antonio de Correa praised Franco and his actions in Spain: "Nine years ago in this same month of October, the dense and thick clouds of the fires . . . projected on Vilafranca a black shadow of shame and adversity, and today, as a contrast, rises above the village restored a prestigious glow that is pointing out to us, day after day, our Caudillo of España who knew how to take his sword to victory; and find the Victory, carrying on his sword the sign of the Cross."[36] During a celebratory banquet, secretary for the exposition Luis Mestre addressed the crowd about the festival's goal the region's desire to save its vitiviniculture: "To that end, patriots mobilized forging this wonderful exhibition, which at the same time fills us with pride because it encompasses . . . with the desire of our Caudillo to allocate work, [and] promotion of industries and work for Spain."[37] This event, then, was not solely about reestablishing the Spanish wine industry in Catalonia, but, as in all dictatorships, honoring the new leader and foregrounding his supposed importance to the local event, especially in a region that had been overwhelmingly against him over the previous years.

The event also sparked a feeling of optimism and religious hope in the region. Bishop Gregorio of Barcelona offered his thoughts: "I have just visited the Vine and Wine Exhibition Organized by Vilafranca de Penedès and I have greatly admired it for its perfection and the agricultural, industrial and commercial wealth of which it is a splendid manifestation. Our Lord God blesses these riches of this beautiful and rich region of the Penedès, may it be pledged, my episcopal Benediction."[38] The connection between faith and the event's success could be seen in other comments written over the days to come. Organizers hoped that the festival could repair the previous divisions in the region. The *Diario* stated, "Without wanting to—so to speak—we have regained our brotherhood and reconciled body and soul, blood and spirit. And it is that the Exhibition is not only about prosperity: it is belief. It is a belief in a perfect harmony of spiritual and material values, of struggle without losing brotherhood."[39] Even though these remarks clearly overestimated the power of one festival in Vilafranca to bring about such a result, it is important to note that this wine event was viewed as a way to heal wounds. Secretary Luis Mestre asserted that the event would "help and profile our unparalleled and magnificent Fair, because in reality it means eagerness; it symbolizes perseverance and optimism, with greater expansive force every day for the good of the country, as a glorious flag of the atmosphere of peace that Spain enjoys in these moments of terrible world struggle."[40] Thus, this festival and the work of its organizers and presenters could act as a shining star of success and hope for the Spanish state after the war; at the same time, this event could serve as an example of peace in a postwar world. While this event indeed supported a nationalist narrative, it boosted the confidence of the country's citizens during a truly terrible period.

While the supposed star of this event was the wine of the Penedès, at this festival wine was spoken about in general terms, celebrated for its positive effects, as natural and helpful for mankind. "Of all the solid and liquid substances that we ingest," the *Diario* suggested, "wine is the one that goes deeper. Wine makes the stingy, generous; to the timid, intrepid; the jovial, sullen; to the quiet, chattery; the short, inspired; the scoundrel, chivalrous; to the warm, passionate; to the shameful, without shame and God knows how many more things."[41] Wine was meant to be celebrated in multiple forms. "Wine," the paper continued, "is an exaggeratedly human element. And, as such, a splendid literary theme. There is hardly any great writer who has not greeted it."[42] Wine did not only affect literature, but it also affected the heart: "Wine and love, love and wine, verb or noun, will always be eternal themes controlled by the heart, because wine encourages or discourages, but always stimulates. Love is also sometimes strong and bitter but like liquor it stimulates."[43] Wine was an element that could affect the drinker, but it was also something that inspired the senses and emotions. As Ramón de Saavedra said of wine during the festival: "Wine is, at the same time, the most spiritual and the most sensual of the gifts of the earth."[44] He continued, "Wine is of a more exalted nature. It is not properly a food. It does not replace, it adds ... Not that wine responds to any purely physical need. It did not satisfy hunger or thirst collectively. The thirst that calls wine is thirst for another fate; spiritual thirst; thirst for perfection, which has its roots in eternal human discontent."[45] Wine offers the drinker its gifts, both physical and spiritual, and, Saavedra continued, "we seek in the wine a second personality, a higher, more noble than the daily of our misery and fatigue.... That is why wine or something equivalent to wine has existed and will always exist on earth. ... We need wine as much as bread."[46] As a central part of life on both the physical and metaphysical planes, wine needed to be exalted. Commentaries like these from the *Diario* showed the reader that this celebration was not solely of an agricultural product but of a substance that made people truly human. Wine brings joy to the drinker and a zest of life for the spirit.

While the 1943 exhibition centered on wine, it offered other reasons to attend. A variety of artistic exhibits opened around Vilafranca to show off the influence of wine in art. "Art—with A capitalized—must not be separated from Enology," the *Diario* explained; "this—it seems—is denoted by the pictorial exhibition that encircles this town."[47] The art at the festival was not meant to be innovative but representative of the historical relationship of art and wine: "This exhibition of paintings is an attempt to present the interest and plastic value that wine can offer to pure artistic creation. It does not pretend to be any innovation. Taking advantage of the conjuncture of the Exhibition and Fair that we celebrate, we wanted to revive a tradition that starts from the most primitive manifestations of art. In effect, wine as a matter of artistic creation is repeated insistently in the bacchanalian themes of the most ancient antiquity; fresh with great brilliance in the bacchanals of Renaissance painters."[48] By connecting wine and art, participants at the event could celebrate multiple aspects of the festival and the Penedès' regional identity. At the same time, by viewing historical depictions of wine within art, the viewers could see these connections as part of a long tradition between the two elements rather than a new phenomenon.

The combination of wine and the other festivities in Vilafranca created a perception of the event as a success for the community, offering good publicity for the place and its products. By October 13, festival organizers estimated, over fifteen thousand visitors had come to the city to share in the revelry.[49] The festival was not only a physical event; it also represented the rising hopes of a region that had been recently devastated. As the *Diario* wrote, "The Exhibition and Official Fair of the Vineyard and Wine is an unprecedented success in Spain. A population, a region surpassing itself, giving all of itself, with the frank thankfulness that can be admitted in an industrial and commercial town; breaking the possible monotony of mercantile facilities with fantastical lights and wonderful water games, and putting up to now forty thousand people . . . to make them come out optimistic, smiling, conquerors of never imagined gaps."[50] The small city was proud of its accomplishments, which some who had left the agricultural region years earlier had returned to see. "The observer was able to see the pupils lit with emotion from people who never remembered that they had been born on this soil," the *Diario* reported. "We have seen those who for twenty years left the village as a prodigal son, have entered it, finally, through the main door. . . . Old friendships that time had endured have been restored. Distant relatives have been reconciled by familiar words."[51] The pride generated by the festival for this small city sparked optimism and encouraged reconciliation while showing attendees the vital role of wine in the local economy, culture, and identity.

Conversations began about the economic importance of wine to the larger Spanish economy and the necessity of exportation. The *Diario* republished an article from Barcelona's *La Prensa* that discussed the economic value of this event for the region and country. The newspaper noted the current economic concerns for wine as "our viticulture production, better and with greater volume as time goes by, crosses a delicate situation today, in which the excess of the production—result of good harvests and technical improvements—must be understood, with insufficient internal consumption and difficulties of demand from abroad. Our wines, even those of a purely foreign style, today enjoy a predicament beyond our borders, as proven by the fact that before we sent them in barrels, to undergo elaborations and label changes, and today they leave bottled and directly directed for sale." Even with the current crisis for wine, there was hope for growth: "The improvements made and the constant and uninterrupted increases, foretells, for another state, a future of strength, in which the improvement and the best conditions of elaboration and commercial method, can render unbeatable results.... Our natural wealth, less subject than our industry to the hazards of the time, has motivated in Vilafranca an Exhibition of which by force will produce benefits to the zones and regions interested in this class of credits and in its exploitation on a large scale."[52] Wine was a form of wealth and an asset with growth potential after the subsiding of global conflicts. A successful festival and growth in the Vilafranca wine industry for both national and international consumption would benefit other locations in the Catalan region, especially cities like Barcelona. Because wine as a crop was inextricably tied to the identity of the larger region, success in one place could have spillover effects.

As the festival came to an end in late October 1943, the staff of the *Diario* reflected upon its successes and the lessons learned. The wine festival was not only about the production and consumption of wine, but about what wine and the creation of this event offered the people of Vilafranca. The *Diario* wrote:

> The Exposición is all that. And, when we speak of political values, the word political should be understood in its pristine name, that is to say: as an expression of the will of a social nucleus that struggles to put harmoniously into shape the most diverse and heterogeneous activities of its life. Now it will be understood why we said at the beginning that the Exhibition could not be considered—it started because it was not—as something superimposed on Vilafranca, not detached from the Municipality, nor did it see in it a vertical imposition. ... The exhibition has emerged from a perfect conjunction of what is in Vilafranca an integral part of the superior national unity.[53]

The event created some unity amongst the denizens of the city, which presented a good image both for the community and for visitors. These outsiders could visit "with increasing influx, the visits of the most diverse people and geographically more contrasting places. . . . For many, for most, the visit has been a discovery. They have even come to discover in us—a question of perspective—traits in which we had never restored."[54] The event "strengthened that spirit of continuity and responsibility, that spirit of union and politics."[55]

At the close of the event, the *Diario* wrote, "It will be very difficult to return to ordinary life and wander under the porticos as a normal year, as if Vilafranca had not had a month of October of transcendence, crossed by people from all regions and latitudes and rocked by all imaginable caresses."[56] This event had been scheduled as a one-time exposition to show off the great successes of the Penedès and its viticulture; now that it was over, the city would return to normal. Even though this festival was not meant to repeat, it did bring success to the region. Tens of thousands of visitors came to the city, drank its wines, and bought its products. Twenty years later the *Diario* described it as the festival of "Confidence"—and, indeed, one can argue it was. During such a dark period in Spanish and European history, this small city used its wine production to offer hope to the people of Spain. Even with the region's long history of wine production, this festival could be seen as a reopening of the wine economy and all it represented to the scarred Catalan region, which created an identity for its wine through these celebrations. As contemporary researchers have argued, these wine festivals can offer economic, social, and cultural advantages for their locations. At the same time, just like with champagne, in creating a perceived identity for the Penedès and its wines, the festival's hosts established the ideas of patrimony and national or regional pride for this product. While not a major success, this first festival sparked optimism in the region trying to reestablish its identity as a cultural and economic touchstone for agricultural products.

1953: OPENING

A decade after the first Exposición y Feria de la Viña y del Vino, the second opened in October 1953 in Vilafranca. The 1943 festival had been set against the backdrop of the Spanish Civil War and at the height of World War II; by 1953 the Franco regime had moved away from its pro-fascist foreign policy and tried to move toward a Western sphere of influence in hopes of normalizing relations with its neighbors and the United States while working to contain the spread of global communism. In 1943, following the Civil War, the Spanish economy was in tatters; a decade later the national economy was still weak, with Spain not seeing the postwar economic development experienced in other western European states. This second Exposition—themed by the *Diario* as an "opening"—welcomed foreign involvement to save the national economy, as a successful festival could act as a form of international propaganda to attract foreign investment. At the same time, the conversation surrounding this event focused on strengthening the identity and consistency of Spanish products, which needed serious improvements to enable the future success of the country.

On October 4, the city greeted the fair with great celebration, and for a second time a daily *Diario* highlighted the main events. The *vilafranqueses* would show their "unparalleled civic virtues" by welcoming visitors "who have wanted to honor us with their presence."[57] The newsletter's opening editorial acknowledged the decade-long hiatus between events: "The II Exhibition will be inaugurated today . . . when the ten years of the first one had just finished. A lapse of ten years between the fairs can be a lot or a little, depending on how one looks at it; a lot, because a decade is enough to cool the most united in terms of continuity and organization; little, because such a gigantic effort should demand the relief. . . . But, between one extreme and the other, there is no doubt that the decade reaches a conciliatory midpoint."[58] There seems not to have been any particular reason for holding this new festival a decade later, but the likelihood exists that it served as a chance for the Spanish state to showcase one of its most important agricultural products and create for it a higher standard to gain greater market share. Jokingly, the *Diario* stated that the period in between events gave more time to prepare wine: "And speaking of wine. . . . It seems that the Fair, after having meditated for ten years, this time has been proposed to be more generous with friends."[59]

Just like the 1943 event, this fair began with political conversations, offering thanks to the national government. Vilafranca mayor Manuel Guilamany Poch mentioned Franco, promising that the wine growers of the region would offer "the vitiviniculture of Catalonia [to] him to contribute to the greatest splendor and greatness of Spain."[60] The governor of Barcelona, Felipe Acedo Colunga, came to Vilafranca and spoke to the crowds, expressing to them the need to help the working class gain access to this "healthy drink because of its high cost" while assisting regional producers and merchants.[61] Festival director Martín Güell stated: "This second Fair is an exponent of the vitality of Vilafranca, the Catalan trade and viticulture, which, in moments of crisis, knows how to galvanize its energies, trusting that with the help of God, the government and its own force will emerge triumphant of these periods as evidence that are undoubtedly necessary to temper our spirits after uneasy times."[62] This second festival would be an opportunity to show the strength of the people of the region and highlight its wine. As all these leaders mentioned, times had been tough for Spain, and a successful festival could foster an inspirational attitude for the region and hopefully for the country as a whole.

Whereas the 1943 exposition focused on projecting confidence and a sense of welcome to those who were supposedly returning home (which can be debatable, as allies and exiles of the Republic would not be welcomed), the reports about this second festival had a noticeably different theme: of gastronomy and the establishment of a better identity for regional cuisine and wine. A series of interviews in the *Diario* discussed the role of food and wine in regional identity for the Catalan people. Author Juan Ramón Masoliver spoke of Catalan cuisine, with its mixtures of seafood and land animals, combined with the agriculture grown in the region.[63] Catalan cuisine acted as this supposed bridge between the peninsula and sea—a unique conversation point under the Franco regime. Even under dictatorships like those of Primo de Rivera and Franco, regional cuisines did gain traction in terms of quality in a larger national conversation.[64] Masoliver stated: "A kitchen supported by wine and dyed in oil, aromatic with garlic, onion, with the coastal products of the Hellenic Sea. In short, succulent, appeasing, confident and well cared. Exactly what corresponds to the best virtues of the Catalan people."[65] These strong, appetizing Catalan flavors, which offered a great deal to the world of gastronomy and to the region, should be celebrated.

Even with this positive discussion of Catalan food, there were issues surrounding the development and quality of Catalan wines. As mentioned earlier Penedès wines in the 1950s were still sold primarily in a bulk format, more often as simple table wine. Regional cava was beginning to grow in popularity, but there were still problems trying to sell quality bottled wines. Master of gastronomy at the Hotel Colón Juan Cabané in Barcelona offered his thoughts about gastronomy and wine in Catalonia, with some interesting opinions about its disadvantages. When asked if Catalan wines could be considered "gastronomic," Cabané replied,

"Gastronomy is based on classic norms and the wines to some equally distinguished types, known throughout the world, which are: The Bordeaux, Burgundy, Rhônes or other styles. It is necessary that Catalan wines try to be cataloged in these types, if they wish to acquire fame in international gastronomy; otherwise, although very exquisite, they will only have a local category."[66] In the early twentieth century, the French had defended their regional wines, creating clear rules for their production and regional identities; even earlier the French had established clear regulations for its champagne. These regulations and constructed identities allowed the French to claim for their wines a particular standard, meaning that regional producers could sell their products for higher prices, and French wines could dominate the idea of "quality." France had been able to set the rules, while Spain had to play catch-up to gain respect on the international market.[67] Until the Spanish—or at least the Penedès—could accomplish this, only Riojan wines (with their heavy French influence) and the unique wines of Jerez would be identified as special. Once again a benefit existed in copying a process developed in France to support a Spanish product.

When asked if Catalan wines could be recommended to his foreign customers at the hotel, Cabané responded, "Roundly, no. They lack that classification and they are excessively strong. Proof of this is that we never recommend a wine to that man, as there are many who, after having had an opinion, still want to taste some cheese; This gentleman will ask for a *tinto* wine, light, aromatic and acid, of which, frankly, we lack. Curious thing is that many foreigners ask for Muscat with their meals and, naturally, they are not satisfied. They come badly informed and they do not know that Muscat is a dessert wine."[68] Without clearly defined rules and regional identities for wines, it was difficult to recommend a specific Catalan wine to a foreign customer who might have heard of a grape like Muscat but was unsure of anything else. Cabané did state, however, that some regional Catalan wines were quality and had good flavor—for instance, the white wine that won the exposition award "can be cataloged very well in a Barsac (white Bordeaux). It has excellent properties to form the basis of a type of wine to be taken with oysters, crustaceans and fish dishes, whose base fuses flavoring with butter."[69] Similarly, cava was a good choice, as it was "excellent with fruit and with some sweet flavor. Our sparkling is exquisite, although very different from French champagne, which are lighter, fruitier and more acidic."[70] There were good choices from the Penedès, but, as Cabané explained, the lack of regional identification and rules made consistency and choice very difficult.

While a lack of regional rules presented a serious problem for Spain, simple knowledge of the rules of gastronomy and taste seemingly prevented the Spanish from enjoying their products. When asked what country knows the most about gastronomy, Cabané responded, "No doubt, France. The French birthed 'gourmet' and the French 'cordon bleu'. Its refined cuisine is the result of a tradition of knowing how to eat and how to cook."[71] The French had the advantage of gourmet identity: they had created the rules, and their people knew how these rules worked. When asked if he could offer an anecdote about this, Cabané told this story:

> I'm going to tell you one story about wines, which happened to me recently. . . . A foreign man, who in his favor had not come from a wine country, asked me for a bottle of the best wine in the world. . . . From our cellar, we took an old bottle of "Chateau du Pape," uncorked it very carefully, because the stopper was already deteriorated by time, gently warmed it to increase its aroma, and served it with the intimate emotion of the one who served a nectar of the gods. "Well"—the guy told me—"now bring me an ice-cold siphon to mix the wine."
>
> Some Frenchmen who were next to me made observations, accompanying me in a [similar] feeling.[72]

The Spanish drinkers were not the only ones with difficulties understanding how to drink great wines, but Cabané's story does highlight the pervasive confusion or ignorance even in Barcelona's finest hotels, and the fact that French visitors were the first to note and sympathize!

Essayist, historian, and gastronome Joaquín de Entrambasaguas visited the Penedès festival days later. He offered his thoughts about wine and the event, first stating, "Wine is always a party. A full party when it accompanies a good meal, and only a good meal without wine is a semi-party. In addition, it is always *fiesta* since it awakes the joy like a Sunday morning. I, personally, distrust those who do not like wine, because he has to lack the joy of the heart that requires deep action."[73] He expressed personal pleasure with the festival: "Your Wine Fair is magnificent, and I am surprised that a population like Vilafranca has been able to organize it with so much energy, taste and detail."[74] Entrambasaguas, who had traveled to Vilafranca to speak about his wine knowledge and discuss the benefits of Catalan wines, told the *Diario* that "the Day of the Doctor and the Gastronomic Days, I think are a great success. We constantly see that snobbery only praises the French wines, as if in Spain we did not possess in an extensive spectrum of exquisite wines for all the gastronomic dishes."[75] Spain, according to Entrambasaguas, possessed quality wines on par with those of other countries, but improvements could be made:

> Yes, I recognize that these wines are not always made with the conditions required to obtain the qualities of which they are capable.
>
> I also recognize that the necessary care for nurturing is laborious and not cheap and, therefore, have to be paid. When there is a gastronomic education in a country, as in France, there is a sufficient consumer mass to make rearing lucrative, which unfortunately does not happen in Spain, where a large part of the winemakers is more for the love of art rather than representing or creating a type of wine and a brand that becomes famous, that the profit that brings them as a business.
>
> It is necessary that the Spanish learn to drink, and the best way to educate it is, as you had started when organizing this Exhibition and Wine Fair, with gastronomic days and conferences.[76]

Once again the main issue facing Spain's wine production appeared to be education. Anyone could make wine, and anyone could drink it, but until the Spanish producers learned to establish rules like the French, and until the Spanish consumer learned to drink with élan, Spanish wine would remain almost invisible on the national and international market. Education, and imitation of the French model, seemed to be the way for these wines to improve the image of their quality.

Other interviews in the *Diario* suggested that the Spanish wine industry needed to adapt to a changing world to make their beverage fit a new modern style. The *Diario* wrote, "The wine crisis in the main vinicultural countries, rather in the aspect of the withdrawal by the consumer who, in his life, puts beer, Coca-Cola and lemonades before wine. . . . a wine crisis, it is a lack of adaptation of this classic and noble drink to the rhythm and tastes of the new times."[77] When asked what else was needed to improve the production in the Penedès, oenologist Enrique Feduchy explained, "More to learn, you need to be able easily to acquire the most modern material both for warehouses and for laboratories, and to make more intimate the relationship between technical centers and those of elaboration, to facilitate the realization of modern advances that in other countries are in practice."[78] All aspects of the Penedès—its producers, sellers, and drinkers—needed to educate themselves and adjust to changes in style and technique. Simply "doing things the same way" would not help Spanish wine gain any increase market share: if it had not been successful before, it would not be successful now.

As the second Exposición y Feria de la Viña y del Vino ended, the *Diario* had some closing words for its readers in thanking them for their participation and offering some inspiration for the future in "the knowledge that Vilafranca and the wines of Penedès work, fight, and conquer the positions from which to defend their agricultural prosperity and economy."[79] The Exposition Executive Committee wrote:

> The Executive Committee of the II Exhibition and Fair is pleased to give public testimony of its gratitude to all those who in a personal way intervened in the set-up of the Fair, to the exhibitors who attended with their brands, to those who contributed to the organization of the various events and exhibitions, the organizations and institutions that presented their support and care, as well as the artisans who, with the best zeal and dedication, worked for the brilliance of the Fair. Nor can we forget, in this recount of gratitude, the population that has uninterruptedly given to foreign visitors the most precious stamp of the Exhibition: that of the active and alert vineyard tradition.[80]

Just like in 1943, the festival's organizers saw the event as a great success, helpful for Vilafranca and the Penedès. While the 1943 festival might have been viewed as a demonstration of confidence, it was more an event of hope: that maybe things could return to normal in a world and country devastated by war. While 1953 could be seen as a fair of openness, the primary discussions surrounding it concentrated on education: how the many layers of wine production and consumption could be learned to create a better product and consume it in a more refined manner. France seemed to offer a model for this. In the end the authors of the *Diario* and the interviewees saw the problems facing Spanish wine production and attempted to offer advice as to how to fix them, even as Spain existed in a unique global position in the 1950s.

1963: FRIENDSHIP

In August 1963 Vilafranca hosted its third Exposición y Feria de la Viña y del Vino. While, this time, the festival would be framed by the theme of friendship, the true underlying theme was the Spanish Plan de Desarrollo (Development Plan) of the 1960s, which used technocrats to modernize the Spanish economy, hoping to take advantage of the successes of other Western European states and improve the country's living standard. At this festival wine was utilized as a tool of modernization. As regional wines improved, they could be exported at higher rates, achieve an image of quality and consistency, and garner more international investment for the Spanish economy.

Spanish secretary for the Commission for the Plan of Economic Success Santiago Udina Martell attended many events at the exposition and offered public speeches and interviews. At the opening Udina Martell spoke to the crowds about the festival's importance and the necessity of the Development Plan for the region. The *Diario* summarized some important points: "Before the industrial revolution, our country was on the same level as the other countries of Europe. And yet, our income is currently below. It could be argued as main causes that our country has been burning in continuous wars, with short periods of tranquility that kept Spain backward from the innovations of the industrial revolution that meanwhile was developing in Europe."[81] According to the secretary, Spain was on par with others in Western Europe, but war had hurt its cause. In 1963, twenty-four years after the end of the Spanish Civil War, Spain could now work on development. Udina believed that "the Development Plan needs intercommunication, understanding, dialogue, [and] friendship. . . . It is not a socializing plan, but an expressive one, that is, that the Government indicates what its purposes are, decisions, the logical paths that must be followed, and then the private sectors, are their spirit of innovation and freedom, act suitably."[82] The state would take the lead in the country's economic planning, but local and private companies would carry out those decisions. In the case of wine, "he explained how it is necessary to provide agriculture with an industrial sense. He gave as an example the case of the fruit growers of the province of Lerida, who went to the markets to learn about the tastes and desires of the public they had to sell to, and according to these tastes channel their fruit production."[83] One of the complaints about Spanish wines from the 1953 festival was that they were good, but hard to identify, and that their consistency could not be guaranteed, which meant they were difficult to recommend to consumers. Also, in 1953 consumers were abandoning old drinks for new ones like beer and Coca-Cola. As consumer demands changed, producers needed to change, too. Wine and food festivals were chances for regions to create or recreate identities for their products, and, in a changing society, this third festival could be a good place for regional wine producers to adapt. For the Development Plan to succeed, it was necessary "to create more teaching positions, in media, university and professional training, because it has been shown to be the most profitable investment for the future of the country."[84] In 1953 men like Juan Cabané and Joaquín de Entrambasaguas had argued that the average consumer needed to become more educated about their food and wine, and now, in 1963, the government wanted more formal education throughout the state to protect the economy. If farmers and vintners could get a better education and learn newer techniques based in science, they, too, could increase their production and develop a quality drink.

Following his speech Udina Martell talked with the *Diario* about the fair and the Development Plan, stating, "The Wine Fair is in line with the Development Plan as it is an effective incorporation of the Penedès wine economy into the spirit and purposes pursued in the economic development policy."[85] The increase in the production of wine could also support the production of other alcohols made through distillation, such as industrial alcohols that could be sold internationally. "In the industrial aspect," Udina Martell said, "I believe that the demand for alcohol has to increase considerably, given the prospects of expansion of the industrial sectors that use it as a base material for their productions."[86] Interestingly, while there was a conversation about improving the quality of Spanish wines for sale, industrial alcohol produced through distillation would not rely on quality but quantity. The aim of the Development Plan was adaptation to market needs, something that Spanish wine producers had seemingly ignored, save the wine plague crises of the late nineteenth century. Udina ended his interview by explaining: "The orientation of the Market in the Economic Development policy requires, by the Spanish production in general, a strict adaptation to the demand. If the producers follow this orientation . . . no foreign competition is to be feared, and, being vinicultural products, the Penedès is in a privileged situation not only for a defensive attitude, but for an offensive action, which affects both the Internal Market and the increase in exports."[87] Adaptation to modern demands would be crucial to a successful future for the Spanish economy and agricultural industry, and wine could be a key to this growth. Santiago de Cruylles, a Catalan on the Development Plan committee, agreed with the necessity to follow the government's ideas. "Our region must and can use the Development Plan to strengthen its own welfare," he stated, "making progress in its economy and making the most of its enviable location."[88] Cruylles suggested that the Spanish could follow French economic expansion committees in making connections between the public and private spheres to increase economic development for Catalonia. This third wine festival, he said, had been "a great opportunity taken advantage of by the wine sector and by the Penedès Region."[89]

Within this talk of economic development, wine was the subject of many conversations. The *Diario* interviewed James Griffin, captain of the U.S. Navy ship *Enterprise*, which was docked in Barcelona during his visit to the festival. When asked about the Penedès's *champán* (a complicated term for Catalan sparkling wine, as French producers despised their mimicry), the navy man responded that he enjoyed the local beverage, but was generally unfamiliar with the drink, as in the United States it was expensive and usually made in France or New York State.[90] The *Diario* also asked Spanish actor Enrique Guitart about the sparkling wine of the Penedès. He told them, "I recognize that the champagne, infuses a euphoria . . . with joy."[91] When asked for an anecdote about wine, Guitart replied, "Well . . . they ask me '. . . Is it French champagne?' I always answer 'No, it's Catalan champagne. The best of the world!' Today I'm going to specify a little more, I'm going to say '*Champán* del Penedès!'"[92] Even though the French had laid down clear rules for the production and defense of champagne, the word was still used in Catalonia to describe its sparkling wine. During neither conversation did anyone use the word "cava," which highlights the fact that the Catalan wine industry was still trying to create an appropriate identity for it.

In conversations about Spanish wine, the primary discussions in the *Diario* most frequently revolved around economic issues. Again, the *Diario* suggested, "the defense of wine production from the Penedès is, above all, a problem of quality and perfect marketing."[93] For success in the region, "the solution to the current problems must be found in the Internal Market, in the Catalan region and, very particularly, in Barcelona. . . . The official statistics of the City Council of Barcelona indicate a consumption of everyday wines, in the year 1961 of 75,892,782 liters; fortified wines 4,314,793; champagnes 2,538,624; vermouth 750,627; and alcohol 10,125,117."[94] The Penedès needed to increase consumption in major cities like Barcelona to boost the overall economic growth of the region. This *Diario* note includes a particularly useful and telling discussion:

> The Penedès must undertake a true exemplification of our wines, quality campaign and efficient commercialization; The public has been served with wines of all kinds and qualities. The excellence of its wines, its aroma, flavor and balanced composition make Penedès wines an insurmountable beverage, stimulating, digestive, healthy and nutritive.
>
> If the consumption, in Spain, has not corresponded to the increase of its population, it has been because, in a depressed economy—in an era of economic difficulties—the first thing that is eliminated from a table is wine. The qualities in use, in these times, have not responded to the interest of the public; its marketing has been quite deficient, and to find a guaranteed and quality wine was very difficult.
>
> The circumstances have changed, and its evolution has been advantageous. The highest level of life today is felt in most consumer products, and wine corresponds to occupy, again, a place of honor at every table.
>
> That the consuming public can taste the fine wines of macabeo and xarel·lo, that in other times made famous the wines of the region of Penedès, and the miracle of the absorption of the current surpluses will have been realized![95]

Wine was not only a product to enjoy (or simply drank as needed), but also a vital part of the economy of Catalonia. By 1963 the Spanish government, Catalan authorities, and regional producers all understood that a successful wine economy could improve the lives of all people in Spain.

The three Exposiciones y Ferias de la Viña y del Vino celebrated in Vilafranca all occurred because the region produced wine, but each festival had different and clearly defined goals. The 1943 festival tried to raise confidence in a country and region suffering the effects of war, disease, and starvation, with the *Diario* focusing on the importance of wine to the culture of the region. By 1953 the festival's goals had changed. With Spain slowly making connections with other western states, this event was intended as an opening to new markets. In addition to the cultural connections with wine, the *Diario* featured conversation meant to show readers the importance of drinking good wine. Improved understanding of wine could not only assist the consumers, but, by creating an educated purchaser, winemakers could create better wine and charge more for their product. Finally, while the 1963 festival celebrated the Penedès and its wines, the main point of the event was to preach the goals of the Spanish Development Plan. In 1953 improved wine quality could make a better educated consumer; in 1963 improved wines could save the Spanish economy. Wine remained a cultural good, but its identity had shifted from merchandise to a cultural element. Wine could be used to improve the lives of the Spanish public.

The articles, interviews, and editorials in the *Diarios* confirmed a series of assumptions about the power of food festivals and regional identities. Food and wine festivals can create an identity for a particular product. Penedès wines went from a local cultural item to a quality good to an economic success story over a twenty-year period. As with a variety of French regions, at each festival the Penedès was able to construct an identity for itself and its wines. Each incarnation of the fair wanted to present the best possible image of the regions' products; they brought tens of thousands of visitors from across Spain and around the world to spend money, helping the local economies. Once these visitors left, they brought the ideas and identities of Penedès wines home with them, possibly looking for those items in stores. Although it would be impossible to identify the exact economic effect of these festivals for the Penedès and its wine producers, the fact that they were celebrated three times shows that they were believed to benefit the region. After each event the identity of the Penedès grew stronger, and the perceived quality of the wines continued to grow, offering pride and economic support to its residents.

6

Making Friends with Wine

INTERNATIONAL TRADE IN THE
FINAL YEARS OF FRANCO

In January 1967 the Comité de Vinos de España (Committee for Spanish Wines) compiled a report about the November 1966 IIº Salon Internacional de la Alimentación (Second International Food Show, or SIAL) in Paris, which was celebrated November 13–21 and that highlighted the agricultural and food goods produced in Europe for the French market. For this second Parisian event, the Spanish Wine Committee chose to take the lead and assume responsibility for the "Spanish Pavilion": a 226 m² location secured by the Spanish embassy for the event, in which Spanish wine would occupy 200 m². The embassy reserved the remaining space for presentations on fruits, legumes, and preserves by Casa Pascual Hermanos de Valencia and Camille Tabar y Campillo. Clearly Spanish wine and liquors would be the centerpiece for this event, amid rising hopes that the French would purchase more. Because the event was expensive, the Ministry of Commerce, the General Directory of Commercial Expansion, and several wine Consejos Reguladores (Regulatory Commissions) offered to finance it. Each participant or bodega received a 10.45 m² area to decorate and display their goods, while the Consejo Regulador de Jerez received the largest space, at 21 m².[1]

Spain's main Consejos Reguladores for Jerez, Rioja, and Cariñena attended the event along with representatives from some of the largest Spanish bodegas: Pedro Domecq, Sandeman, Lopez Heredia, Miguel Torres, La Vincola Ibérica, Hijos de José Suarez Villalba, Emilio Hidalgo, Hijos de A. Barceló, and Cavas del Conde de Caralt. The space contained an exposition on the history and diversity of Spanish wine bottles. During the event the general public and wine connoisseurs could obtain portfolios from the committee and various

Consejos; information on where to find Spanish wines in France; and material from Iberia Airlines about travel in Spain. Visitors also experienced the art of the Jerez venenciador don José Ortega while sampling some of the 137 liters of sherry or the 2000 liters of Riojan wine brought to the event. To remind the Parisian community of the SIAL and the Spanish pavilion, the committee produced radio and newspaper advertisements.[2] The event was a success, with only one complaint about the design: "Finally, the place attributed to Spain was not satisfactory, since our Pavilion was in the second row. For the year 1968, it will be advisable to act, with sufficient advance and it is indispensable to demand from the Organizing Committee, a space located in the first place and then in the first row."[3]

This Salon Internacional de la Alimentación represents an important moment for the Spanish wine industry and its producers in the 1960s. With the signing of the Treaty of Rome in 1957, the European Economic Community reduced tariffs for many goods within the zone, but, since Spain fell outside the region, Spanish producers often found themselves at a disadvantage and in need of creating their own demand. Protected by the EEC, Italian wine could enter French markets with little to no tariff implications, and Spanish wine producers had to find access to these EEC and other European markets.[4] Additionally, Spain's public relations sector remained weak well into the 1960s, hindering the marketing of Spanish goods.[5] With the lack of clear messaging, growing external competition, and previous disorganization, it was necessary for Spain's wine industry to work very hard in the 1960s and early 1970s to construct a clear identity for its products on the international market.

This chapter explores the relationship between Spanish wine and foreign states during the last decades of the Franco regime. First, I look at a sample of issues between Spain and France. As France remained the world's largest consumer of wine, the country needed imports to meet demand, but Spanish producers were overlooked. Spain's wine producers, concerned that their products were not penetrating the French market, grew angry with the unfair playing field. Second, I will look at the relationship between Spanish wine and the United Kingdom, the largest importer of Spanish sherry. Sherry producers feared that fraud would undermine authentic Spanish sherry in their most important market, leading to a major legal battle between Spanish sherry and "empire sherry." To guarantee their future market share, Spanish producers needed to distinguish their products from imposters. Spanish companies like Burdon's Sherry ran advertisements in wine trade journals with characters like Sherlock Holmes stating, "Which is the best reason for stocking Burdon's. With a steady demand from discriminating sherry-drinkers, and advertising to increase the demand, the monetary advantages of catering for the needs of the tassel seekers [the scarlet tassel symbol of Burdon's] are obvious."[6] In a later advert, Sancho Panza stated to Don Quixote: "In faith it is, sir. Would that we were wine sellers that we could profit handsomely from stocking [Burdon's]. Those with a fine palate demand it. And advertisements are constant in proclamation of its virtues, that the demand may be increased. Rely on it, your Graceship, Burdon's brings great rewards."[7] Next, this chapter will explore the development and successes of the 1970 Spansk Vinefestival in Copenhagen, Denmark, which the Spanish wine syndicate viewed as a possible location to expand its markets for both sherry and table wine. A great deal of effort went into this event to introduce Spanish wine to the Scandinavian market and create a new identity for the beverage. Finally, this chapter will examine the relationships between Spanish wine and a number of other states. Overall, I argue that, due to previous failures, the 1960s were a critical time for Spanish wine producers, as they needed to strengthen the identity of their wines to establish better markets overseas.

The wine industry had a great impact on the Spanish economy and its exports. In 1967 the export of grape wine and grape must with alcohol accounted for 3.78 percent of total Spanish exports, bringing in 3,202,995,049 pesetas. On its own sherry accounted for 2.36 percent of exports, bringing in 1,996,166,872 pesetas.[8] Over half the value of all wine exports, therefore, came directly from the Jerez denominación de origen. In terms of bottled exports, Jerez sold 3,888,652 liters internationally, representing 33.36 percent of all wine sold by volume in bottles. Riojan wines sold 3,450,444 liters, representing 29.6 percent of all exports; Tarragona wines 1,158,112 liters, or 9.94 percent; and sparkling wines sold 457,944 liters, or 3.93 percent of sales. In total Spain sold 11,657,316 liters of bottled wine in 1967, earning 429,053,145 pesetas.[9] In other containers (to be bottled in international markets), Jerez sold 54,435,613 liters, or 21.54 percent; Tarragona 33,342,878 liters, or 13.19 percent; and generic white wines represented 11.6 percent of sales, at 29,320,846 liters. In other formats Spain exported 252,685,892 liters of wine, earning 2,761,136,202 pesetas. Jerez sold 58,324,265 liters, Tarragona 34,500,990 liters, generic white wine 29,697,968 liters, and Rioja 19,675,632 liters. In total Spain exported 264,343,208 liters of wine.[10] Spanish wine thus remained a central element of the national export economy.

Wine production and exports contributed significantly to the economic development of many countries across the world. In 1967 Spain produced 22,660,394 hectoliters of wine and exported 2,667,091 hl. Spain's neighbor and closest competitor, Portugal, produced 9,858,596 hl and exported 2,523,164 hl. Italy was the world's largest producer, with 75,025,000 hl, but it only exported 2,590,259 hl. France produced 65,025,000 hectoliters of wine and exported 3,341,593 hl. Argentina was the largest producer in the western hemisphere, producing 27,839,915 hl, but only exporting approximately 6,000 hl. The United States produced 6,905,200 hl and only exported 10,784 hl. The Soviet Union, likely in the historical wine areas of Georgia and Armenia, produced 17,032,990 hl, with no reported exports. Other Eastern European countries produced and exported substantial amounts of wine: Romania produced 6,500,000 hl and exported 463,000 hl; Yugoslavia made 5,320,000 hl and exported 452,158; Hungary produced 4,789,383 hl and exported 675,267; and Greece made 3,869,138 hl selling 462,690 internationally. Even in 1967 the former French colonies of the Maghreb continued to produce and export substantial amounts of wine. Algeria produced 6,273,263 hl of wine, exporting a whopping 5,300,000 hl, making it the largest wine exporter in the world. Morocco produced 1,087,405 hl and exported 335,455 hl, while Tunisia produced 924,800 hl and exported 711,000 hl. Former British colonies also continued to produce substantial amounts of wine. South Africa made 4,324,705 hl and exported 144,380 hl; Australia made 1,603,806 hl and sold 80,828; Canada produced 441,520 hl; and Cyprus made 410,000 hl, exporting 166,300 hl.[11] A variety of countries produced and exported reasonably significant amounts of wine, which meant that Spain had competition on many fronts. In total 20,294,036 hl of wine were exported globally in 1967, and Spain in third place, controlling 13.14 percent of the market; with France as the second largest exporter; and Algeria as the global leader, with 26.12 percent of all exports.[12]

Just as important to wine production was the wine consumption levels in 1967. In France the average person drank 117 liters of wine a year for a grand total of 57,800,000 hectoliters annually. Italians drank 112.5 liters per person, totaling 58,900,000 hl. The Portuguese drank 84.5 liters per person, totaling 7,962,039 hl. The Argentines were fourth in consumption at 82.8 liters per person. Spanish internal consumption was fifth, at 62 liters for a total of 18,366,000 hl. To round out the top ten consumers, Chileans drank 50 liters per person, the Swiss 40.2 liters, Greeks 38.7 liters, Austrians 31.9 liters, and Hungarians 31 liters. Other notable countries for 1967 include: West Germany with 15.1 liters per person for 9,021,000 hl; Belgium 9.1 liters for 870,252 hl; Denmark 3.9 liters for 188,382 hl; Holland 3.8 liters for 478,700 hl; the United States with 3.7 liters for 7,235,700 hl; and the UK with 2.8 liters per person for 1,256,800 hl.[13] As French, Italian, Portuguese, and Argentine consumption levels were much higher than any other country in the world, the Spanish could try to target those markets for their excess wine exports.

Wine importation numbers are important to understanding the internal demand of countries. Even with their massive wine production, France still imported 4,923,000 hl of wine in 1967, making it the world's largest importer of wine. West Germany was a close second, importing 4,561,008 hl. The UK was third, importing 1,423,980 hl, which was more than its entire internal consumption for 1967. Switzerland imported 1,611,386 hl; Belgium 988,868 hl; the United States 714,490 hl; Sweden 403,000 hl; Denmark 207,200 hl; Holland 575,500 hl; and Italy still needed to import 111,243 hl. In the same year, Spain only imported 4,442 hl, while Portugal registered no wine imports at all.[14] These numbers make it clear that France had the highest demand for imports and was the greatest prize for exporters, yet, as will be explored later, their connection to the Maghreb gave them an unfair advantage. A strong demand existed in northern European countries that could not produce wine, and that the Spanish could target to increase market share. In 1967 Spain produced 22,660,394 hl, consumed 18,366,000 hl, and exported 2,667,091 hl—therefore, 1,627,303 hectoliters of Spanish wine had nowhere to go and might not be consumed.

THE ISSUES WITH FRANCE

As discussed in previous chapters, the relationship between Spanish wine producers and France had fluctuated greatly since the nineteenth century. When oidium and phylloxera devastated French vineyards, France needed to import large amounts of wine from other countries, with Spain often a beneficiary. When French markets stabilized, however, French vintners worked overtime to protect their economic interests, and Spanish wines suffered. French wineries claimed that their products were of a higher quality and safer to drink, as they did not contain chemicals like gypsum, and that French identity was inextricably tied to drinking French wine. At the start of the twentieth century, French imports of Spanish wines dropped precipitously, not because the French produced enough of their own wine, or that their consumption subsided, but because French producers had a weapon for meeting demand: the Maghreb. French colonies in North Africa supplied millions of hectoliters of wine to mainland France during colonialism, and even after. Spanish producers viewed this "special connection" between France and the Maghreb as unfair. This section will explore a selection of commentary in Spain about the perceived unfairness of French practices and the rising concerns in Spain about lack of access to this vital market.

On September 17, 1964, the Spanish Ministry of Commerce representatives in France sent a note to the Spanish National Syndicate for Wine, Beer, and Beverages about new French regulations on wine sales. According to the *Journal Officiel de la République Française*, Decree no. 64902, September 1, the government would establish new terms and rankings for wines sold in France. Previously, wines in France were ranked as either "bad" or "good" after being reviewed by the regulators. With this new decree, "when new standards are applied, all wines of 'good quality' for present consumption and only those that deserve this qualification, can be sold benefiting from support prices."[15] Wines would be classified by a variety of standards: region, acidity, and levels of sulphuric anhydride (a state of sulphuric acid). If wines did not meet them, they could not be sold for consumption and only be sent to distilleries or used for vinegars. The French had once again created new standards for the sale and consumption of wine, and the Spanish would have to adjust if they were going to penetrate the market.

The main complaint for Spanish producers, however, remained Algeria. Even after the bloody Algerian Revolution (1954–62), France relied on millions of hectoliters of Algerian wine to meet national demand. According to Spanish commercial attaché M. Albizu Alba, France would continue to allow the importation of Algerian wine below tariff levels, yet they would pay low prices to the Algerian producers. This being said, however, due to postindependence tensions between the two states, the Algerian government authorized a cessation of shipments to France until prices could be renegotiated.[16] Therefore, Spanish producers believed they could fill this void if they could negotiate some new treaty to reduce tariffs on their wines.

Spanish wine trade journals also spoke of this problematic relationship between Spanish wine producers and France. On August 29, 1964, *La Semana Vitivinícola* of Valencia published an opinion piece denouncing the possible accord between Spain and France (along with the EEC), on the grounds that it made Spain a "client for France" rather than equal trading partners. Spanish wine producers offered an interesting example about failed trade relationships: on June 5, 1964, the French government authorized a supplementary import of 450,000 hectoliters of wine from Morocco, but it was wine "that nobody had ordered!"[17] If France had wanted to improve relations, then why did the wine that had been ordered not come from Spain?

In its September 19 issue, *La Semana Vitivinícola* continued its discussion of French actions regarding imports. One article complained of the tariff situation between France and Spain, as a 35.50 franc-per-hectoliter cost was added to Spanish imports, but wines from the Maghreb only paid a 3.50 tariff.[18] If France intended to foster better connections among its European trading partners, this action would not help. In the previous eleven months, France had imported 11,395,000 hl of wine, with almost 11,300,000 coming from North Africa alone. Even more insulting, France imported only 9,358 hl from Spain during the period. In comparison the much smaller producer, Greece, had sold 8,057 hl to France, and the Eastern Bloc country of Bulgaria had sold France 6,000 hl of wine in 1963.[19] Spanish producers were furious that their closest neighbor had bypassed their wine to purchase from North Africa and Eastern Europe. Again, the question was raised: How could France claim to care about European cooperation if they were unwilling to purchase wine from their European neighbor, who produced such a large sum? For these vintners it was clear that the French did not see the Spanish as equal participants in trade.

Rodolfo Argamentería García, the vice-secretary of economic management, spoke with the Spanish national vice-secretary about the upcoming trade accord with France and about the role of wine sales with France. While some winemakers had published op-eds against the signing of this new accord, the Spanish government took the position that the accord was necessary because "a rejection would suppose a hostile gesture with a neighbor." Even though it was going to be signed, this did not mean that the economic relationship between France and Spain was a good one. The national vice-secretary stated, "The total balance [of trade] is very unfavorable for Spain," but that the growth of tourism in

Spain was beginning to help Spanish finances, maintaining a close connection between the countries was important in making future advancements.[20] One future hope involved wine. As the letter states, "To the confidential commercial agreement in which it was said that if France had to import ordinary wines from outside the franc zone, prudential amounts would be reserved for Spain."[21] For years Spanish exporters had wanted to crack the French market, but Maghreb wines stood in the way. In conclusion the letter suggested, "If there really exists the climate of goodwill pointed out by the Commerce official, it seems that France would have no problem in facilitating the entry of Spanish wines at the expense of those that have been exported from Algiers until now."[22] Spanish wines needed their import tariffs slashed, and the countries' proximity and improving relations meant that Spain should be treated the same way as others. In the end, however, the accord was going to be signed no matter what, as Spain seemed to need France more than the other way around.

The Commercial Office of Spain in Paris continued on October 20 with commentary about the relationship between France and Spain in relation to Algerian wine. Wine issues did have an effect on Franco-Spanish negotiations. The Commercial Office stated, "The virtual maintenance of an Algerian monopoly on this matter is in contradiction with the liberalizing spirit that presides over Spanish-French commercial relations. Algeria has ceased to be a French department and today there is no reason why Spain should not be accorded equal treatment in all exchanges."[23] If France had been espousing the benefits of a common European economic zone and worked for free trade among those states, then it was counterfactual to allow Algeria to control French wine imports for no reason other than the historical connection. The letter continued: "This year the Spanish harvest of wine may exceed 28 million hectoliters, it would be a great advantage for our economy to have possibilities of placement in the French market." As one of the world's largest producers of wine, therefore it would make sense for Spain to export its products to its close neighbor. According to the letter, Spain imported 1.5 billion francs of French goods; therefore, France should allow more Spanish wine into their markets. The note then stated: "Although the question of wines is a subject of marked internal political sensitivity, complicated by Franco-Algerian relations, which are extremely delicate, it is essential to create an atmosphere in all sectors of French life so that our wines can recover the position they lost."[24] The question of wine was unique in

France: as French wine was central to national identity, and Algeria had once been considered part of France, then drinking Algerian wine could be construed as drinking "French wine." Now, only a few years after the failed French military action in Algeria, relations between the two states were strained, yet the French still wanted this particular crop. This letter concluded: "The current situation is one of manifest injustice toward Spanish interests and it is necessary to take advantage of all the occasions that are offered to highlight this discriminatory situation."[25] The Spanish government must push for greater economic inclusion for wine while, as always, paying special attention to the attitudes of the French, so as not to alienate them.

Almost two years after the accord with France, the Campaign for General Propaganda of Spanish Wines in France began a combined effort with the Federation of Importers of Foreign Drinks; the General Direction of the Commercial Expansion; the Spanish embassy in Paris; the Spanish National Syndicate of Wine, Beer, and Beverages; the Wine Regulatory Commissions; and the National Confederation of Wine and Spirits of France. On July 16, 1966, the campaign held a cocktail party to celebrate the beginning of the event at the Spanish chamber of commerce in Paris. Beginning on August 15, the campaign would begin distributing portfolios of Spanish wines to all French tourists visiting Spain that they could bring home with them.[26] Also, the Campaign was sponsoring a series of events in Biarritz, France to exhibit the wines of Spain. On August 11, the campaign sponsored a working session and a cocktail party featuring an introduction by Nicolás Castejón y Paz-Pardo, the general delegate of Spain for the promotion of Spanish wines in France; an exposition of the campaign and Spanish wines; and the distribution of detailed portfolios and other materials for the attendees.[27] On August 11, the campaign hosted a dinner titled "Spanish Wines and Bulls" at the Casino de Bellevue to honor bullfighting and Spanish wine, costing five hundred pesetas per person.[28] The following night a gala was held at the Hotel du Palais in Biarritz, costing one thousand pesetas per person.[29] From November 13 to 21, the campaign supported the Spanish wine section at the Salon Internacional de la Alimentación in Paris. As Nicolás Castejón y Paz-Pardo writes, "All the European buyers of food products come to this International Show and, of course, those who trade in the line of wines. Therefore, I consider in principle that this promotion is carried out in the SIAL not only has interest for the French market but also for the other European markets."[30] Any event that could present Spanish wines in a positive light and find new purchasers was important. Overall, this committee looked to find inroads with the French market, targeting the growing French tourist segment in Spain, nearby cities to the Spanish border, and international events in Paris.

The sherry market in France had a difficult time over the years. At the end of the nineteenth century, the French government prohibited the importation of wines with excessive levels of gypsum, which Jerez used to clarify its wines. From there Spain saw a slow increase in sherry imports to France once the Jerez regulatory commission worked to improve production. The belief in 1967 was that while France was a small market (in comparison) for the consumption of sherry, it was a place for growth. One problem facing sherry shipments to France was tariffs. Wines with 15–18 percent alcohol had tariffs of 74.05 pesetas for up to two liters, 59.24 pesetas for containers between two to five liters, and 36.98 pesetas for larger containers. Sherry, however, usually had alcohol percentages between 18 and 22 percent and therefore paid higher tariffs: 181.43 pesetas for bottles up to two liters, 172.05 pesetas for bottles between two and five liters, and 77.70 pesetas for larger containers.[31] These extremely high tariffs made sherry more expensive than other imported wines. Sherry producers saw other problems exporting to France (similar to all Spanish producers): Algeria and Tunisia had unfair tariff exceptions, Morocco had quotas for the French market, Greece had negotiated preferential treatment, with countries like Portugal, Italy, and Germany posing threats as well.[32] Sherry imports still remained small to the overall French consumption of 57,800,000 hectoliters in 1967. In 1960 France only imported 579.31 hl; 657.92 hl in 1961; 840.26 hl in 1962; 1,150.05 hl in 1963; 956.81 hl in 1964; 1,134.46 hl in 1965; 1,665.54 hl in 1966; 1,286.33 hl in 1967; 1,536.46 hl in 1968; and 1,322.9 hl in 1969.[33] This infinitesimal importation and likely consumption rate of sherry in France must have been frustrating for the producers, as one of their closest neighbors disregarded Spain's oldest quality exported alcoholic beverage.

In general Spanish wine producers must have been frustrated with France. The world's largest consumer and importer of wine barely acknowledged its southern neighbor. Historically, with French fields in chaos, Spain represented a close and cheap market from which to obtain table wine, but, when French vineyards recovered, France more or less cast Spain aside. French producers were able to maintain their perceived identity of quality and class, while demoting Spanish wine to a second-rate commodity. France also seemed to have undue advantages, as its vestiges of colonialism and emigration to Northern Africa established thousands of vineyards in the Maghreb and allowed for cheap wine to be sold. Even as France spoke of European integration under the auspices of the European Economic Community, Spain seemed to be an afterthought. High tariffs on quintessentially Spanish beverages like sherry meant that the drink would always be more expensive than North African low-tariff table wines. Even with these disadvantages, Spanish organizations did try to penetrate the market in the 1960s, with some small successes.

SHERRY AND THE UNITED KINGDOM

The British alcohol trade magazine the *Wine & Spirit Trade Review* contains reports on alcohol sales, information for distributors, and various advertisements for a variety of liquors and wines available for sale in the United Kingdom. While Spanish sherry companies like Williams & Humbert, Harvey's, and Valdespino advertised their products, so did companies located outside of Jerez de la Frontera, Spain, who made a product under the umbrella term "empire sherry." These fortified wines were produced outside of sherry's historical home yet still aimed to equate to this culturally Spanish product. In an advertisement the Cyprus Wine Board claimed: "A Toast to Cyprus Sherry. Good Sherry is no longer the privilege of the few, for Cyprus Sherry is within the means of all your customers. Make sure you have some—always."[34] While Cyprus was not the home of sherry, its sherry-like product occupied the same pages as traditional sherry and claimed to be comparable to the real thing at a lesser price. In the same edition, Monte Cristo Cream Cyprus Sherry announced: "'Big news about Monte Cristo Cream for *everyone* in the wine trade,' said the Count. 'You'll see Monte Cristo Cream in vast advertisements in the *Sun*, the *Mirror*, and the *Express*, from October 22. I shall be so popular.'"[35] While later the advert does describe the product as "Cyprus sherry," the national origin of the beverage is mentioned only once; thus a cursory glance could make one assume it was real sherry.

In November 1964 the Emu Imperial Bond announced its new campaign for its Australian Sweet Sherry: "Throughout your peak selling time right up to Christmas, forceful publicity for Emu Imperial Bond will build even greater sales. At main viewing times there will be arresting spots on no less than 8 stations.... Millions will see and respond to the Imperial Bond message. It stresses the sweetness and value of this unique Australian Sherry at 11/- a bottle."[36] Airwaves would be flooded with the news of this faux Australian "sherry," promoting its quality and, more importantly, its low price. In an earlier edition, Sherries by Burgoyne's introduced its "Cyprus sherry" in a full-page advertisement: "For the past ten years the demand for full-strength Empire Sherries has been growing. This demand should continue to grow during the rest of 1964. Shortages may occur later this year because demand may out-run supply."[37] Burgoyne's claimed that its product would be the next big thing, touting its knowledge of Empire Sherries: "We, at Burgoyne's, have long been planning on this moment. We have been selling 'South African' full-strength sherries for years. Keeping growth potential in mind, we commissioned the maturing of a small range of Cyprus Sherries convinced that they would immediately win approval in a very critical market."[38] Importers of these empire sherries knew the game well: find cheaper product and try to get it into the UK market. As a final example, RSVP Medium and RSVP Cream Sherries tried to make their cases to the liquor community, with the word "British" in much smaller letters in the ad, which claims, "These two superb British Sherries are proving triumphantly successful. People like them because they're good value for money—and because they make entertaining so easy . . . there will be a powerful boost for RSVP MEDIUM and CREAM with striking full-colour insertions in 'Weekend', 'Women's Realm' and 'Women's Own' at Christmas."[39] Yet again the major draw for this empire sherry was its lower price than real sherry, and, in this case, women were the primary market for the product.

As discussed previously, sherry had been Spain's largest wine export to the UK for centuries, as the fortified wine could survive the longer sea journey without spoilage. Even in the 1960s, Britain was the largest global consumer of sherry. In 1960 Spain sent 218,705.48 hectoliters of sherry; by 1962 this number increased to 258,410.32 hl; in 1964 293,932.7 hl; in 1966 320,306.14 hl; in 1968 426,342.9; and dropping to 409,112.36 in 1969. Therefore, nearly 27 percent of all British wine imports in the 1960s were sherry from Jerez. By 1968 sherry earned 1,542,146,144 pesetas for Spain in the UK—a truly massive sum.[40] After arriving in the UK, 4.79 percent was reexported to the United States, 1.84 percent to Canada, and 2.68 percent to other countries, meaning that 9.31 percent of sherry was resold through British corporations.[41] Even with these large numbers, sherry researchers in the 1960s were nervous about continued international success, mainly due to fears relating to perceived fraud from "Australian Sherry," "South

African Sherry," "Californian Sherry," "Cyprus Sherry," and "British Sherry."[42] As mentioned earlier, these imposter sherries had tried to take portions of the market, and a battle would occur for the future of the beverage. The influx of these imposter sherries combined with a steady demand for the beverage at any level created pricing concerns. For real sherry producers, a twofold danger loomed: the need to maintain high standards of production to bolster their products' strong identity, and the need to reduce prices in order to compete with the imposters.[43] This new pressure from outside forces could harm the economic prospects for sherry throughout the UK.

The most important moment for the future of authentic sherry in the UK did not begin as a conversation about the Spanish product, but about French exports. In December 1960 French champagne producers took legal action in British courts against a perceived imposter. In 1927 the French government passed a law delineating the region where champagne could be made, and in 1935 the Appellation d'Origine Contrôlée, was formed creating a series of rules and quality expectations for champagne, which meant that it had to be produced within this geographical region and follow specific regulations. In *Bollinger v. Costa Brava Wine Co. Ltd.* (1961), French producers sued a Spanish producer who had been selling "Spanish Champagne." In this case it was determined that champagne was a protected product that had established an image of quality over many decades, and that this new product from Spain attempted to use this earned term, which could damage the identity of the original product. Also, and importantly, this Spanish product had only recently entered the British market and therefore had no historical claim to use the word "champagne." French champagne won its case, and now enjoyed a monopoly of this title in the UK.[44]

On July 12, 1963, following the French victory in the *Bollinger* case, attorneys for sherry shippers in the UK wrote to a series of British sherry importers, stating, "We are instructed by the Sherry Shippers of London and Jerez with reference to the advertisement and sale of your 'British Sherry.' We would observe that your advertisements for this product and the labels used upon the bottles are couched in such terms as to indicate that it is sherry."[45] Just as French producers had claimed that the labels for "Spanish Champagne" were created to trick consumers into thinking the product was truly "champagne," these sherry shippers viewed the use of the term "British sherry" as an attempt to obfuscate the true nature of the beverage. The letter continued: "The word sherry can properly only be used upon or in relation to wine made from grapes grown in the Jerez district of Spain, and blended and matured under the control of the Council of Denomination of Origin 'Jerez-Xérès-Sherry.'"[46] Just as the Appellation d'Origine Contrôlée established the protection for champagne, the denominación de origen for sherry created in 1933 clearly demarcated the geographical region where sherry must be produced. In response to this letter, attorneys for the British sherry importers wrote, "We have assumed, however, that this is not what you intended, and that you are not in fact requesting on behalf of your clients that our clients should now abandon the right to use these common descriptions which have been in constant use for very many years and in the case of 'British Sherry' for hundreds of years."[47] On July 30, sherry attorneys responded rather pointedly:

> The undertaking which we are seeking is in respect of the sale of "British Sherry" or "English Sherry" by your clients. We are instructed to ask whether your clients will give to our clients their undertaking and not hereafter advertise, offer for sale or sell any of their products under or by reference to the words "sherry" "British Sherry" or "English Sherry" or any other word or words likely to indicate or enable other to indicate the belief that such products are wines from grapes produced in the Jerez district of Spain.
>
> We think that this clarification will make it unnecessary at this stage to reply in detail to the other points you have raised, except to say that our clients are all the shippers of sherry wine from Spain to this country. If your clients are willing to give to such an undertaking as we have mentioned we will, of course, let you have a list of their names, as the undertaking will be made with each of them; if your clients decline, we shall give you particulars of the facts on which our clients rely in the writ and statement of claim which we are, in the absence of a favourable reply, instructed to issue and serve, and in respect of which we should be glad to have your confirmation that you will accept service.[48]

The sherry producers wanted an end to the use of the word "sherry" for any product not made in Jerez, which constituted a serious attack against the British industry, but this agreement was based on the *Bollinger* case that was only settled a few years earlier. How could "vino de Jerez" not come from Jerez, Spain?

In response to this letter, the British sherry importers acted. Wisely, these importers did not wait to become defendants in a case about the word "sherry" and filed paperwork as plaintiffs on August 9, 1963. The statement of claim reads:

> The plaintiffs, Vine Products Limited, sell, offer for sale, and advertise for sale in (inter alia) England wines under the descriptions "British Sherry," "English Sherry," "Cyprus Sherry" and "Australian Sherry." The plaintiffs, Whiteways Cyder Company limited, sell, offer for sale and advertise for in (inter alia) England wines under the description "British Sherry." The plaintiffs, Jules Duval & Beaufoys Limited, sell, offer for sale and advertise for sale in England wines under the descriptions "British Sherry," "South African Sherry," "Cyprus Sherry" and "Australian Sherry."[49]

The defendants named in the case were Mackenzie & Company Limited, Williams & Humbert Limited, and González Byass & Company, English companies that shipped sherry from Spain to Britain. Pedro Domecq SA, a Spanish corporation, was also named as a defendant. Martin Silva & Company Limited was originally named as well, but, as this was in error, they were soon removed from the case.[50] The battle lines were drawn; both sides in this case would have to provide evidence of their proper understanding of the meaning of the word "sherry" to the English-speaking world. Spanish producers feared their identity and reputation could be destroyed by the term's improper use, and British importers believed their long-term use of the word would suffice for the case.

The case between British sherry and authentic sherry began in February 1967 on the question as to whether the former product was trying to use unfair trading practices to sell their good in Britain. The plaintiffs based their case on certain central facts. First, they claimed that the issue of the product's quality was "wholly irrelevant" because they were not trying to "pass off" their product as authentic sherry. Second, they stated that the term "sherry" had been used for many decades in conjunction with other geographical locations, and, therefore, there could be no confusion, as the product was clearly marked. Lastly, they stated that since this "empire sherry" had been sold in the British market for an extended period of time, during which the Spanish made no complaints, the wait had been too long. The Spanish had no defense for this.[51]

Attorneys for the defense mounted a strong case, stating that there were nine questions that needed to be addressed by the court to side with the plaintiffs— first, whether the word "sherry" when used in England meant wine from a particular region, or if it could be produced in other locations. Second, was the English word "sherry" derived from the Arabic word *Sherrish*, which was the name of a geographical region in Spain? Third, had this wine, known as sherry and from southern Spain, developed a positive reputation in English markets? Fourth, was the defendants' wine strongly associated with the Jerez region of Spain? Fifth, were the wines made outside Jerez produced by similar grapes and under controlled conditions within the specific region? Sixth, had the plaintiffs sold wines with no connections to the geography of the Jerez zone? Seventh, did the use of geographical terms like "Cyprus" or "South Africa" clearly distinguish these wines? Eighth, had the plaintiffs obtained the right of the use of the term? And, finally, did the defendants already lose their opportunity to complain about this use, and, if so, why?[52]

The defense also asserted that because sherry is a geographical name reflecting a product from that area and not simply a common word, then "it is a part of the goodwill and a right of property belonging to every person who makes that class of goods in that area, and any act which takes a part of that right of property or injures that right of property is actionable," thanks to *Bollinger v. Costa Brava Wine Co. Ltd.* and other precedent.[53] The defense stated: "Once it is shown that part of the complainants' goodwill has been taken, the onus lies with the taker to show that no deception has been caused."[54] The defense claimed that because British producers took the already established word "sherry" for their product, it was in fact their responsibility to prove that they had caused no harm to its already established identity. The defense continued that three conditions must be met before the plaintiffs could proceed with their claims: 1) "the person who invades the right of another must not be aware that he is doing so"; 2) "the person whose right is invaded must have done something to encourage the other to continue in his course of action"; and 3) "the person whose right is being invaded must be aware of the existence of his right."[55]

In response the plaintiffs claimed: "Trade marks apart, there is no such thing as a monopoly in the use of a name save that no one may make, either directly or indirectly, a false representation that his goods are the good of another."[56]

The attorneys contended that "if there is no evidence of deception or of intention to deceive, the court should not find that there is likelihood of deception, particularly where goods have been on the market for a long time."[57] They also stated that the use of an ordinary English word such as "sherry" cannot be used to deceive, especially if other words accompanied it. Lastly, the plaintiffs responded that even though *Bollinger* had been recently decided, it did not create new precedent, and that the defendants had been ignorant of previous British law and, therefore, had waited far too long to advance their complaints against "empire sherry."

The plaintiffs outlined other aspects of their claim as well. Their attorneys claimed that the average person did not understand that the use of the word "sherry" would specifically mean a wine produced exclusively in Spain from particular grapes. In addition, the term "British sherry" had been used in the UK for over a hundred years, and other "empire sherries" had been imported for years without problems. At the same time, Spanish producers, knowing of these trends, had not acted earlier to end this usage, and their entire complaint relied on *Bollinger*. By using the geographical location of the "empire sherry" in the name of the wine meant that there could be no confusion by the purchaser.[58] Due to this evidence and other statements, the British sherry producers and importers wanted the court to find:

1. A declaration that each of the plaintiffs is entitled to continue to sell, advertise and offer for sale any wine heretofore sold by any of them respectively under any of the descriptions "British Sherry," "English Sherry," "South African Sherry," "Cyprus Sherry," or "Australian Sherry" and is entitled to sell, advertise or offer for sale any similar wine under which such descriptions without infringing any right of any defendant.

2. A declaration that none of the defendants have any such right as would entitle them either severally or in conjunction with all other shippers of sherry wine from Spain to England to restrain any of the plaintiffs from selling, advertising or offering for sale any such wines as aforesaid, or similar wine under the respective descriptions as "British Sherry," "English Sherry," "South African Sherry," "Cyprus Sherry," or "Australian Sherry;" thirdly they claim an appropriate injunction; further or other relief; and costs.[59]

For these British producers, the idea was simple: in no way was their product meant to deceive the consumer, as they clearly identified the location of production, and, as their product had been sold in Britain for many decades, the Spanish producers could not suddenly be concerned now. These producers wanted the court to prevent any future actions by Spanish companies attacking the idea of "empire sherry." If the court would offer this ruling, then British sherries would be allowed to continue sales in the UK without any future impact to their businesses.

In response to these claims, the defense amended its previous statements to offer additional information for their case: "The word 'sherry' is and always has been distinctive of a wine fortified, matured and blended in the Jerez district in Spain and produced from the juice of specified varieties of grapes grown in the Jerez district."[60] The defense suggested that because sherry had been produced under these tight regulations for over two hundred years in the region, and that "such control has been exercised since 1934 under the Ministerial Order of 14th July 1935 by the control board for the Denomination of Origin 'Jerez-Xérès-Sherry,' the word in question was inextricably bonded to Spain."[61] They continued: "Sherry is sold and bought in the United Kingdom, by both the trade and the public reputation established by the wines made as aforesaid, and the reputation attaching to the word 'sherry' has by reason of the care taken in the production of sherry been for many years a very high one."[62] For Spanish producers the careful management of their product had created a positive identity for it, and these imposter wines could destroy this hard-won reputation. Finally, the defense claimed that the creation of these "empire sherries" was "calculated to deceive and cause confusion and to lead the trade and public to believe that the beverages offered for sale and sold by the plaintiffs and each of them are sherry, that is to say wines produced in manners specified."[63] The use of labels with "rather small letters" identifying the geographical location served as proof of obfuscation. The defense stated that these loose standards of "empire sherries" were harming the identity of authentic sherry and therefore harming the financial stability of Spanish wines. The defense looked for the judge to rule on their counterclaim against the British producers:

> An injunction to restrain the plaintiffs and each of them, whether by their servants or agents or otherwise howsoever, from passing off or enabling or assisting others to pass off as and for sherry beverages which are not wines

fortified, matured and blended in the Jerez district of Spain under the control of the Council for the Denomination of Origin "Jerez-Xérès-Sherry," and produced from the juice of specified varieties of grapes grown in the Jerez district supplemented under specific circumstances with wines from the neighbouring provinces of Huelva, Sevilla, and Cordoba, and brought into the Jerez district under controlled conditions, by offering for sale or selling the same under or by reference to the word "sherry."[64]

This injunction would allow Spain to defend the usage of the word "sherry" throughout the British market. As a side note, the Spanish also asked the court to offer financial damages to the defense for previous attacks against sherry's reputation.

Judge Justice Cross delivered his ruling on November 27, 1967. In his opinion the judge outlined his understanding of the history of authentic sherry and British sherry to explain his ruling. He identified the beginnings of the Arabic period of the town when it was called "Shereesh" and was then reconquered by Christian knights in the thirteenth century, and that over time the name of the town was converted to "Jerez." Spain exported wine to England in the sixteenth century, sending 40,000 butts of wine annually. The judge identified the first English dictionary reference to "Sherris, Sherris sack, Sherry" in Johnson's *Dictionary* in 1757: "From Xeres, a town in Andalucia in Spain: a kind of sweet Spanish wine."[65] The importation of Spanish sherry increased over the centuries. On all authentic sherry bottles, the words "Product of Spain" appeared in small letters, but, as the judge pointed out, never did the words "Spanish Sherry" appear on the labels for the beverage. Cross therefore understood the long-term historical relationship between sherry and Spain as well as sherry and its exportation and labeling in Britain.

After discussing authentic sherry, Cross turned his attention to British sherry and its history, which was vital to his final determinations. In 1635 a Francis Chamberlayne was given the monopoly of making wine in England from "dryed grapes or raysons."[66] The first reference to "British sherry" came in 1852, when the House of Commons had records for a Mr. Walker and a Mr. Frith and their conversation about 600,000 gallons of wine being made in Britain, some of it labeled "British sherry," as it was sweet wine. After the 1875 Trade Mark Act, various companies received trademarks for "British sherry." By 1900 Alexander

Metzotakis (a co-founder of Vine Products Ltd., a plaintiff in this sherry case) created a system to make wine from dehydrated grape juice, a process that spread quickly to make less expensive wines. In 1928 Britain made 2,272,593 gallons of wine, a number that later rose to 9,182,860 gallons, with almost all coming from importation of either juice or grapes.[67] The plaintiffs in this current case produced between 65 to 70 percent of all British wine, with just over half being considered "sherry type." Since the 1875 Trade Mark Act, however, sherry produced in Britain was always called "British sherry" and had never been advertised or sold as simply "sherry" in any significant quantities.[68] This history was very damaging for Spain's case, as a central factor in *Bollinger* was the fact that Costa Brava had only recently begun to sell its "Spanish Champagne" in the UK, and that Bollinger quickly sued. In the sherry situation, beverages called "British Sherry" had been sold for close to a century with protected trademarks; therefore, it could not come as a surprise that these products existed.

Another blow to the Spanish argument came from the 1925 *Corke v. Pipers Ltd.* case, where the Spanish Sherry Shippers' Association sued Pipers Ltd., who were selling wine made by Vine Products Limited labeled as "Corona Pale Sherry." The judge in that case "found as a fact, on the evidence before him, that 'sherry' meant wine produced in the Jerez district of Spain and that by selling British wine under the label in question the defendants were applying a false trade of their good."[69] When the judge was shown a bottle marked with the term "British sherry," he concluded that the label would not confuse the consumer and was therefore acceptable. The magistrate ruled that "British sherry" was appropriate, whereas just labeling it as "sherry" was not. Seemingly, the Sherry Shippers agreed to this ruling and never filed other suits against any companies for using the term "British" or "Empire" until this case in 1963.

Other historical events influenced the case for British producers. In the 1920s it was often common to call these wines "sherry style," but over the years, the better-sounding "British sherry" title was used. As for South Africa, grapes arrived there as early as the seventeenth century with the Dutch settlers, which meant that the region had a long period of wine production. During the Napoleonic Wars, England could not access wine from the continent, so "Cape ports" and "Cape sherries" entered the market at large numbers. At the start of the twentieth century, Australia began to produce larger amounts of wine, and as Britain passed laws to give preferential treatment to Commonwealth countries, the

Australians had a legal advantage to enter Britain. By the 1930s British Cyprus began to produce larger amounts of wine, which could also enter the British market more easily.[70]

Judge Cross discussed issues relating to labeling in wine catalogs as well. According to his research, the category of "sherry" was used exclusively for products made in Spain, with separate categories in the catalogs housing sherries from the other states. That being said, the wine distributers were not trying to pass their wines off as authentic, and wine purchasers would know the origin of their purchase by simple checking. Interestingly, the use of the word "sherry" among the general public was less clear. According to Cross there could be ambiguity for the average purchaser, as the word "sherry" had been used interchangeably in common conversation. However, a solution to this would come from the actual purchase of the product: "The witnesses all agreed that if a customer previously unknown to them asked for a bottle or a glass of sherry in a shop or a bar they would assume without question that he meant a wine from Spain unless it was clear from the price which he expected to pay that he must mean a British or Commonwealth sherry."[71] While the historical evidence presented earlier greatly helped the British arguments, one can assume this last assertion was tenuous at best. If this judge were to believe that every salesman or barkeep in Britain was always honest with his sales to every customer, then, clearly, he was being naive or had never drank at a bar. However, this testimony helped to support the belief that a clear distinction between sherry and "British sherry" did exist in the minds of the experts, and, as they were the ones who sold the product to the nonexpert, if they were being honest, then the system was working.

After all the evidence had been presented and reviewed, Justice Cross presented his final orders to the case:

> This Court doth declare that each of the Plaintiffs is entitled to continue to sell, advertise and offer for sale any wine heretofore sold by any of them respectably under any of the descriptions "British sherry," "English sherry," "South African sherry," "Cyprus sherry," "Australian sherry" or "Empire sherry" and is entitled to sell, advertise or offer for sale any similar wine under such descriptions without infringing any rights of any of the Defendants.
>
> And this court doth declare that none of the Defendants has any such rights as would entitle them either severally or in conjunction with all

other shippers of sherry wine from Spain to England to restrain any of the Plaintiffs from selling, advertising or offering for sale any such wines as aforesaid or similar wine under the respective descriptions "British sherry," "English sherry," "South African sherry," "Cyprus sherry," "Australian sherry" or "Empire sherry."

And this court doth order that the plaintiffs and each of them be restrained (whether by their respective directors, officers, servants or agents or any of them or otherwise howsoever) from using in the course of trade the word "sherry" in connection with any wine not being wine coming from Jerez district in Spain otherwise as part of one or more of the phrases "British sherry," "English sherry," "South African sherry," "Cyprus sherry," "Australian sherry" or "Empire sherry."

And it is ordered that the Defendants do pay the Plaintiffs one quarter of their costs of this Action and the said Counterclaim such costs to be taxed by the Taxing Master.[72]

Authentic sherry lost the case. British producers were able to show that they had used the word "sherry" for an extended period of time, and that they only did so in conjunction with the geographical location from where the wine came. For Spain to have won the case, they would have had to have acted much earlier, as "sherry" had entered common parlance and changed its meaning. As was stated frequently by the plaintiffs, the Spanish should have sued earlier if they actually saw serious interest in the name identity. Even with this legal loss, Spanish sherry would continue to be the largest wine import to Britain for years.

On March 9, 1970, deputy commerce counsel for the Spanish embassy in London Víctor Audera wrote to Pío Miguel Irurzun, president of the Spanish National Syndicate for Wine, Beer, and Beverages about the condition of Spanish wine sales in the UK. The letter opened with a discussion about the problems facing Spanish wine and sherry in the market. Audera believed it would be a good idea to find some individuals who could help promote the beverages in the British market, presumably spokespeople outside the wine industry. Another issue was import taxes; Audera joked that they ought "to invite the Chancellor of the Exchequer and all the administrative apparatus" to drink Spanish wine and get "so conveniently drunk they were convinced that they had to lower taxes."[73]

Clearly this was a witticism, but it is interesting to see the Spanish desire to lower these tariffs. The real conversation was about showing the British the great value associated with Spanish wine. The problem, which has been true for decades for Spanish wine, was that purchasers thought "Spanish wine is synonymous with cheap and bad wine."[74] There was a need to show the value of Spanish wine when compared to the wines of other countries. The idea of spokespeople, or at least casual allies, was again raised: "The best use that could be given to the invitations was to make people who were in a position to be able to say with authority good things about our wines, production areas, qualities, etc., etc., and that . . . influence the general opinion, thus giving more strength to our exporters negotiating."[75] Audera suggested a series of people who should be invited to the Third Gala of Wine and Fashion: the president and members of the British Wine and Spirit Association; members of the Wine Development Board; the editors of *Wine Trade Review*, *Harpers*, and *Financial Times*; and other figures associated with taste-making. If these individuals attended the event in Madrid and saw the quality of Spanish wines, they could act as unofficial spokespeople for the beverages when they returned to the UK.

The British interaction with Spanish wine was vastly different than that of France. Britain did produce some "wine," but it came from imported juice and often was of exceptionally low quality, whereas French identity has become tied to quality wine. The British also had a long history of purchasing Spanish wine, particularly sherry, and consuming it in large amounts; in fact Britain was the largest purchaser of sherry in the world. Even with this close connection, Spanish wines did not receive the respect producers believe they deserved from the British. The sherry legal case was striking because sherry had become so ubiquitous in English that the consumer assumed all sweet wine of a particular color and taste was sherry, even though this was not true. At the same time, this case and the Aubera letter bring up a strange irony about Spanish wine: Spanish sherry was more expensive and of a higher quality than its impersonator, but overall Spanish wine had to combat the impression that it was simply cheap and, therefore, of low quality. The question seems to have haunted Spanish wine throughout its export history: How can one prove that a wine can be good and yet less expensive than others? This was a struggle without a clear answer, even in a country that drank so much sherry.

Denmark was not a major wine consumer in the 1960s, but, as previously shown, the average citizen did drink 3.9 liters of wine a year (more than the United States) for a total of 188,382 hectoliters. To meet this demand, wine needed to be imported for a total of 207,200 hectoliters. In 1960 20,141.23 hl of sherry entered Denmark, but that number reached 30,900.41 hl in 1969, for about 15 percent of all imports. Denmark imported 5.79 percent of global sherry production, making it the third largest consumer.[76] Spanish wines did have a consistent presence in Denmark, but it was a wonderful location to increase exports. In the 1970 Spansk Vinefestival in Copenhagen, the Spanish wine industry wanted to take advantage of early success in the region and persuade this Nordic country to drink more of its wine.

On March 3, 1970, Antonio Riaño, commercial advisor in Denmark, sent a note to the director general of Commercial Policy about sponsoring a wine festival in Copenhagen. This celebration would be a good idea, he thought, as "the Danish interest for our table wines remains enormous, and therefore I am very glad that we can take the tasting in Denmark. Now, this tasting must take place as soon as possible, because it is now when the Danes newly acquire wines in Spain, and therefore it is also now, when they need our support, in the form of propaganda or tasting."[77] The president of the Spanish National Syndicate of Wine, Beer, and Beverages had already extended invitations to Sigurd Muller, president of Danish Wine Importers, and Gunnar Buchwald, a journalist and the president of the Confederation and Friends of Wine, to attend the Gala of Wine and Fashion in Madrid. Another individual who should receive an invitation was Poul Møller, a Danish journalist for *Berlingerske Tinende*, who had written positively about Spain over the years, as compared to others in the Danish press, "since until now the press has been rather hostile toward Spain," likely due to the political differences in democratic Denmark versus dictatorial Spain.[78]

As for planning the event, Riaño suggested that it would be easy to put together with the help of Spanish wine producers and hotels in Copenhagen. The primary tasting could take place in the Hotel Royal, featuring appetizers and wines from Jerez, diverse plates of vegetables and meats paired with white and red wines, and desserts and cheese such as manchego served with brandies and sweet sherries.[79] The event would work as a buffet for visitors to sample a variety of Spanish products. Other than the men already mentioned, "all the major importers of wine in this country, journalists, officials of the Ministry of Foreign Affairs and Commerce and some other personalities will be invited."[80] With some of Denmark's leading politicians and celebrities in attendance, the word of the quality of Spanish wine could spread to many important decision-makers. Even though sherry would be served, as it was a known commodity, the tasting needed to celebrate other wines as well. "Finally, it is only necessary to add," Riaño said, "what matters most are the table wines, since those of Jerez have always been sold and are still selling well in this market, while those table wines due to the preferential tariff rights of the EFTA, practically they had disappeared."[81] The European Free Trade Association, which was created in 1960, included Denmark as well as the wine-producing powerhouse of Portugal. This pact allowed the Danes and Portuguese to negotiate prices on tariffs, giving Portugal an advantage over Spain in the market. Spain did not have to worry about Portugal taking the market for sherry (even though some saw port as comparable to a sweet wine), but table wine needed to be helped. Riaño continued: "Other wines that should be included in the tasting are the whites of Galicia, to be able to demonstrate to the Danes that, even if they stop buying white wines in Portugal, they can find them in Spain, which also produces them, a fact little known in this country."[82] The proposal to push Galician white wines is an interesting one. Because of Galicia's location north of Portugal, similar styles of wine were produced there. Also, as mentioned in chapter 2, Galician wines had suffered in the nineteenth century under the plagues oidium, mildew, and phylloxera and were very slow to recover, with demand at that time primarily for red wine. It was not until 1988 that the Rías Baixas denominación de origen for albariño was established. Therefore, this Copenhagen event could have been one of the first main attempts to push Galician wines as an option to Portuguese wines. Lastly, Riaño considered it a good idea to send maps and books and guides on wine to Copenhagen to be given to the importers and visitors so they could understand the vast production of Spanish wine. Overall, this *Spansk Vinefestival* could be a fantastic opportunity to introduce Denmark to new wines while celebrating the historical connections with sherry and the Danes.

Planning for the wine festival continued as the National Syndicate of Wine, Beer, and Beverages organized in Copenhagen. Juan Antonio Domingo and José Antonio Lopez Cascante, commissioners for the National Group of Exporters of Wine, traveled to Denmark in March to begin the process. The men met with Juana Heimann and A. Kapp of the Hotel Royal to schedule the event for June. The tasting schedule for regional wines was as follows: June 2, Priorat, Tarragona, and Penedès; June 3, Valencia, Utiel, Requena, Cheste, and Valdepinas; June 4, Alicante, Jumilla, and Cariñena; June 9, Malaga, Montilla, and Navarra; June 10, Rioja; and June 11, Jerez.[83] This event did not focus solely on the largest regions, but would allow Danes to try wines from throughout the country. The Ministry of Tourism and the National Hotel Syndicate scheduled food, music, and folkloric events for the attendees and launched an advertising campaign. The men mention that in 1969 Portugal initiated an advertising campaign for their wines in Denmark at approximately forty million pesetas. From 1968 to 1969, wine imports to Denmark purportedly increased by 17.2 percent, with a whopping 95 percent of those imports coming from Portugal. The Spanish desperately wanted to experience this increase as well. The Spanish representatives began to confer with local Danish advertising agencies, creating a traveling mural showcasing wines and brochures with a drawing of Denmark, a Spanish sun, and a bottle of wine pouring its happiness onto the country. These materials could be sent to other cities like Aalborg and Aarhus to announce the arrival of the event.[84] This advertising firm would also produce a film on wine to be screened at the event and send invitations to personalities in Denmark and other Nordic countries. José Antonio Lopez Cascante again wrote to the syndicate on May 8 with an update on their progress. Plans had been finalized to host the event on June 2–4 and 9–11 at the Royal Hotel in Copenhagen; each of the regions previously mentioned had confirmed their tastings. The Consejos Reguladores had confirmed their placements; local Danish tourism boards were notified about the event, posters sent to grocery stores throughout the country, and advertisements placed in print and on radio. Invitations were also sent to the press and Danish Diplomatic Core.[85]

On June 30 Luis Medina, commercial advisor for Spain in Denmark, sent a letter to the director general for Commercial Policy and the General Commission of Festivals to report on the wine festival. According to the advisor, reviews of the event were "frankly favorable"; there had been growing interest in Spanish wines in the months leading to the event, with Spanish wine imports increasing one million krone over the first three months, compared to 1969, for a total of 3,987,000 krone by the end of the festival. Expectations were that imports could reach seventeen million krone by the end of the year.[86] In the week of June 15–21 the Danish supermarket IRMA reported sales of twelve thousand bottles of Spanish wines. This connection with a supermarket chain was quite advantageous: "As the Portuguese 'danger' always stalks us, I think it is an opportunity to continue with the propaganda of our wines, and the offer of IRMA is very appropriate for this purpose."[87] By making connections with IRMA, Spanish producers could access Danes across the country and present strong competition to the Portuguese.

The restaurant publication *Danmarks Restaranter* created a special edition of their magazine on Spanish wines and sent 5,700 copies to restaurants and hotels across Denmark. It featured articles on how to properly serve and pair Spanish wines for the consumer. This special edition was a serious success. Medina wrote, "As the impact of our festival has been very strong, we have managed to awaken the interest of directors and owners of hotels and restaurants, with the help of the aforementioned articles in the professional magazine, in the future they will surely include them in their wine list."[88] If consumers could try Spanish wines while out to dinner and learn about them, if they enjoyed them they could purchase them in stores—a highly effective way of infiltrating the Danish market.

Medina stated, "Finally, I can only add that not only has the organization been perfect on the Spanish side, the wines arriving with enough time to select them, but also without [broken bottles] is worth mentioning."[89] Even with these direct successes from the event, it was necessary to keep working in the Danish market. Medina continued: "As a final point, I just want to insist, in the absolute necessity of continuing with the propaganda of our wines in this country, either through this Commercial Office or directly by the different Regulatory Councils, taking into account that autumn is when the consumption of wine in Denmark increases."[90] This success could not be a one-time thing, left to wither on the vine; Spanish agencies needed to continue to work. There was a major problem, however, that the Spanish government and trade representatives still needed to address: Spanish wines still had a customs tax of 1.36 krone per liter, while Portuguese wines, due to trade agreements, did not have to pay one at all. Another problem was how Spanish wines were sold and taxed once entering the market. Bulk Spanish wine paid an additional internal tax of 6 krone per liter, but bottled wine paid an additional 3 krone and then an internal tax of 20 krone per liter, which made purchasing bottled Spanish wine problematic.

Until these fees and taxes were reduced, putting Spanish wines on equal footing with the Portuguese, there would always be inequity in their interaction. At the same time, until taxes on bottled wines were reduced, it was cost preventative for many Danes to buy these Spanish wines. As the average person likely bought wine in individual bottles and not in bulk, this problem needed to be addressed.

The estimated cost of the *Spansk Vinefestival* was approximately 4,457,428 pesetas.[91] The successes in the weeks following the event raised the hopes of the Spanish for conquering this market. Luckily, Spanish producers, especially those of sherry, were already known entities in Denmark, giving them some footing there. Clearly, the most problematic factor was Portuguese wines in Denmark. Due to the EFTA, Portuguese wines had an advantage of less or no tariffs or import taxes, making them a cheaper commodity. In this case the best strategy was to export the sunshine and happiness of Spain along with the improved quality of its wines to bolster their stronger identity for the consumer.

A SAMPLING OF OTHERS

In this section I will briefly explore communications regarding wine concerns between Spain and other states. The Archivo General de la Administración contains material about attempts by the Spanish industry to access and send their products internationally. An article in *Arriba* from November 6, 1966, talks about the importance of the Second International Food Show (mentioned at the beginning of this chapter), which the Spanish should use to take advantage of European markets. Tourism had been the initial economic foray for Spain as Europeans from the cold and dark north traveled to sunny Spanish beaches to enjoy their vacations. With tourism off to a good start, Spain could show Europe how to purchase the goods they enjoyed while on their trips. Quality agricultural products, particularly wine, could help the Spanish grow economically. Once again the main issue for Spain was that other countries had been outselling them. Portugal seemed to be the main thought for the Spanish. In 1966 France consumed six million bottles of port, but only two hundred thousand of sherry—a dramatic difference.[92] As Portugal exported fifteen million bottles of wine to France, clearly Spain needed to improve in this area. Generally, Spanish producers needed to target any market they could.

In July 1966 Pío Miguel Irurzun wrote about the possibility of exporting more wine to Switzerland. The National Subgroup of Producers and Exporters of

Wine had contacted the director general of Commercial Policy to open negotiations to increase the 30,000 hectoliters of wine that had been sent annually. Irurzun wrote, "The moment seems to be the most opportune, given the better quality of the wines sent to Switzerland, the situation of the Balance of Payments between the two countries and above all the difficulties experienced by Switzerland at the moment . . . [as] its regular suppliers of wines belong to the Common Market."[93] As the European Economic Community gave priority to the signatory states, those who were not part of the agreement were excluded from these deals. As the Swiss and the Spanish were outside this agreement, there was a hope that they could agree on a project. At the same time, Spanish producers noted the improvement in their wine qualities that could allow them to compete with others.

In November 1968 Irurzun wrote to the president of the National Subgroup of Sparkling Wines to discuss the possibility of a celebration for Spanish agricultural products in West Germany. This event, which would be planned for either March or April 1969, would allow Germans to try products from Spain and feature discussions about agriculture, with sections celebrating sherry and sparkling wines.[94] West Germany was a growing market for wine consumption, going from 7.3 liters consumed per person in 1951 to 15.1 liters in 1967.[95] With imports of 4,561,008 hectoliters, this market would be a hot target, but, as late as 1969, the Germans only imported 20,303.56 hl of sherry, representing only 0.3 percent of the market.[96] This small celebration for Spanish wine could be repeated in other countries, as it neither took much effort nor cost very much, and any new consumers would be a win.

The U.S. market—also growing rapidly in the 1960s—was a target for Spain. Americans still did not drink a great deal of wine, only consuming 3.2 liters per person in 1951, but this did rise to 3.7 liters in 1967. Even with these low numbers per capita, the United States imported 714,500 hl by 1967.[97] In the same year, Americans bought 98,783,000 gallons of table wine, 95,154,000 gallons of fortified wine, 10,669,000 gallons of sparkling wine, and 9,742,000 gallons of vermouth, for a grand total of 203,403,000 gallons of wine or 769,964,113 liters.[98] This was a 28.9 percent increase in wine consumption from 1960 to 1968. Clearly Americans did not drink a lot of wine individually, but, collectively, this was a lucrative market. In November 1969 Irurzun wrote to Russell G. Hopkins, the executive secretary for the National Beer Wholesale Association in Chicago, about selling more wine. Irurzun raised the idea of the Beer Wholesalers helping to sell Spanish wine throughout this large market.[99] The Archivo General de la Administración also contains information about wine distributors in the United States who had been selling various types of Spanish wines and the connections they made with Spanish bodegas, listing sellers in major cities like New Orleans, Chicago, San Francisco, New York, and Washington DC.[100] With a large population and a strong economy, it should not come as a surprise that the United States was a key location for Spain.

A much smaller country, Belgium, began to worry Irurzun in 1969. Belgian wine consumption in 1967 was 9.1 liters per person—a low number, but not terrible.[101] The problem for Irurzun, however, was the producers of these imports. In 1965 Irurzun estimated that Belgium imported 1,008,000 hectoliters of wine, with 244,134 hl coming from Spain and 16,908 coming from Algeria. By 1966, Spain sent 78,253 hl to Belgium and Algeria sent 99,224 hl. In 1967 Algeria exported 134,515 hl to Belgium and Spanish exports had dropped to 73,743 hl![102] This dramatic decrease in Spanish exports had been directly caused by the rise of Algerian wine in Belgium. Irurzun surmised that the increase of Algerian wine was clearly political, as Belgian inclusion in the European Economic Community meant that agreements helping France import Algerian wine were extended to Belgium, putting Spain in a disadvantageous position. Irurzun wrote: "There is no doubt that the reduction of rights to the importation in Belgium . . . has already been shown, this produces great upheavals to the imports of Spanish wines, which are displaced from a traditional market for political reasons, completely unrelated to export activity."[103] It seemed that every time Spanish producers gained a foothold in one country with their wines, along came a battle in another market. As long as Spain was not allowed to participate in the European Economic Community, they could not receive the benefits of the trade pact and the protections associated with it.

THE CHALLENGES TO EXPORTS

In the 1960s wine exportation was clearly an important part of the Spanish economy, accounting for 3.78 percent of all exports by 1967. As Spain was one of the largest wine producers in the world and had a comparably low consumption rate (when compared to the other major producers), wine was an area with growth potential. Even with this surplus of product, Spanish wine producers found it a challenge to sell their goods internationally. Selling wine was not the same everywhere, and the Spanish had to find ways to improve their identity while carving out more market share. Clearly, however, this was often not easy. The French required large amounts of wine imports in the 1960s to meet their high demand, but, even so, Spain was often overlooked. Historical connections with the Maghreb gave the French an inside track to their wines. The Spanish were often at a loss as to how to deal with this problem, and, when Belgian wine importers began to rely more on Maghreb wines, a true crisis arose. The Spanish tried to work themselves into the French market, attending food and agricultural festivals in France and hosting events for French wine buyers, but with little return. These problems from the 1960s were nothing new for the Spanish in France: when France was desperate for cheap wine, they turned to Spain, but the moment the markets and production stabilized, the French quickly abandoned their southern neighbor. The French pegged Spanish wine as cheap and low quality, not like the great wines of France, and if the French wanted cheap wine, they had their own access to it in North Africa.

The situation with sherry in Britain was different. Spanish sherry was an authentic product with a long history in Britain, but many viewed this Spanish good as an expensive commodity. The empire sherries were cheaper and of a lower quality, but they were also more easily accessible to the average consumer. *Vine Products v. Mackenzie & Co. Ltd* was a turning point for sherry in Britain. According to the case, Spanish shippers waited too long to challenge the creation and usage of empire sherries. By the time the Spanish challenged the British use of this terminology, other sherries had become well known in Britain and already carved out their niche. Unlike in France it was the Spanish product that was high quality, and Spain wanted to defend its identity. In the end, however, these Spanish producers would now have to compete legally against these imitations. The British market for sherry was vital, which dealt a major blow to sherry's global identity.

By the end of the 1960s, political tensions in Western Europe were growing, with the tide turning against Francoist Spain. To combat this negative image of Spain, tourism and festivals were instrumentalized to change minds. Spain needed to get other markets to try their wines and appreciate them apart from politics. The Spanish Wine Festival in Denmark was a way to get Danes to see Spain for its sun and wine and not its right-wing authoritarianism. Spanish wine makers needed possible buyers to see their products as quality alternatives to other, less expensive wines, but they also needed stronger reception. What better image could there be for cold Denmark in autumn then uncorking and drinking a glass of warm Spanish sunshine? Foreign consumers needed to associate Spanish wine with good things for Spain to earn more market share.

Spanish wine in the 1960s was a blended bottle. On the one hand, Spain was producing better wine and in larger quantities; therefore, it could export more. Moreover, global wine consumption was increasing, so there was a strong possibility this product could work well. On the other hand, preconceived notions about Spain and its wines were hard to shake. Spanish producers had to find a middle ground: explain to the consumer that the country had a strong history of wine production with quality outcomes while highlighting the commodity as something new, reasonably priced, and interesting that people should try. Having the best of both worlds proved difficult, but Spanish producers would continue to try to set their wines apart.

7

What to Know about Spanish Wine Today

MODERNIZATION OF WINE IDENTITY
UNDER DEMOCRACY

On the inside cover of his 2012 book, *A Traveler's Wine Guide to Spain*, Harold Heckle writes, "Spain has more land under vine than any other country in Europe, and over the past thirty years has transformed its wine industry into one of the greatest in the world. Using a unique combination of native and imported grape varieties, Spain now produces a wide range of quality wines. Yet its wine regions and villages—many of which are located in unspoiled and remote areas—remain relatively unknown."[1] This statement sums up one of the greatest problems when discussing Spanish wine and its history: Spanish wine remains generally unknown or misunderstood outside of Spain. With nearly 1.2 million hectares of wine-producing land and eighty-one *denominaciones de origen* (designation of origin geographical and regulatory zones) by 2012, one might assume that Spanish wine should be universally understood across all markets, but this is still not true. Heckle notes that even though many large producers have created fantastic wines and offer tours, in general "the Spanish wine industry has not yet fully woken up to wine tourism."[2] At the start of the twenty-first century, Spanish wine remains an enigma, which presents a problem for both producers and consumers.

This chapter explores recent literature about Spanish wine: its quality, its consumers, its producers, and the development of wine tourism. To compete with an ever-growing list of international competitors and historical rivals, Spanish producers need to introduce—or reintroduce—their products to the world market. This chapter consults studies on enotourism (wine tourism), guidebooks for oenology travel in Spain, and literature about Spanish wine regions to examine the changes that producers have tried to make to create a new identity for their products. First, I explore the idea of the "wine route" in Spain and the goals of these tourist-driven activities for visitors and hosts. Next, I look at some recent literature on sherry, which was once the grande dame of Spanish exports, but has since become less popular; sherry aficionados need to reintroduce sherry to new drinkers, not just to their grandmothers. From there, I investigate contemporary literature on Spain's sparkling treat, cava. After years of arguing with France and ultimately losing the ability to call their beverage *xampany* in Catalan or *champán* in Castellano, cava is now one of the most popular sparkling wines in the world, and its producers and their allies need to let the world know what it actually is and why it is such a great drink. Finally, this chapter notes other issues and changes in some of Spain's many regions, such as Rioja. In each case, as global tastes changed, these producers looked to find a way to fit in the new world. Even with numerous adaptations and well-thought-out plans, Spanish wine still does not have the international popularity it deserves, and its producers must continue to adjust for future survival.

The relationship between wine and the consumer has changed tremendously over the past decades. For much of history, wine was viewed as either a medicinal or nutritional commodity needed for a healthy lifestyle. As previous chapters have shown, it was not until after World War II that a serious conversation began about the health risks of drinking too much wine. In this contemporary period, wine is no longer seen as necessary, but as compatible with a new lifestyle.[3] As wine is now a choice and possible sign of class knowledge, wine drinkers see the product differently. As Alan Young surmised in 2000, "It is fair to say that today's consumer is better educated, and more discriminating, than ever before" and that they will seek out new and more interesting varietals that meet their needs and interests.[4] As technology has made the world smaller, many new options have come within the reach of consumers. When they do find a wine or a wine region they like, they can now spend hours researching it online. Because of this new connection to products, wine can take a new position in drinkers' lives, and to learn more these wine enthusiasts may want to travel (which has never been easier) to see where these wines are made.[5] A consumer who lives thousands of miles away can appear one day and explore the bodega, the vineyard, and the community.

Even though Spanish wine still remains underrepresented in the American market, wine experts have spoken about certain regions for years. Damià

Serrano Miracle suggests that, recently, writers and journalists have begun to mention Spanish wines more frequently, thereby increasing knowledge of the drink and the interest in enotourism to Spain.[6] Cava Paul Cheneau of Cigravi SA won the Gold Medal for sparkling wines under twenty dollars at the New York International Wine Center in the late 1980s, defeating 150 others. At the same time, it was classified as "exceptional" by *Time Magazine*, a "best buy" by *Wine Spectator*, and a "fantastic buy" by *Vintage Magazine*.[7] After American wine critic Robert Parker once gave one of his highest reviews to 2002 Las Rocas Garnacha from Spain, the bottles flew off the shelves.[8] In drawing their attention to certain Spanish wines, wine writers interested consumers in learning more about the regions they came from. During the early 2000s, Spanish chefs began to hit the world stage, as their restaurants won major prizes and their cooking staffs appeared on American television. New Spanish restaurants that opened in larger American cities served authentic wines. As Liz Thach and Steven Cuellar propose, the popularity of Italian food in the United States meant that consumers became familiar with Italian wines, and new foodies could try Spanish wines at Spanish restaurants and tapas bars.[9] While still nowhere near as popular as Italian restaurants, these Spanish restaurants could inspire guests to consider making a trip to Spain.[10] Advertisements, like those mentioned in the previous chapter, worked to establish an image for the locations where the wine was produced. As consumers' palates adapt and change, especially in a faster-paced world, people can try different foods more easily and desire to learn more about them.

Specifically, the relationship between the United States and Spanish wine, which has never been perfect, is slowly improving. Thach and Cuellar report that between 2001 and 2005 Spanish wine imports increased 61 percent, which is substantial, but Spanish wine often does not exceed 1 percent of American consumption—a low rate.[11] One problem for Spanish wines at the start of the twenty-first century was competition at lower price points, especially from countries like Chile and Australia.[12] Lower price-point wines may cost less and therefore may carry the stigma of being "low quality," or, simply, "cheap." Thach and Cuellar suggest that Spanish wines, fortunately, avoided this issue and were perceived as having "a reputation of quality and value," while Chilean and Australian wines were not so lucky.[13] There did exist, however, a problematic dichotomy for Spanish wines: as new technology and grape varietals became successful in Spain, wine styles began to change to adapt to international tastes. While this would seem like a gain, some wine critics feared that too many new techniques would ruin the "artistry of their traditional methods, [which] would be distressing."[14] Spanish wines had—and still have—a difficult path to take: maintaining their traditional style, which earned them international acclaim, or adapting to changing tastes in hopes of finding new consumers. In reality Spanish wines need to do both.

TOURING FOR WINE

While it is important for wine producers to get global consumers to purchase their products at home, they also need to encourage tourists to travel to their bodegas to learn about the wine process. If consumers or casual tourists can make a special connection with a wine and a location, then the vintners might be able to sell more. This section considers the recent benefits of enotourism in Spain. Large-scale wine tourism, along with food tourism, is a relatively recent phenomenon that has grown steadily around the world. Countries like the United States, Australia, and New Zealand led the way, but over time Spain began to develop this industry as well.[15] Vacationing in Spain has been popular since the 1960s, for its beaches and sun; now visitors can also come to experience the wine.

Traveling for leisure now is tied to food and drink, as visitors often come to a place to experience local life.[16] Gastronomy forms part of the larger cultural identity of a region and can act as symbols of a place. When tourists have an interest in food, they can travel to a location known for its fine dining, local food, or attend festivals known for a particular product.[17] A newer style of food tourism is the "food and wine trail" (or "route" or "tour"). Robb Mason and Barry O'Mahony describe this trail as "an itinerary, self-directed or pre-determined, through a well-defined area the aim of which is the exploration and understanding by tourists of the products, cuisine, and culture of the area."[18] Visitors leave the city and spend time in rural regions where, often, they can see the production of the commodity. By traveling to the site of production, the visitor can get a firsthand experience and also perhaps learn how the product fits into local culture. A visit to a bodega gives the traveler sights, sounds, smells, and experiences they would never have had if they stayed in the city, giving the tourist the opportunity to discover connections to aspects of rural life.

In trying to raise awareness of their goods, the sponsors of these cultural events are interested, of course, in economic gain. At the same time, the events they host have cultural value and establish a traditional encounter for the visitor to experience.[19] At times these supposedly traditional events might be invented so they can be better connected to the changing identity of the location. The main factor is the connection that gets made between a region's traditions and contemporary visitors. As Christina Ceisel writes about Galicia, "We also see a commitment to Galicia and the land as a means of remembering a community's history and developing a future. It is this duality—our interest as consumers in supranational high-end food marketing and our increasing awareness of the ethic of consumption."[20] Consumers are becoming more interested in knowing how their purchased good was made, and they want to see that process firsthand; by traveling to the locality, the tourist can interact with various aspects and people involved in its production. In our modern society, there is a certain romance to traveling to the countryside to see rural life, as this "leads us to consider the rural space as a place to find compensation for lost identity."[21] Therefore, regardless of the location, people from urbanizing environments look to the rural as something lost, and a trip there can be a refreshing visit to the pleasant past. There the experiencing of food is necessary. According to Jacinthe Bessière, food (and, to an extent, wine) holds symbolic meaning for the tourist: as a symbol of values, as a representation of the ideals of community and sharing, as a class signifier, and as a sign of cultural heritage.[22] The experience of consuming a particular good in a particular place is not simply "eating" but the creation of a unique experience for the consumer. Similarly, the consumption of a product viewed as traditional in its native environment can give "certain symbolic characteristics: one appropriates and embodies the nature, culture and identity of the area."[23] There is nothing more "local" than eating the food or drinking the wine of a particular place. If food tourism sites and events can harness these ideals, they can attract visitors, who, if they enjoy themselves, may be more likely to purchase those goods before they leave or when they return home.

The wine route or trail is a perfect way to experience the culture of a region and the local products made there. These trips allow tourists to access the rural in a controlled way with scheduled paths. These routes can work in a variety of ways: as a day or weekend trip to an area known for wines from a specific denominación de origen; as "circular routes" for the tourist to experience the wider wine zone and its culture; or as urban explorations in specific cities.[24] In each case the tourist makes a connection with the local identity and its wines while, intentionally or not, experiencing local culture. A series of producers and regional elements need to come together to create and sponsor the tour so visitors know where to go. For example, in 1994 producers founded the Asociación Española de Pequeñas y Medianas Ciudades Vitivinícolas (Spanish Association of Small and Medium Wine Cities, or ACEVIN) to help bodegas in smaller regions of Spain develop wine tourism, thereby serving a public relations function for these producers.[25] By working together these producers in small and medium-sized cities could draw tourists while creating regulations for a positive experience. ACEVIN later developed the Rutas del Vino de España (Wine Routes of Spain), which directed visitors through planned routes. Interestingly, these routes could not simply be slapped together. Denominaciones de origen needed to be measured by size and from there follow requirements for the number of bodegas participating, cities involved, and housing and eating options. A denominación de origen with twenty-six to fifty bodegas needed at least seven bodegas on the route, with between one and five municipalities each having four restaurants, three hotel options, and one wine shop.[26] There would be nothing worse for a wine route than a shortage of wineries and housing. If the route was shoddily put together, then visitors would complain and perceive the product associated with the region as poor quality. Developing these routes was a success for Spain, as in 2023, thirty-six routes, from the Penedès to Rías Baixas, currently exist.[27]

What type of consumer would participate in enotourism? First, and expectedly, the tourist might have an interest in the rural aspects of Spain and the production of wine. As this is experiential tourism, the participants must want to experience the creation of the product.[28] At the same time, the tourist should have an interest in nature and the environment.[29] Moreover, the tourist should also be interested in history and culture, as these wine routes are designed to highlight historical locations in the countryside.[30] While these are the tours' basic goals, there needs also to be constant adaptation and new things for people to experience or see on each route, or there could be no way to differentiate one trail from another. Each route needs to offer a variety of activities for the various arrivals: singles, couples, families, or large tour groups. Outside of the normal wine-based experiences, some bodegas along these routes have come up with events such as bottling your own wine, eating at a bodega restaurant, or even bathing in wine at an on-premise or nearby spa.[31] Nearby golf courses, commercial centers, museums, and nightlife are also important options for visitors.[32] As these wine routes could be multiday and involve traveling to rural locations without visits to large cities, tourists should have many options on their trip so that it can be a fully experiential visit. At the same time, connections between the bodegas and the local community can help multiple groups economically. The more options presented to the traveler; the more people may come. In a study from 2015, the average person participating in enotourism was middle aged, with about 70 percent being coupled and over half having a university education with upper-middle-class incomes.[33] As for visitors' wine knowledge, this same study suggests that only 24.4 percent were "highly knowledgeable and interested," 48.2 percent had an "intermediate" knowledge of wine, and 27.4 percent had a "limited knowledge of and interest in wine."[34] This study shows that knowledge about and interest in wine were not necessarily the reasons for participating in the wine routes. This would mean that the more "nonwine" activities presented could draw more participants. At the same time, the average visitor does skew older, creating an interesting paradigm: Does the route sponsor events for that specific age group, or create new events hoping to attract a younger audience? This is a decision for the routes to make over time.

There are benefits to the producer in these events. Showcasing the local product is a useful step in trying to build market share.[35] Since wine tourism has been growing in Spain, it is better to participate than not. In 2013, 7.4 million tourists went to bodegas and wineries in Spain, and by 2014 that number had reached 9.5 million.[36] As more tourists from far-off locations, like North America, come to Spain, they often prebook their trips; therefore, bodegas can know how many people may attend and plan accordingly.[37] Other advantages for the bodegas are better knowledge of the brand, larger sales margins, increased sales, direct marketing and immediate responses from visitors, and more knowledge for the consumer.[38] There are some inconveniences to joining a wine route: greater investment, the preparation of activities, the personnel planning, and the logistics of showing visitors the workings of the bodegas.[39] These inconveniences, however, could be small if enotourism continues to grow in Spain and more tourists with more money arrive.

Sociologist Lluís Tolosa has written numerous books on the wine tourism and culture in Barcelona, Catalonia, the Penedès, and other regions.[40] His 2017 book, *Marketing del enoturismo: 12 errores habituales, 12 propuestas alternativas*, explores the problems associated with wine tourism, with special attention paid to the mistakes made by producers. After hundreds of visits to bodegas, Tolosa highlights the twelve errors associated with wine tourism and offers possible solutions. On many occasions I have also experienced some of these issues while visiting bodegas. If these errors could be corrected, Tolosa thinks, then wine tourism in Spain can be improved. At the same time, Tolosa notes that some of the suggestions made by enotourism associations may offer mixed messages to the visitors, reducing the success of wine tourism.

The first two errors noted by Tolosa deal with the type of visit presented by the bodega. For Tolosa the fact that producers concentrate too much on the production side at the winery and on the creation of the wine itself creates problems. As he explains, on many occasions the tour of the cellars and wine production areas are the same at each location, so the tourist is not really getting anything new on a visit. Similarly, spending too much time talking about the wine-making process can get repetitive: Why visit more than one bodega just to hear the same story? Tolosa explains that the goal of these visits is to sell wine and make some extra money from tourism. To fix these two concerns, Tolosa suggests that visits center more on the tasting areas for wine and, rather than merely offer an explanation of wine making, focus more on the location's nature and history.[41] After traveling to numerous wineries in Spain, I have heard many such stories about the wine-making process, but have only spent a small amount of time in tasting rooms, unlike in the United States, where many wineries concentrate more on the drinking of wine versus the process.

Other concerns revolve around how the visits are designed for the guests. Tolosa rejects the idea of offering many other activities, especially because of the difficulty of knowing just how many guests may arrive. Rather than offer a wide variety of events, these locations should offer fewer, well-planned activities.[42] And, rather than advertise a bodega as an "experience," the wineries should strive to do their best to be kind and gracious to the guests and offer a carefully planned visit.[43] These trips can be improved, according to Tolosa, if bodegas remember the big picture of enotourism: that anything on the property associated with wine is part of the culture. The bodega's history, its archeology, and buildings should be integrated into the event. This is easier to do, of course, than open spas for the visitor.[44] Frequently I have found that the trips to bodegas do not focus on a variety of wine-related cultural opportunities. By concentrating on the culture that already exists, these bodegas will not have to make major changes. Tolosa also recommends that these visits be basic in nature and not overwhelm the average visitor. Most visitors go to a bodega to try wine and have a good time; wineries should not compel their visitors to learn a great deal about the wine before they sample it. Rather than spend too much time talking about the formal rules of wine tasting, allow the visitors to try the wine and see what they like.[45] All in all, in Tolosa's opinion, these visits should be simple and direct, explore more than the wine-making process, and allow the visitors to try the wine. Rather than pay for special on-site events, if bodegas offer a relaxing and interesting location for people to visit, then it would be worth their time to return.

As Tolosa notes, bodegas also had to take serious steps in establishing their identities and understand marketing to succeed at enotourism. Many bodega visits seem to be very similar in nature; why would a guest stop at one bodega when they could simply visit another? Too often bodegas do not communicate a clear message about what their location means and why it is different than another, and visitors want to know what makes a location unique.[46] Similarly, bodegas need to learn more about their visitors. As shown by research from Genoveva Millán and Eva Agudo, as well as by Arturo Molina, there seems to be an even distribution of visitors by factors such as age and gender. Tolosa suggests, however, that this is not the kind of information that a bodega really needs. Bodegas should internally create four separate types of visits, not centered by age or gender, but on the interest of the visitor: standard visits for general tourists, visits for enotourism specialists, visits for alcohol professionals, and visits for business.[47] This idea makes sense; at some bodegas I wanted to know specifics about the winery's history while other tourists wanted to try the wine. Different tourists will have different interests, and the more the bodega can prepare for these, the better. While this may appear basic, Tolosa is also concerned with the scheduling and publication of visitation hours. On more than one occasion I have scheduled a visit weeks in advance and from thousands of miles away, only to have an email sent the day before, telling me that the guide has taken a vacation. Tolosa advises that all visits should be firmly scheduled and offer a variety of tours; he also thinks that bodegas should be open on Sundays, and that staying closed on Sundays could lead to lost revenue and create an unwelcoming environment.[48] While the advice may sound harsh, it does underscore one of Tolosa's main points: that enotourism is meant to help the bodega, so the bodega needs to be flexible and professional with its clientele.

In the area of professional marketing, Tolosa is very clear. One error he sees is that bodegas simply "hope" to sell wine as guests leave. These bodegas, he says, need to get better at collecting visitors' information, such as email addresses, so they can contact them later to try to sell more wine. Because the goal of these visits is to make money for the bodega, plans need to be in place to sell wine after the tour ends.[49] Similarly, bodegas should make connections with groups, like ACEVIN, to work together to bring tourists to the area. These organizations can cooperate with other agencies globally to attract visitors through a wide variety of marketing tools. By having this support, bodegas could also plan their arrivals more effectively and be better prepared for the different types of visitors they will receive.[50] Finally, Tolosa asserts that bodegas must understand that, while they have competitors for visitors, smaller wineries should work together to attract tourists to their area. Having local competition could mean making improvements to each bodega that, in sum, could lift the quality of the entire region.[51] Tolosa offers concrete advice for these bodegas to improve their visitors' experiences, which could assist the long-term success of enotourism for Spain.

The growth of enotourism in Spain is logical. For the country with the most land devoted to winemaking, it would make sense to use it for multiple purposes with minimal negative impact to the land. Traditional tourism in Spain has been centered in the beach areas and larger cities, often leading to the overcrowding of many sites, which weakens local identity. With the creation of enotourism and wine trails, other parts of Spain can see this tourism money, too. True, enotourism can be frustrating for the bodega—visitors who do not care about wine production and only want to drink (or get drunk) can be problematic if not obnoxious. But they do spend money, and, hopefully, they purchase something in the gift shop on their way out. If even a few of these "noninterested" people learn to like Spanish wine and the product of a specific bodega, they may order some in the future. If these wine tours are run well and offer quality visits to tourists, this improves the image of Spanish wine in general. Very importantly, though, as Tolosa explains, enotourism cannot rely on old patterns, uninspiring visits, or wacky sideshows to gain more visitors; these locations need to be very clear about what their bodegas mean and offer friendly and professional visits to all types of guests.

Before I begin to discuss the changing modern identity of sherry, I think it might be worthwhile—and comical—to tell three stories of my interactions with it. In June 2015 I was at an upscale experimental restaurant in Barcelona. After a particularly good dinner, it was time for dessert. I asked the bartender, who was likely in his mid-twenties, for a sweet sherry. He seemed perplexed. After a few minutes searching in the cooler, he found one open bottle. He took the ubiquitous Spanish water glass and began to pour, almost to the top. The sherry was not a sweet Pedro Ximénez, but a dry fino. I was shocked by the pour size—well over the typical three ounces or two hundred milliliters. When I asked if he knew anything about sherry, he said no. In May 2017 I was in Jerez de la Frontera, the home of sherry, to do some research. After a long day of work, I went to my hotel bar for a quick nightcap. I ordered a Pedro Ximénez. A few minutes later, an English woman, presumably in her sixties, sat at the bar and ordered a port. I was beyond shocked. This woman was with a larger tour group of sixty-somethings who were spending a few nights in Jerez. Likely she had visited a few sherry bodegas that day and tasted the various types, even those sweeter varieties similar to port. I could not believe that in the city of sherry she would choose a port. After a few moments, the bartender explained that there was no port in Jerez, and that she had to have a sherry. A minute later her friend joined her and ordered a prosecco. Once again I was bewildered that she would not choose a native product. Of course I understand that people should drink what they like, but the problem, I think, was that these women did not know why the bartender was so confused by their requests. Finally, in May 2018 I joined a colleague for a drink at a new, swanky hotel bar in my American city. After a quick look at the menu, I noticed that they offered dry sherries for aperitifs; excitedly, I ordered one. The bartender found a chilled bottle and opened it. Then he picked up a regular-sized wine glass and asked if I wanted a six- or nine-ounce pour. I chose the six-ounce, knowing full well that this was larger than the traditional size. In the end I only had to have one drink. All in all, these experiences made me wonder: "Why does no one seem to understand sherry?"

Manuel González Gordon's 1935 masterpiece, *Sherry: The Noble Wine*, was updated and rereleased in 1990 with additional commentary by John Doxat. This book is the central resource for learning about the production and creation of sherry. In the 1990 edition, Doxat highlights some of the problems facing sherry at the end of the 1980s. One of Doxat's goals was to challenge the perception of sherry as a generic drink, to make it clear that sherry is truly a special and protected beverage. Additionally, he made these updates for the sake of Spanish citizens, to emphasize the importance of sherry for them, because many Spaniards were ignorant of it and its identity for Spain.[52] Doxat's goals were admirable, as he saw that sherry was becoming less popular. While every year environment and weather play a role in the success of sherry growth, the numbers in production were problematic, going from 322,021 butts (200-liter cask) in 1979, 252,149 butts in 1986, to 194,028 butts in 1989.[53] The decrease was not a good sign.

John Radford's 1998 book, *The New Spain: A Complete Guide to Contemporary Spanish Wine*, discusses all of the major wine-producing regions, including Jerez. Radford notes that it was not until January 1, 1996, that the European Union finally protected the name "sherry" throughout the zone. While discussing the problems in the history of modern sherry, Radford writes, "In many ways, the sherry industry was the architect of its own downfall. It had become complacent after centuries of unending prosperity, and unwilling to change and react to the market. There was also far too much poor-quality wine overloading the market and being shipped around the world."[54] Throughout the 1980s things got worse, as there were too many vineyards and a glut of wine. Labor issues created economic problems, and many producers either got bought out or consolidated during this period. By 1989 sherry production stood at only 783,000 hectoliters—half its total from a decade earlier.[55] According to Radford, the 1990s, however, were better for sherry. Less wine was being made, but it was of much higher quality, restoring its illustrious identity. At the same time, modern drinkers were avoiding the sweet sherries and turning to the dry aperitif styles, creating innovation in that market.[56] The 1980s almost destroyed sherry completely, but it slowly stabilized and seemed to recover, although still nowhere near the levels of earlier years. These producers began a slow process of diversification as well, introducing white and red wines to the market.[57] It was time for sherry producers to think about a world where sherry was not as popular as it used to be.

In her 2014 book, *Sherry: The World's Best-Kept Secret*, Talia Baiocchi offers a modern look at sherry. Even the title is striking: while sherry was once a huge commodity, now it is a "secret." In her introduction Baiocchi writes, "Despite its storied pedigree, however, sherry has been maligned in America for decades—so misunderstood that one wonders whether it was the victim of an elaborate smear campaign involving all of the grandmas, everywhere."[58] Baiocchi's assumption might be correct; at some point someone made sherry "uncool" in the American market. She does assert, however that "sherry has, in short, been reborn. And with this rebirth, it's time that sherry's story is told."[59] As Doxat mentions in 1990, one of the goals of his book was to teach the younger generation about sherry, and Baiocchi aims to do that as well.[60] One common misconception about sherry is that it is always sweet. Most Americans might think of the syrupy blended cream sherries, popular with grandmothers. While Pedro Ximénez is a very sweet drink, 40 percent of all the sherry produced is either fino or manzanilla, which are considered the driest wines in the world.[61] Baiocchi postulates that because Americans seemingly prefer dry wines, like Pinot Grigio or Rosé, if the drinker assumes that all sherry is sweet, they will not try it.[62] This is, therefore, a self-fulfilling problem. If Americans assume all sherry is sweet, even though most of it is not, then they will not want it. Apparently, education is lacking.

Harold Heckle offers some easy-to-understand descriptions of sherry. The main grape is the palomino fino. Fino is "pale and bone dry" and light in color. Manzanilla is also a dry sherry but made in Sanlúcar de Barrameda. These two sherries have the lowest alcohol contents, of 15.5–17 percent. Amontillado is "amber in color, with more body," with greater intensity and a possibly "nutty flavor," with 16–18 percent alcohol. Oloroso is "dark gold in color, very aromatic . . . full bodied and dry," with 18–20 percent alcohol. Sweet sherries like cream are blends of oloroso and Pedro Ximénez and were invented for the British market, with 18–20 percent alcohol.[63] Pedro Ximénez is made from its own grape and is sun dried before juicing to increase the sugar content; in the end it usually has an alcohol level between 17–18 percent.[64] The wines are placed in oak butts that are not filled completely. From there a *flor* (yeast) develops on the surface, protecting it from the air. While the flor is alive, finos and manzanillas are produced. As the flor dies, oxidation can occur, darkening the wine, and lending it other notes. Storage of sherry is also unique in the solera system. New wine is put in the top barrel to age. When needed for bottling, wine is taken from the bottom or third butt. Wine from the second butt replaces that taken from the third, and wine from the first replenishes the second. This fascinating process means that portions of the wine in the third butt may be partially decades old. At the same time, this means that sherry is inherently mixed, as parts of many harvests create the finished wine.[65] These unique processes, grapes, environment, and history create a truly distinct wine that cannot be created as successfully elsewhere.

In the recent American market, sherry can be best described as a specialty drink highly influenced by whims and trends of tastemakers. As *Wine Spectator* author Ben O'Donnell writes, "In 2002, the United States imported 2.3 million liters of Sherry; by 2011, the most recent year for which there are figures—and which arguably predates the recent Sherry wave—that number had fallen to 1.4 million, a 38 percent drop."[66] He continues, "So I had to ask: Are we looking at a fad, or something with more permanence?"[67] Baiocchi writes about rumors in 2006 that sherry would have a resurgence. Sherry imports to the United States did increase 25 percent from 2012 to 2013—a good sign, but, still, it was overall a small import.[68] But if there has been an increase in sherry consumption in the United States, where is it? The average American liquor store might carry a bottle of cheap sherry (or even fake sherry), but quality sherries are hard to find. As Baiocchi suggests, sherry is not only being drank alone, but also mixed with other ingredients to make cocktails. At the end of her book, she offers dozens of recipes that contain sherry or that have been restyled to include it.[69]

Sherry is a special wine; no one can doubt this fact. Its location, the process of its production, and its styles are like nothing else in the world. For decades, if not centuries, sherry was the primary wine export from Spain to the UK, and it created a unique identity. Market share meant financial success in Jerez. The problem, though, is that all commodities can fall out of favor. Products that are seen as "old" or unfashionable can simply fall away, yet those that become nostalgic or kitsch may come back. While sherry producers relied on a long tradition of consumption, once "the next big thing" came along, sherry, apparently, did not adapt. Now sherry is playing catch-up to try to regain market share. Should sherry market itself as a great wine of tradition and only produce expensive, quality bottles to target the wealthy, or should sherry reduce its prices—and, therefore, quality—to reach a lower price point? Can sherry serve both as a stand-alone drink and an ingredient in cocktails? In the years to come, sherry producers need to address these questions to help this magical beverage survive in a new world.

In 2015 I traveled to the Penedès to complete research for this project. While there I visited a biodynamic cava producer in the countryside and took a tour. Before the tour began, a travel van with eight Americans arrived from Barcelona, where their cruise ship was docked. From the moment they arrived, it was clear that they knew nothing about cava, but it was a good sign, at least, that they came for a tour. As the tour began, these guests seemed more interested in complaining about the lack of air conditioning in the company van than listening to the tour guide as they wandered around the property. At the tasting they spent more time cracking jokes among themselves than hearing the commentary about the wines. In the end they paid their money and went back to Barcelona. Fortunately, the bodega owner felt sorry for me that the other tourists were so abrasive and did not charge for my visit, even offering me a ride back to the city. In 2017 I visited larger cava bodegas in the same region, where I joined dozens of foreign tourists, taking trams through the underground caves. The day I visited was popular for British bachelorette parties, where numerous glasses of cava were consumed. Again I admit that my interest in those tours was quite different than that of the average tourist, and I am glad they had a good time. But, during all of these trips, the tourists were always confused about what cava was and why it was not called champagne—something that got explained to them many times. As with sherry, it seems that, while this important Spanish export might be familiar to some, most people still are not sure what cava is.

Cava is a sparkling wine made in Spain under the *método tradicional* (same as the *méthode champenoise*), which requires a second fermentation in the bottle that creates bubbles in the wine. Although Spain has made this sparkling wine since the end of the nineteenth century, the idea of cava is rather new. Formally marketed as *xampany* or *champán*, French producers relied upon EEC guidelines to force a name change. When Spain joined the EEC in 1986, cava was recognized as a unique wine and in 1992 had its identity protected as a Quality Wine Produced in a Specific Region.[70] Even as a protected wine, knowledge about cava is low. As Anne Wallner writes, "Cava is after all, the most exported bubbles in the world, and you'll find at most a single page on the subject in the literature on wine."[71] Cava producers exported 244.8 million bottles in 2010, yet, "unlike Champagne, it seems that many people drink Cava without knowing much about the product itself, its history, its geography, production methods, the constituent of grapes or anything that makes this sparkling wine special."[72] Cava prices are usually much lower than well-known champagnes, making them a value buy to many customers who do not actually know what they are buying. Wallner makes some interesting points about the relationship between French and Spanish sparkling wines: "Since [cava] nudged the same price range as the cheapest Champagnes, and due to our history and upbringing, we chose Champagne, and against our better judgment, just because the name is on the label."[73] In her opinion people do this "frankly because we as consumers in this case have been more interested in what it says on the bottle, than in the contents of the bottle itself, and because we do not know any better."[74] In Wallner's opinion—and in mine—cava has been misunderstood not because it is a bad wine, but because French champagnes have been more successful in legally and culturally defending their name. People buy champagne because it is special; people buy cava because they can.

The cava denominación de origen is unique in Spain, since it is not geographically determined, even though the overwhelming majority is produced in Sant Sadurní d'Anoia and the Penedès region of Catalonia. For cava the rules of production are key. The grapes used are the Spanish macabeo, xarel·lo, and parellada, but they can also include small amounts of chardonnay and garnacha.[75] After harvest the grapes are juiced and first fermented in large tanks. Afterward the wines are bottled with small amounts of yeast and allowed to ferment again, to create bubbles. The bottles are stored in large underground tunnels and caves (hence the name *cava*) to mature. After the cava ages for the appropriate time, the bottles are slowly turned at angles in *pupitres* (stands) to let the dead yeast settle. When the yeast has reached the cap area, the bottle top is quickly frozen and opened so yeast can fly out in a block of ice in a process known as *degorgement*; then small amounts of wine are added (some with sugar) in a process known as *dosage* to create the appropriate sweetness level. In the end a real cork *tapón* is added; at this point, the bottle is almost ready.[76] If no or little sugar is added, the wine is *brut nature* (three grams of sugar and none added). If the wine contains twelve grams of sugar per liter, it is *brut*; twelve to seventeen grams of sugar makes *extra seco*; seventeen to thirty-one grams of sugar creates *seco*; and over fifty grams makes *dulce*.[77] Therefore, like sherry, cava is quite varied in its taste and can quench many different kinds of thirst. The bottle labels contain a great deal of information for the consumer: the denominación de origen marker, the producer's name and location, the type of wine (level of sweetness), the aging period, the bottle size, and the alcohol content.[78] All this information is helpful to the consumer when choosing the correct wine.

The production of cava has seen a great increase over the decades. In 1920, 4 million bottles of cava were produced, rising to 51 million bottles in 1972, 200 million in 1999, to the aforementioned 244.8 million bottles in 2010.[79] The number of cava producers has also increased dramatically, going from 82 in 1980 to 256 in 2010.[80] Due to these increases, cava now can be bought in over 120 countries. In 2010 Germany, the UK, the United States, and Belgium bought one-third of all cava exports. Another factor that separates cava from champagne is that 60 percent of all cava is exported, whereas only 40 percent of champagne leaves France.[81] This means that, unlike sherry, cava is readily available in stores outside of Spain. However, like with sherry, it still appears that consumers are unsure about what they buy.

Cava is a worldwide beverage. Even with its global reach, it seems many consumers do not really know about the product and only choose it because they want a sparkling wine within a certain price point. With so many choices for wine, it appears that cava is more known for its economical price rather than its heritage, unlike champagne. Anna Wallner writes that cava types make a wonderful addition to any meal, as they balance and support salty, sour, sweet, and bitter ingredients; she also offers recipes for meals to be paired effectively with cava.[82] As with sherry, certain questions remain about cava's future. Companies like Freixenet and Codorníu ship millions of bottles a year from their large bodegas, but smaller companies like Raventós i Blanc, Recaredo, and Blancher produce much less wine but aim for a more expensive price point. Many bodegas offer tours, and some have weekend restaurants for their visitors. Ultimately, each producer must create its own identity, and the Consejo Regulador must continue to push quality wines and work to create for them concrete and clear identities.

SOME OTHER REGIONS TO MEET

In his 1998 book, John Radford writes, "Spain is in the midst of what amounts to a revolution in wine. Those who considered it an unchanging, tractional course for unexciting, traditional wines would be amazed by the dramatic rise in quality and the extraordinary explosion of wine styles that has taken place throughout the country in recent years."[83] Spanish wines have changed a great deal over the centuries, and modern Spanish wines are growing in reputation. As Miguel Torres, one of Spain's greatest winemakers, writes in the foreword to Radford's book, "The boom in wine culture has been a spectacular phenomenon of the late 20th century. Thanks to the rise in interest and enthusiasm, Spanish wines now enjoy a privileged position on the world's vinous stage. Not only does this renaissance represent a public relations victory, it also represents the triumph of conscientious work in the vineyards, in the laboratory, in the marketplace and, indeed, in the world's gastronomic culture."[84] Successful Spanish producers have made adaptations when needed, such as bringing in new foreign grape varietals or trying to revive older, less popular national grapes. While traditional elements still exist, new technologies have also been introduced to improve the quality and consistency of the product.[85] At the same time, "the progress achieved by Spain's wine industry has been impressive in recent years. To help foster improvements, Spanish authorities, encouraged by the European Union, maintain an official system to guarantee minimum levels of quality and provide guidance."[86] These successes have helped Spanish wine become world renowned in expert circles, but Spanish wine is diverse, and many styles are less well known. This section explores a sampling of other regions in Spain to show the changes that have been made there. As will be seen, each unique area has its own advantages and disadvantages when trying to carve out its own future.

While cava is the best known of the wines from Catalonia, a variety of other styles are produced throughout the region. When discussing the Penedès—the home to cava and other still wines—Alan Young writes, "Although the author and contributing writer have had a lengthy and relatively close association with Catalonia through teaching and writing about its wine, we could not have anticipated how little we knew about the Penedès when it came to magnifying the area in depth."[87] At the end of his book, Young notes a series of wine routes and tours that tourists can take to explore the local Penedès producers and better understand their wines. Robert A. Davidson suggests that these denominaciones (or regional Denominació d'Origen Protegida in Catalan) and their relationship with regional terroir have also given power to Catalonia, as the regional government has been able to take its locally identified products and work them into global conversations of protectionism under European Union rules. Therefore, by creating regions in Catalonia for Catalan products, the Generalitat further specializes its region and creates "a form of sovereignty" over their foodstuffs, using them for agricultural and possibly political means.[88] By 2011 the Penedès denominación had 3,750 producers of wine, which equates to about one-third of all in Catalonia. About 23,500 hectares are under cultivation in the region, with 160 bottling companies.[89] The recently formed Catalonia denominación produced 22 million bottles at its start in 2000, a number that had risen to 50 million by 2010. Two hundred wineries with over 50,000 hectares produce wine for this denominación.[90] Recently, the shining star for red wine production in Spain is the Priorat Denominació d'Origen Qualificada (DOQ). The terraced slopes of the region and its high altitude create exceptional red wines that have become renowned around the world.[91] Including cava and the newly created Conca del Riu Anoia, thirteen denominaciones exist in Catalonia, highlighting the diversity in the region. For the outsider, however, these various regions take time to understand.

Often viewed as Spain's most famous region for wine, La Rioja has produced wine for centuries. As previously discussed, this region achieved serious financial growth during the early years of the oidium and phylloxera crises as French producers scrambled to find robust red wines to meet demand. The tempranillo grape is the most famous in the region, where the red wine is often oaked for years. In keeping its identity clear over the decades, Rioja did a better job than most Spanish producers. When producers of bulk wine in Spain lost their identities in the 1960s, Rioja maintained its style and name. As Radford discusses, by the end of the 1960s food experts had again started considering wines from Rioja as quality.[92] By the 1970s prices of French Bordeaux had increased dramatically; when consumers looked for quality alternatives, Rioja was the site. With improved technology and hygiene processes, Riojan wine greatly improved, and demand for it continued to grow.[93] In 1991, when Riojan vineyards covered 63,500 hectares, these wines earned the classification Denominación de Origen Calificada, signifying the highest level of production.[94] In 2005 Riojan wines represented 2 percent of the European Union's wine production, with almost 300 million bottles.[95] While tempranillo is the main grape, producers can also use garnacha, mazuelo, graciano, viura, malvasía, and garnacha blanca.[96] Luckily for Rioja the identity of the product has not changed much, and the knowledge and styles imported from France at the end of the nineteenth century allowed for the cultivation of a quality product. Riojan wines continue to be the most famous reds from Spain—a trend that will likely continue, as the region has successfully defended itself and the identity of its wines.

The north central region of Ribera del Duero in Castilla y León has also seen recent changes in its wine production. Like neighboring zones this region has a history of wine production, but its style changed in 1864, when don Eloy de Lecanda Chaves returned from a trip to Bordeaux, bringing with him the oaking process for local red wines. These oaked wines achieved some success for their flavor, which sparked investment in the region. The greatest problem for Ribera del Duero, however, was its proximity to Rioja. Ribera's wines would never garner the same early prestige as those of Rioja. Following the 1982 creation of its denominación de origen, the region could not find success, and many producers replaced their fields with cheaper grapes.[97] By the early 1990s, however, under the leadership of producers like Alejandro Fernández, local producers realized that they could once again plant better vines and produce a quality product. In the past winegrowers in the region struggled with the varied temperatures and adapted to produce cheaper wines, but by the 1990s they had learned that they could produce strong and quality reds, as "quality sells, even if it does demand a generous admixture of patience."[98] This recent story of Ribera del Duero could serve as an allegory for Spain: while great wine can be produced, it is not easy to do in every region. Often, when Spanish producers found that their quality wines were not selling, they replaced the vineyards with cheaper grapes and made a lower-quality product, ultimately harming the perception of local wines. In the case of Ribera del Duero, however, winemakers realized their error early and worked for quality over quantity. While Ribera del Duero will never be Rioja, if the region can offer a quality product and explain it is comparable to Riojan wine, it can establish a better identity.

Another Castilian wine region, Rueda, has a unique history. Before the seventeenth century, it was a producer of a fortified wine like sherry from white grapes that was considered high quality. As the Jerez region regained its successes from the eighteenth century onward, Rueda's production declined. In the 1970s Marqués de Riscal, a major Riojan producer, began to experiment with the local Ruedan grape, verdejo. Rather than let it oxidize to create a fortified wine, new technologies from Riscal—"stainless-steel vats, cool fermentation and blanketing the grapes, juice, and fermenting wine with inert gas"—helped to create a "crisp, fresh, fruity wine."[99] With the later arrival of sauvignon blanc, the Rueda region has now become famous for its white wines—a fascinating fact, as it is nowhere near the ocean, where Spanish white wines are more common. Before the arrival of Riscal, Rueda was on the verge of collapse; however, this region was willing to adapt to changing styles and technology to make a fantastic wine. Here, the lesson is quite clear: if the process for winemaking that has been followed for centuries is not working, maybe it is best to make a change.

The region of Rías Baixas in Galicia has also experienced major change recently. The oidium and phylloxera outbreaks in the late nineteenth century devastated the production of Galician wines. As mentioned in earlier chapters, at this time red wines began to dominate the export market, and Galicia's whites were all but forgotten, except to small local producers. This region was lucky, as agriculturalists in the 1980s took an interest in exploring wine varietals destroyed due to phylloxera, reviving the albariño grape. Once this grape was rejuvenated, the grape was exposed to modern techniques like stainless-steel fermentation to create a wine that is "relatively low in alcohol and high in fresh acidity, making them crisp, delicate, and often subtly honeyed"; however, "albariño is an expensive grape to cultivate properly, so its wines are not cheap."[100] Even with the expense required to grow the grape, once the albariño grape from Rías Baixas hit the market in 1988, it made a splash as a new style of a unique grape.[101] In Rías Baixas lies a similar lesson to Rueda: sometimes the grape is good, but the process needs help. In this case the albariño grape is an amazing fruit, but modernizing and rebranding can offer great benefits. As I am writing this, if you find a quality Spanish white wine in a generic liquor store, chances are it is from Rías Baixas.

With all of these regions, there seems to be one clear takeaway: produce good wines, and you'll earn a strong identity. When regions tried to cut costs or maintain a failing status quo, the identity of the wines diminished, and collapse loomed on the horizon. As several regions learned, there is nothing wrong with studying new techniques to improve production. While stainless-steel fermentation was never "traditional" in Spain, the incorporation of this technique produced the amazing white wines of Rías Baixas and Rueda. Once-forgotten regions, like the Priorat, if given the proper attention, can create stellar wines to sell at high prices. These regions can produce very special wines, and the adapting consumer wants to buy something wonderful.

The twenty-first century presents some fascinating paths for Spanish wine. On the one hand, after decades of struggling, wines like cava, rioja, and albariño are the faces of Spanish production. They have adapted when necessary to find success, even in niche markets. Other producers, such as in Jerez, are still trying to find their way forward. Once the "noble wine," the sale of sherry has never recovered from its heyday. Sherry needs to find a way to make itself trendy again if it wants to recover market share. There is, though, a danger in adapting too much. As Thach and Cuellar suggest, by 2005 some wine enthusiasts were worried that new technology that made Spanish wine "hip and cool" could destroy the traditional essence of the wine and its true identity would be lost forever. "If the majority of Spanish wine makers were to start adopting the new international wine styles and lose the artistry of their traditional methods," they write, "that would be destressing. Therefore, some type of compromise of marrying the old traditions with the new technology could be in order."[102] I wholeheartedly agree with this conclusion. Without new techniques verdejo would not exist. Without new technology and environmental research Priorat would be avoided. Without mechanization cava could never meet the world demand. This being said, however, it is always critical that these regions remember what made them special to begin with.

When looking at the American market (which is, of course, possibly one of the largest to infiltrate), Thach and Cuellar offer suggestions for Spanish wines. Spain, they believe, should continue to "Maintain & Enhance Quality Levels; Promote Highly Rated Spanish Wines; Support and develop passionate wine importers; and Develop positive relationships with critics, distributors, & retailers." At the same time, these producers should begin to "Conduct Flavor Profiling on American palate; Consider Crianza brands targeted at Millennial Generation, Pursue Market Labeling for U.S. Hispanic market; Develop partnerships with American wineries to sell direct to the consumer; Offer more Spanish wine and food events; and Promote Spanish Wine Tourism."[103] Each of these ideas is solid and could help the American market in a large way. As this chapter has shown, Spanish producers have recently tried many of these techniques, to some success. There will always be problems, however. The 2008 economic meltdown limited purchases of luxury brands, and, frankly, tastes can change over time. As I write this chapter, COVID-19 has left devastating results

182   SPANISH WINE TODAY

in the world, especially in Spain, and there is still not a clear understanding as to how this human pandemic will affect Spanish wine's future. The production of a quality product in a style that no one likes at a period of economic collapse cannot bring success. In the end the best path for all Spanish wine producers is to stay aware of contemporary trends and tastes, always try to learn ways of improving production quality, and remember to highlight the best attributes in their regions to distinguish themselves from their competitors.

Conclusion

In a 2018 piece for *Wine Spectator* about the "extreme virtues" of Spanish wines, Thomas Matthews argues that one of the greatest advantages of Spanish wine was its continued uniqueness. "Some people who love wine fear globalization—in terms of production methods as well as consumer tastes—is imposing sterile standardization of style," he writes. "They may have a point when it comes to Napa Valley Cabernet Sauvignon or New Zealand Sauvignon Blanc or Pinot Noir from Burgundy. It takes close attention to find the differences in wines from these categories. But Spain argues against this fear. Its glorious variety testifies that wine culture is inherently resistant to uniformity. With an abundance of natural resources and talented vintners, Spain cultivates the entire rainbow of wine styles."[1] In the twenty-first century, the variety of Spanish wines made them special for the consumer. When it comes to Spain's traditional red wines, "while elegance has been the traditional template for Spanish reds, it has not become a prison. Tempranillo, Garnacha, Cariñena and Monastrell, all indigenous varieties, have proven their ability to make beautiful wines of power. The attempt to play in the same league as Bordeaux, Tuscany and Napa has required changes in both mindset and technique on the part of Spanish vintners. The effort began in Rioja in the 1990s. . . . They also focused on single-vineyard and, often, single-variety bottlings. The resulting wines were very different from the gran reserva model, but, in my opinion, the best are no less transparent or true to their *terroir*."[2] Spanish wine producers began to adapt the process for wine making to improve the quality of existing styles and to experiment with the creation of new types of wines.

For modern Spanish wines, this creativity has seemed to work. Old wine grapes, traditional processes, experimentation, and new models have created a solid wine industry. For Matthews Spanish wines are varied in quality and price: "This analysis has concentrated mostly on wines that earned outstanding scores of 90 points or higher in our blind tastings. Many of them sell for $100 or more, commensurate with benchmark wines from top regions around the world. But Spain is deservedly known for its abundance of values, and these wines offer a full range of styles as well."[3] Exciting Spanish wines now match quality with higher pricing, allowing them to compete with international powerhouse producers. "Of the nearly 1,200 still, dry wines reviewed for this report," Matthews writes, "about half earned very good scores of 85 to 89 points. Of these, more than 200 cost $15 or less—mostly reds, but also about 50 white wines and 20 rosés. Exploring these wines is a way to minimize risk while maximizing the opportunity of discovering exciting new flavors."[4] Less expensive Spanish wines offer consumers an experience that more pricey regions cannot offer.

Thomas Matthews's kind words for Spanish wine offer a perfect opportunity to reflect about the changing idea of Spanish wine from the mid-nineteenth century to today. Spanish wines might actually be having their moment in the sun, but this ascent to higher status is intricately connected to the industry's history. Now a fear of wine globalization and mass production are taboo for wine aficionados—a modern trap into which Spain is not falling. This was not always the case for Spain, however. As this book has shown, bulk sherry production in the late nineteenth century, the push to produce cheap bulk red wine during the plagues, the government's goal to increase exports quickly, and the attempt to standardize all wines were Spanish wine's true history. From the mid-nineteenth century until the late twentieth century, Spanish producers seemed most interested in profit and competition, not the uniqueness of their product. Rioja's first serious successes came as substitute wines for French markets. In a way Spanish wines—with exceptions like sherry—seemed to copy international tastes for the export market. White wine fields were replaced with red wine vineyards as French demands grew. Matthews credits Spanish wines with not trying to standardize too much, which marks a serious change from the past. What was once a desire to standardize wine has now become a push to stand out from the crowd. Traditional Spanish grapes are coming back, and consumers can now purchase a 100 percent xarel·lo cava or still wine in the United States, something a standardized production would never have aimed to do.

One of the most interesting issues mentioned by Matthews is that of the price and quality of Spanish wines. This had long been a problem for Spain. When sherry prices suddenly spiked in the 1860s and 1870s, cheap and imposter products flooded the British market, and sherry's quality was questioned. From there the Spanish goal appeared to be producing substitute wines for export at a reduced price. While more wine was sold, this process seemed to create a negative image for Spanish wine: that it was cheap. If Spanish wine was an inexpensive replacement, when the genuine product (like French wines) came back into production, the replacement could easily be avoided. At the same time, if a consumer only wanted to buy cheap wine, when a less expensive wine was found, such as from Algeria, Spanish wine could easily be pushed out of the market. Likewise, as Spain did not have any economic community ties until the 1980s, their prices could always be undercut due to trade agreements between other countries. As Matthews believes, however, in a new era when some consumers do not want a homogeneous bulk wine, Spain is a great location. Spanish wines now are part of the spice of life as opposed to standardized beverages.

This book began as a study to track the ever-changing idea of Spanish wine in internal and external markets from the mid-nineteenth century until today. As it has shown, there was a constant battle about what Spanish wine meant to both the producer and the consumer. For much of the time under discussion in this book, Spanish wines encountered difficulty in defining themselves. With the exception of sherry, these modern Spanish wine producers often tried to copy the successes of other nations' wines. The most important conversation for many decades centered around how to produce and sell more wine in international markets. Economically, agriculture was a central part of Spanish exports, and there existed a constant need to strengthen this arena, especially after the loss of Spain's colonial territories. When it was necessary to sell wine for economic growth, speed in production seemed to be the central tenant. By concentrating on speed rather than quality, and by looking to replace the wines of other nations when they were in crisis rather than developing their own varietals, Spanish wines earned the unfortunate identity of being cheap and, in some instances, even dangerous. Quick successes led to long-term struggles. At a variety of points, such as through national and international wine festivals and tastings,

Spanish wine did have some positive achievements, and these wines were able to gain market share globally. Today, however, it seems that Spanish wines have been able to break this pattern of solely producing as much wine as possible, and specialty wines have brought success to Spain. Even today, however, the historical identity of cheap, substitute wine still haunts Spanish vintners and their exciting new products.

Culturally, the idea of Spanish wine can best be described as fluid. From its earliest inception, wine served as a way to preserve grapes, offer nutrients, act as a medicinal agent, and create enjoyment. With the development of modern medicine, the role of wine changed, raising questions about the health risks of alcohol. By the nineteenth century, wine was not seen as a source of nutrition, but developed an identity around culture and class. For some wine-producing nations, like France, wine was a sign of cultural superiority, due to its quality. For Spain it often seemed that copying successful actions of other states was the best policy. As Spanish gastronomes in the mid-twentieth century have noted, the French created gastronomy, and the Spanish needed to understand this concept. There is nothing wrong with the Spanish wine industry imitating foreign concepts; science and technology helped in the development of better and safer wines. At the same time, it was important for Spanish wines to create their own identity, which seems to finally be happening. Spanish wine producers have become prouder of their products and to attach themselves to the uniqueness of Spain.

Throughout this book it has been my goal to show the dramatic changes in Spanish wine identity over the previous decades. Many actors played roles in the creation of this identity. Farmers, producers, shippers, exporters, local and state government agencies, performers, artists, connoisseurs, gastronomes, chefs, sommeliers, alcoholics, advertisers, national and international consumers, event planners, store and bar owners, foreign competitors, foreign governments, trade organization, and others all have responsibility in how Spanish wine is understood. Some of these actors played intentional parts in trying to improve Spanish wine, or they worked to sell more wine or to celebrate the product. Other actors played a more tacit role—choosing either to buy or not buy Spanish wine for a variety of reasons. Ultimately, Spanish wine's history is a sum of these parts. For many decades these activities presented Spanish wine as having different standards from their international competitors. However, because the identity of any commodity is fluid, it makes sense that the image of Spanish wine has improved. My respect for Spanish wine producers has remained strong throughout the course of writing this book. The challenges they faced were significant from the mid-nineteenth century onward, and the fact that their wines have been able to achieve contemporary success highlights the hard work and dedication of these individuals to their craft. Wine is truly Spanish, and Spain should be enormously proud of its wines.

NOTES

All Spanish-to-English translations of source material are the author's.

INTRODUCTION

1. Ulin and Black, "Introduction," 1.
2. Holt, "Introduction," 4.
3. Mintz, "Food and Eating," 25.
4. Mintz, "Food and Eating," 26.
5. Mintz, "Food and Eating," 26.
6. Miller, *Feeding Barcelona*, 106.
7. Miller, *Feeding Barcelona*, 107.
8. Miller, *Feeding Barcelona*, x.
9. Miller, *Feeding Barcelona*, 244.
10. Miller, *Feeding Barcelona*, 246.
11. Miller, *Feeding Barcelona*, 248.
12. Parkhurst Ferguson, *Word of Mouth*, xvii.
13. Parkhurst Ferguson, *Word of Mouth*, xxi.
14. Parkhurst Ferguson, *Word of Mouth*, xxi.
15. Parkhurst Ferguson, *Word of Mouth*, 53.
16. Parkhurst Ferguson, *Word of Mouth*, 71.
17. Parkhurst Ferguson, *Word of Mouth*, 141–42.
18. Parkhurst Ferguson, *Accounting for Taste*, 12.
19. Anderson, *Cooking up the Nation*, 146.
20. Anderson, *Cooking up the Nation*, 147.
21. González Turmo, *Sevilla*, 31.
22. González Turmo, *Sevilla*, 129, 54.
23. González Turmo, *Sevilla*, 115.
24. González Turmo, *Sevilla*, 143.
25. González Turmo, *Sevilla*, 145.
26. Guy, "Rituals of Pleasure," 38.

27. Guy, "Rituals of Pleasure," 44.

28. Parker, *Tasting French Terroir*, 1.

29. Parker, *Tasting French Terroir*, 5.

30. Parker, *Tasting French Terroir*, 3.

1. HOW TO SELL WINE

1. Nadeau, "*Moscatel morisco*," 156.

2. Fernández-Pérez, "Challenging the Loss," 72.

3. Fernández-Pérez, "Challenging the Loss," 73.

4. Fernández-Pérez, "Challenging the Loss," 84.

5. Manjarrés y de Bofarull, "Revista agrícola," 297.

6. Manjarrés y de Bofarull, "Revista agrícola," 297.

7. Manjarrés y de Bofarull, "Revista agrícola," 302.

8. Manjarrés y de Bofarull, "Revista agrícola," 302.

9. Manjarrés y de Bofarull, "Revista agrícola," 302.

10. Manjarrés y de Bofarull, "Revista agrícola," 302.

11. Manjarrés y de Bofarull, "Revista agrícola," 303.

12. Manjarrés y de Bofarull, "Revista agrícola," 303.

13. Valls-Junyent, "Compitiendo con el *champagne*," 52–53.

14. Manjarrés y de Bofarull, "Revista agrícola," 335.

15. Manjarrés y de Bofarull, "Revista agrícola," 335.

16. Llansó, "De la vinificación," 59.

17. Llansó, "De la vinificación," 59.

18. Llansó, "De la vinificación," 59.

19. Llansó, "De la vinificación," 59.

20. Llansó, "De la vinificación," 60.

21. Llansó, "De la vinificación," 60.

22. Llansó, "De la vinificación," 60.

23. Llansó, "De la vinificación," 60.

24. Llansó, "De la vinificación," 62.

25. Llansó, "De la vinificación," 61–62.

26. Ulin and Black, "Rethinking Terroir," 11.

27. Ulin, "*Terroir* and Locality," 68.

28. Ulin, "*Terroir* and Locality," 72.

29. Ulin, "*Terroir* and Locality," 81.

30. Trubek, *Taste of Place*, 19.

31. Trubek, *Taste of Place*, 22.

32. Trubek, *Taste of Place*, 24.

33. Foxá, "Del cultivo" (August 1, 1860), 169.

34. Foxá, "Del cultivo" (August 1, 1860), 170.

35. Foxá, "Del cultivo" (September 1, 1860), 193.

36. Foxá, "Del cultivo" (September 1, 1860), 194.

37. Foxá, "Del cultivo" (September 1, 1860), 194–95.

38. Foxá, "Del cultivo" (September 1, 1860), 196.

39. Foxá, "Del cultivo" (October 1, 1860), 229–30.

40. Simpson, *Creating Wine*, 172.

41. Simpson, "La producción," 166–67.

42. Plasencia, *Los vinos de España*, 147; Simpson, "Adapting to International," 208.

43. Simpson, *Creating Wine*, 178.

44. Simpson, "La producción," 170.

45. Simpson, "Selling to Reluctant," 81.

46. Simpson, "Adapting to International," 209.

47. Simpson, *Creating Wine*, 179.

48. Simpson, *Creating Wine*, 179.

49. Simpson, *Creating Wine*, 177.

50. Simpson, "Selling to Reluctant," 91.

51. Espigado Tocino, "Exportación y fraude," 36.

52. Simpson, *Creating Wine*, 180.

53. Simpson, "Adapting to International," 212.

54. Simpson, "Too Little Regulation?," 379.

55. Simpson, "Selling to Reluctant," 82.

56. Simpson, "Too Little Regulation?," 375–76.

57. Simpson, "Too Little Regulation?," 380.

58. Girón Sierra, "El marco de Jerez," 179.

59. "Cuadro gráfico de las cantidades de vinos exportados desde 1850 a 1883 según resumenes facilidades por la dirección general de aduanas," May 13, 1884, MAPA, Fondo Antiguo AC-31235/1.

60. Consejo Superior de Agricultura, Industria y Comercio, May 1, 1884, MAPA, Fondo Antiguo AC-31235/2.

61. Consejo Superior de Agricultura, May 1, 1884.

62. Consejo Superior de Agricultura, May 1, 1884.

63. Consejo Superior de Agricultura, May 1, 1884.

64. Consejo Superior de Agricultura, May 1, 1884.

65. Consejo Superior de Agricultura, May 1, 1884.

66. Consejo Superior de Agricultura, May 1, 1884.

67. Consejo Superior de Agricultura, May 1, 1884.

68. Consejo Superior de Agricultura, May 1, 1884.

69. Consejo Superior de Agricultura, May 1, 1884.

70. Albacete, MAPA, 1885, Fondo Antiguo AC-31235/1.

71. Ávila, MAPA, 1885, Fondo Antiguo AC-31237/2.

72. Badajoz, MAPA, 1885, Fondo Antiguo AC-31238/1.

73. Barcelona, MAPA, 1885, Fondo Antiguo AC-31238/3.

74. Cáceres, MAPA, 1885, Fondo Antiguo AC-31239.

75. Cádiz, MAPA, 1885, Fondo Antiguo AC-31237/4.

76. Ciudad Real, MAPA, 1885, Fondo Antiguo AC-31238/4.

77. Girona, MAPA, 1885, Fondo Antiguo AC-31240/4.

78. Logroño, MAPA, 1885, Fondo Antiguo AC-31244/1.

79. Málaga, MAPA, 1885, Fondo Antiguo AC-31244/4.

80. Orense, MAPA, 1885, Fondo Antiguo AC-31244/7.

81. Palencia, MAPA, 1885, Fondo Antiguo AC-31244/9.

82. Tarragona, MAPA, 1885, Fondo Antiguo AC-31235/4.

83. Valencia, MAPA, 1885, Fondo Antiguo AC-31246.

2. EL LABORATORIO DEL VINO

1. Amor, "Sobre el azuframiento," 206.

2. Amor, "Sobre el azuframiento," 206.

3. Farré Huguet, "Del arte," 23.

4. Farré Huguet, "Del arte," 35.

5. Piqueras Haba, *From the American Pests*, 21–22.

6. Piqueras Haba, *From the American Pests*, 22.

7. Piqueras Haba, *From the American Pests*, 20.

8. Piqueras Haba, *From the American Pests*, 21.

9. Piqueras Haba, *From the American Pests*, 23.

10. Piqueras Haba, *From the American Pests*, 35–37.

11. Piqueras Haba, *From the American Pests*, 57.

12. Piqueras Haba, *From the American Pests*, 27–28.

13. Farré Huguet, "Del arte," 26.

14. Foxá, "Noticias," 102.

15. Foxá, "Noticias," 102.

16. Llansó, "Sección práctica," 221.

17. Llansó, "Sección práctica," 221.

18. Llansó, "Sección práctica," 221.

19. Llansó, "Sección práctica," 221.

20. "El azufre empleado," 171–72.

21. Piqueras Haba, *From the American Pests*, 45.

22. "El azufre empleado," 172.

23. "El azufre empleado," 172.

24. "El azufre empleado," 172–73.

25. Llansó, "Sección práctica," 220.

26. Llansó, "Sección práctica," 220.

27. Llansó, "Sección práctica," 221.

28. Piqueras Haba, *From the American Pests*, 56–57.

29. Amor, "Sobre el azuframiento," 206.

30. Amor, "Sobre el azuframiento," 207.

31. Amor, "Sobre el azuframiento," 207.

32. Amor, "Sobre el azuframiento," 207–8.

33. Piqueras Haba, *From the American Pests*, 29–30.

34. Granett et al., "Biology and Management," 392.

35. Piqueras Haba, *From the American Pests*, 63.

36. Granett et al., "Biology and Management," 389. Clearly this is a complicated process best described by scientists, but it is necessary to get an overview of the unique, diverse, and complex existence of this insect.

37. Granett et al., "Biology and Management," 393.

38. Piqueras Haba, *From the American Pests*, 66–67.

39. Granett et al., "Biology and Management," 395.

40. Ley de defensa contra la filoxera promulgada, 30 June 1878, Real Jardín Botánica, https://bibdigital.rjb.csic.es/idurl/1/15740 (accessed July 5, 2022).

41. MAPA, July 18, 1879, Fondo Antiguo 15/8 AC-31137/1.

42. MAPA, July 21, 1879, Fondo Antiguo 15/8 AC-31137/1.

43. MAPA, August 9, 1881, Fondo Antiguo 15/10 AC-31137/1.

44. Piqueras Haba, *From the American Pests*, 77.

45. Parada y Barreto, "Discurso," 15–16.

46. Parada y Barreto, "Discurso," 22.

47. Consejo Superior de la Agricultura, Industria y Comercio, "Dictatem."

48. Badia-Miró et al., "Grape Phylloxera Plague," 40.

49. Consejo Superior de la Agricultura, Industria y Comercio, "Dictatem."

50. Badia-Miró et al., "Grape Phylloxera Plague," 42.

51. Piqueras Haba, *From the American Pests*, 72.

52. Colomé Ferrer and Valls-Junyent, "Las consecuencias demográficas," 49, 68.

53. Molleví Bortoló and Serrano Giné, "Impacto de la filoxera," 134.

54. "Bodega," Bodegas Franco Españolas, May 5, 2019, http://francoespanolas.com /history/?lang=en.

55. Piqueras Haba, *From the American Pests*, 65.

56. Molleví Bortoló and Serrano Giné, "Impacto de la filoxera," 135.

57. Farré Huguet, "Del arte," 37–38.

58. Colomé Ferrer and Valls-Junyent, "Las Consecuencias Demográficas," 48.

59. Badia-Miró et al., "Grape Phylloxera Plague," 44.

60. Badia-Miró et al., "Grape Phylloxera Plague," 46.

61. Planas, "State Intervention," 184–85.

62. Planas, "State Intervention," 186.

63. Planas, "State Intervention," 185.

64. Planas, "State Intervention," 186.

65. Phillips, "Wine and Adulteration," 33–34.

66. Phillips, "Wine and Adulteration," 32.

67. Holmberg, "Wine Fraud," 106.

68. Stanziani, "Information, Quality, and Legal Rules," 269.

69. Phillips, "Wine and Adulteration," 34.

70. Piqueras Haba, *From the American Pests*, 124.

71. Stanziani, "Information, Quality, and Legal Rules," 280.

72. Stanziani, "Information, Quality, and Legal Rules," 280–81.

73. Stanziani, "Information, Quality, and Legal Rules," 281.

74. Planas, "State Intervention," 177–78.

75. Stanziani, "Information, Quality, and Legal Rules," 269.

76. Stanziani, "Information, Quality, and Legal Rules," 274.

77. Stanziani, "Information, Quality, and Legal Rules," 275.

78. Piqueras Haba, *From the American Pests*, 123; Stanziani, "Information, Quality, and Legal Rules," 277.

79. Planas, "State Intervention," 193.

80. Holmberg, "Wine Fraud," 109.

81. Planas, "State Intervention," 202–3.

82. Stanziani, "Information, Quality, and Legal Rules," 269.

83. Stanziani, "Information, Quality, and Legal Rules," 269.

84. Planas, "State Intervention," 193.

85. Stanziani, "Information, Quality, and Legal Rules," 278.

86. Stanziani, "Information, Quality, and Legal Rules," 278.

87. Piqueras Haba, *From the American Pests*, 123.

88. Comisión de Vinos, MAPA, 1878–1892, Fondo Antiguo 70A/70B AC-31217.

89. Ramón de Manjarrés y de Bofarull, "Informe sobre el medio de descubrir la fuchsina en los vinos," MAPA, 1879, Fondo Antiguo 70A/70B AC-31217.

90. Manjarrés y de Bofarull, "Informe."

91. Manjarrés y de Bofarull, "Informe."

92. Manjarrés y de Bofarull, "Informe."

93. Institute San Isidro to Ministry of Development, April 28, 1879, MAPA, Fondo Antiguo 70A/70B AC-31217.

94. MAPA, October 31, 1886, Fondo Antiguo 70A/70B AC-31217.

95. MAPA, October 31, 1886.

96. MAPA, October 31, 1886.

97. MAPA, October 31, 1886.

98. Piqueras Haba, *From the American Pests*, 123.

99. Piqueras Haba, *From the American Pests*, 111–21.

100. MAPA, May 23, 1887, Fondo Antiguo 70A/70B AC-31217.

101. MAPA, May 23, 1887.

102. MAPA, May 23, 1887.

103. MAPA, June 6, 1887, Fondo Antiguo 70A/70B AC-31217.

104. MAPA, June 6, 1887.

105. MAPA, June 6, 1887.

106. MAPA, October 21, 1887, Fondo Antiguo 68B/8 AC-31217.

107. MAPA, October 21, 1887.

108. MAPA, October 21, 1887.

109. MAPA, October 21, 1887.

110. MAPA, June 6, 1887.

111. MAPA, June 6, 1887.

112. Farré Huguet, "Del arte," 52.

113. MAPA, October 21, 1887.

114. Farré Huguet, "Del arte," 52.

115. Granett et al., "Biology and Management," 402–4.

3. *SABER BEBER*

1. "Un vino para cada hora y una hora para cada vino," *Fotos*, October 6, 1952, n.p.

2. Anderson, "Recipe," 77.

3. Albala, "To Your Health," 11.

4. *Galen on Food*, 188.

5. Grieco, "Medieval and Renaissance Wine," 19.

6. Grieco, "Medieval and Renaissance Wine," 20.

7. Grieco, "Medieval and Renaissance Wine," 21.

8. Timón Tiemblo, "El patrimonio inmaterial," 19.

9. Grieco, "Medieval and Renaissance Wine," 17.

10. Grieco, "Medieval and Renaissance Wine," 22.

11. Grieco, "Medieval and Renaissance Wine," 28–29.

12. Grieco, "Medieval and Renaissance Wine," 30.

13. Albala, "To Your Health," 11.

14. Albala, "To Your Health," 15.

15. Albala, "To Your Health," 16–17.

16. Albala, "To Your Health," 17.

17. Varriano, "Wine and Death," 11.

18. Alfredo Marquerie, "Defensa del borracho," *Fotos*, December 1, 1945, n.p.

19. Marquerie, "Defensa del borracho."

20. Marquerie, "Defensa del borracho."

21. Marquerie, "Defensa del borracho."

22. Marquerie, "Defensa del borracho."

23. "Los peces de colores: Ya que nos hemos metido en juerga," *Fotos*, December 1, 1945, n.p.

24. "Los peces de colores."

25. "Los peces de colores."

26. "Los peces de colores."

27. Haine, "Drink, Sociability," 130.

28. Haine, "Drink, Sociability," 133.

29. Kneale and French, "Moderate Drinking," 112.

30. Kneale and French, "Moderate Drinking," 112.

31. Kneale and French, "Moderate Drinking," 112–13.

32. Kneale and French, "Moderate Drinking," 113.

33. Munholland, "Mon docteur," 77–79.

34. "Los peces de colores."

35. F. Hernández Castanedo, "El vino corriente: Bebida de moda," *Fotos*, December 1, 1945, n.p.

36. Hernández Castanedo, "El vino corriente."

37. Hernández Castanedo, "El vino corriente."

38. Hernández Castanedo, "El vino corriente."

39. "La producción vinícola española: Exportación de nuestros vinos y sus problemas, entrevista con el jefe del Sindicato Nacional de la Vid," *Fotos*, December 1, 1945, n.p.

40. "La producción vinícola española."

41. Fernando Castan Palomar, "Los vinos preferidos por las personalidades," *Fotos*, December 1, 1945, n.p.

42. Castan Palomar, "Los vinos preferidos."

43. Castan Palomar, "Los vinos preferidos."

44. Castan Palomar, "Los vinos preferidos."

45. Bohling, "Drink Better," 504–13.

46. Puig, "El mercado vinícola," 246.

47. Bohling, "Drink Better," 506, 509.

48. Alonso Fernandez, "State of Alcoholism," 235.

49. Alonso Fernandez, "State of Alcoholism," 236.

50. Alonso Fernandez, "State of Alcoholism," 235.

51. Alonso Fernandez, "State of Alcoholism," 237.

52. Alonso Fernandez, "State of Alcoholism," 238–39.

53. Pozo Andrés and Rabazas Romero, "Exploring New Concepts," 221–25.

54. Alonso Fernandez, "State of Alcoholism," 241.

55. Bohling, "Drink Better," 503–9.

56. Bohling, "Drink Better," 517, 522.

57. Puig, "El mercado vinícola," 243.

58. Puig, "El mercado vinícola," 244.

59. Puig, "El mercado vinícola," 246.

60. Timón Tiemblo, "El patrimonio inmaterial," 5, 16.

61. Timón Tiemblo, "El patrimonio inmaterial," 16.

62. Anderson, "Recipe," 80–81.

63. Anderson, *Control and Resistance*, 69.

64. "Escoja su bebida y tome con nosotros una copa," *Fotos*, December 4, 1948, n.p.

65. Rafael Garcia Serrano, "Laude del vino y elogia de la sed," *Mundo Hispánico*, February 1951, n.p.

66. Castillo Puche, "El arte y los modos de beber," *Mundo Hispánico*, February 1951, n.p.

67. Joaquin de Entrambasaguas, "La rioja en la mesa," *Mundo Hispánico*, February 1951, n.p.

68. Entrambasaguas, "La rioja."

69. Entrambasaguas, "La rioja."

70. "Saber Beber," *Diario de la Feria*, October 9, 1953, 4.

71. "Saber Beber," 4.

72. Curro Sanchez, "Beber vino con 'palada,'" *Fotos*, December 8, 1956, n.p.

73. "Adecuación de los vinos con los platos," *Destino*, October 1, 1966, n.p.

74. Francisco Rodríguez Alverez, "Acta de la reunion del Comite Nacional de Propaganda Correspondiente al día 16 de junio de 1966," AGA, Sección: Sindicatos, Caja 5478, 1.

75. Rodríguez Alverez, "Acta de la reunion," 1.

76. Rodríguez Alverez, "Acta de la reunion," 1.

77. Rodríguez Alverez, "Acta de la reunion," 2.

78. Rodríguez Alverez, "Acta de la reunion," 2.

79. Rodríguez Alverez, "Acta de la reunion," 2.

80. Rodríguez Alverez, "Acta de la reunion," 3.

81. Francisco Rodríguez Alvarez, "Memoria—Resumen de acivitidades desarrolladas por la Comisión de Propaganda en Favor del Consumo del Vino, Zumos y Mostos— del Sindicato Nacional de la Vid, Cervezas y Bebidas," June 23, 1966, AGA, Sección: Sindicatos, Caja 5478, 1.

82. Rodríguez Alvarez, "Memoria," 1.

83. Rodríguez Alvarez, "Memoria," 2–3.

84. Rodríguez Alvarez, "Memoria," 3.

85. Rodríguez Alvarez, "Memoria," 3.

86. Anderson, "Recipe," 83–86.

87. Rodríguez Alvarez, "Memoria," 3.

88. Alonso Fernandez, "State of Alcoholism," 241.

4. WINE GOES TO THE FAIR

1. Mintz, "Food and Eating," 26.

2. Mintz, "Food and Eating," 29.

3. Mintz, *Tasting Food*, 97.

4. Harrington, "Defining Gastronomic Identity," 131.

5. Johnson Morgan, "Food Festivals," 59.

6. Johnson Morgan, "Food Festivals," 60.

7. Harrington, "Defining Gastronomic Identity," 141.

8. Johnson Morgan, "Food Festivals," 61.

9. Harrington, "Defining Gastronomic Identity," 141–42.

10. Harrington, "Defining Gastronomic Identity," 143.

11. Johnson Morgan, "Food Festivals," 61.

12. *España en forma*, 4.

13. *España en forma*, 4.

14. *España en forma*, 4.

15. *España en forma*, 7.

16. *España en forma*, 7.

17. *España en forma*, 7.

18. *España en forma*, 7.

19. Anderson, "Recipe," 76.

20. Johnson Morgan, "Food Festivals," 63.

21. Vizconde de Trueste, "Exposición Universal de Chicago de 1893," MAPA, November 1892, Fondo Antiguo 68B/8.1 AC-31217, 1.

22. Trueste, "Exposición Universal," 1.

23. Trueste, "Exposición Universal," 2.

24. Trueste, "Exposición Universal," 2.

25. Trueste, "Exposición Universal," 2–3.

26. Trueste, "Exposición Universal," 3–5.

27. Guy, "Rituals of Pleasure," 38.

28. See chapter 3 for an in-depth discussion of the "drink better" movement in France.

29. Guy, "Rituals of Pleasure," 39.

30. Guy, "Rituals of Pleasure," 39.

31. Guy, "Rituals of Pleasure," 40.

32. *Catalogue des exposants*, 13.

33. *Catalogue des exposants*, 5.

34. *Catalogue des exposants*, 13.

35. *Catalogue des exposants*, 13.

36. *Catalogue des exposants*, 13.

37. *Catalogue des exposants*, 13.

38. *Catalogue des exposants*, 13.

39. Raventós, "Codorníu, la historia," 126.

40. Raventós, "Codorníu, la historia," 126.

41. *El cava y sus elaboradores*, 70.

42. *El cava y sus elaboradores*, 71–73.

43. *El cava y sus elaboradores*, 75.

44. The seven sages were the men of Sant Sadurní who saved the wine industry from the serious plagues of the late nineteenth century. "Festa de la Fil·loxera," https://www.festadelafiloxera.cat/la-festa-de-la-filloxera/ (accessed December 8, 2022).

45. *El cava y sus elaboradores*, 76.

46. *Visita de S.M. el rey don Alfonso XIII a las Cavas Codorníu*, ARB, April 17, 1904, 82.

47. José Montserrat, "Al Lector," in *Visita de S.M. el rey don Alfonso XIII a las Cavas Codorníu*, ARB, April 17, 1904, ARB.

48. *Visita de S.M. el rey*, 14, 21.

49. *Visita de S.M. el rey*, 36.

50. *Visita de S.M. el rey*, 23.

51. *Visita de S.M. el rey*, 21.

52. *Visita de S.M. el rey*, 29.

53. *Visita de S.M. el rey*, 68.

54. *Visita de S.M. el rey*, 14–15.

55. *Visita de S.M. el rey*, 82.

56. *Visita de S.M. el rey*, 89.

57. *Visita de S.M. el rey*, 89.

58. "The Vendemia Festival," Andalucia.com, http://www.andalucia.com/festival /vendimia.htm (accessed July 3, 2020).

59. Duarte Alonso, "Stakeholders, Collaboration," 175.

60. Duarte Alonso, "Stakeholders, Collaboration," 186.

61. Stilling Blichfeldt and Halkier, "Mussels, Tourism," 1588.

62. Filippo Fontefrancesco, "Of Grape," 80.

63. Filippo Fontefrancesco, "Of Grape," 81.

64. Anderson, *Control and Resistance*, 24.

65. Filippo Fontefrancesco, "Of Grape," 84.

66. Filippo Fontefrancesco, "Of Grape," 84.

67. Filippo Fontefrancesco, "Of Grape," 85.

68. Laferté, "Folklorization of French Farming," 703.

69. Laferté, "Folklorization of French Farming," 706–7.

70. J. F. Avellaneda Lucas, "El teniente de alcalde presidente de la fiestas jerezanas, al habla," *Fotos*, September 8, 1956, n.p.

71. Avellaneda Lucas, "El teniente,"

72. J. F. Avellaneda Lucas, "Jerez de la Frontera, ciudad única en el mundo," *Fotos*, September 29, 1959, n.p.

73. Avellaneda Lucas, "Jerez de la Frontera."

74. J. F. Avellaneda Lucas, "Don José María Pemán habla de Jerez, el vino y su literatura," *Fotos*, September 14, 1957, n.p.

75. Avellaneda Lucas, "Don José María Pemán."

76. Avellaneda Lucas, "Don José María Pemán."

77. Avellaneda Lucas, "Don José María Pemán."

78. Rodrigo Molia, "Venenciar es, también, un arte," *Fotos*, September 14, 1957, n.p.

79. Molia, "Venenciar."

80. Molia, "Venenciar."

81. Laferté, "Folklorization of French Farming," 681.

82. Laferté, "Folklorization of French Farming," 692.

83. Laferté, "Folklorization of French Farming," 692.

84. "Proyecto para la instalación del Museo Nacional del Vino," AGA, Sección: Sindicatos, Caja 5476, 2.

85. "Proyecto para la instalación," 2–3.

86. "Proyecto para la instalación," 3.

87. "Proyecto para la instalación," 4.

88. "Proyecto para la instalación," 5.

89. "Proyecto para la instalación," 5.

90. "Proyecto para la instalación," 6.

91. "Proyecto para la instalación," 6–7.

92. Pio Miguel Irurzun, AGA, March 29, 1969, Sección: Sindicatos, Caja 5476, 1.

5. EXPOSICIÓ I FIRA OFICIAL

1. "Esta es la Feria de Amistad," *Diario*, August 14–15, 1963, 4.

2. Cazorla-Sánchez, "Family Matters," 78.

3. "Esta es la Feria de Amistad," 4.

4. "Esta es la Feria de Amistad," 4.

5. Soler Becerro, "From Trade," 7.

6. Young, *Wine Routes*, 39–40.

7. Young, *Wine Routes*, 16.

8. Young, *Wine Routes*, 16.

9. Soler Becerro, "From Trade," 10.

10. Soler Becerro, "From Trade," 9.

11. Soler Becerro, "From Trade," 27.

12. Soler Becerro, "From Trade," 14.

13. Soler Becerro, "From Trade," 13.

14. Bonfanti, Castellani, Rossato, "Developing Territorial Identity," 46.

15. Bonfanti, Castellani, Rossato, "Developing Territorial Identity," 47.

16. Bonfanti, Castellani, Rossato, "Developing Territorial Identity," 47.

17. Bonfanti, Castellani, Rossato, "Developing Territorial Identity," 47.

18. Bonfanti, Castellani, Rossato, "Developing Territorial Identity," 47–48.

19. Christensen, Kenney, and Patton, "Regional Identity," 85.

20. Christensen, Kenney, and Patton, "Regional Identity," 85.

21. Laferté, "Folklorization of French Farming," 681.

22. Guy, *When Champagne*, 4.

23. Guy, *When Champagne*, 6.

24. Bohling, "Drink Better," 521–22.

25. Duarte Alonso and Bressan, "Stakeholders' Perspectives," 324.

26. Chang, "Spillover Effects of Wine," 690.

27. Cavicchi, Santini, and Belleti, "Preserving the Authenticity," 253.

28. Cavicchi, Santini, and Belleti, "Preserving the Authenticity," 257.

29. Cavicchi, Santini, and Belleti, "Preserving the Authenticity," 259.

30. Molina et al., "Market Segmentation," 193.

31. Armesto López and Gómez Martín, "Tourism and Quality," 166.

32. Armesto López and Gómez Martín, "Tourism and Quality," 167–70.

33. Gómez and Molina, "Wine Tourism in Spain," 354.

34. Falange Española Tradicionalista de las Juntas de Ofensiva Nacional-Sindicalista (Traditionalist Spanish Phalanx and of the Councils of the National-Syndicalist Offensive).

35. "Esta mañana tendrá lugar la solemne bendición e inauguación de la exposición y feria con asistencia de las autoridades y jerarquías de movimiento, nacionales, provincials y locales," *Diario*, October 10, 1943, 1.

36. "Editorial," *Diario*, October 11, 1943, 1.

37. "Fiestas y espectáculos," *Diario*, October 12, 1943, 3.

38. "La exposición de pinturas," *Diario*, October 13, 1943, 2.

39. "Vilafranca y la exposición," *Diario*, October 15, 1943, 1.

40. "Vilafranca y la exposición," 3.

41. "Digresión al vino," *Diario*, October 12, 1943, 1.

42. "Digresión al vino," 1.

43. Miguel Utrillo, "Lección de amor y de vino," *Diario*, October 17, 1943, 4.

44. Ramón de Saavedra, "Elogio del vino," *Diario*, October 20, 1943, 2.

45. Saavedra, "Elogio del vino," 2.

46. Saavedra, "Elogio del vino," 2.

47. "La exposición de pinturas," *Diario*, October 13, 1943, 2.

48. "La exposición el vino en as artes plásticas," *Diario*, October 14, 1943, 2.

49. "Raíz," *Diario*, October 13, 1943, 1.

50. "Al cabo de ocho días," *Diario*, October 18, 1943, 1.

51. "Otras de las virtudes de la exposición," *Diario*, October 24, 1943, 1.

52. "Nuestra riqueza natural," *La Prensa*, reprinted in *Diario*, October 19, 43, 1.

53. "Examen," *Diario*, October 25, 1943, 1–2.

54. "Examen," 2.

55. "Examen," 2.

56. "Hoy fiestas, y ¿mañana qué?," *Diario*, October 26, 1943, 1–2.

57. "Hoy se inaugura con la máxima solemnidad la II Exposición y Feria de la Viña y del Vino con la asistencia de diversas autoridades nacionales, provincials y locales," *Diario*, October 4, 1953, 1.

58. "Hoy se inaugura," 1.

59. "Por los corrillos del recinto," *Diario*, October 4, 1953, 3.

60. "El excmo. Sr. secretario técnico del ministro de comercio declara abierta la II Exposición y Feria en nombre del ministro del ramo," *Diario*, October 5, 1953, 1.

61. "Editorial," *Diario*, October 4, 1953, 2.

62. "Sesión oficial de apertura de la feria," *Diario*, October 5, 1953, 2.

63. "Sesión oficial de apertura de la feria," 3.

64. Anderson, "Recipe," 95.

65. "Sesión oficial de apertura de la feria," 3.

66. A. J. M., "El aperitivo con Juan Cabane," *Diario*, October 9, 1953, 2.

67. Anderson, "Recipe," 79.

68. A. J. M., "El aperitivo," 2.

69. A. J. M., "El aperitivo," 2.

70. A. J. M., "El aperitivo," 2.

71. A. J. M., "El aperitivo," 2.

72. A. J. M., "El aperitivo," 2.

73. "El Dr. Entrambasaguas dice. . . . ," *Diario*, October 23, 1953, 2.

74. "El Dr. Entrambasaguas dice. . . . ," 2.

75. "El Dr. Entrambasaguas dice. . . . ," 2.

76. "El Dr. Entrambasaguas dice. . . . ," 2.

77. "El vino en la cátedra," *Diario*, October 13, 1953, 3.

78. "El aperitivo con Enrique Feduchy," *Diario*, October 14, 1953, 2.

79. "Nobleza obliga," *Diario*, October 31, 1953, 2.

80. "Nota del comité ejecutivo," *Diario*, October 31, 1953, 3.

81. "Esta es la Feria de la Amistad," *Diario*, October 14–15, 1963, 4–5.

82. "Esta es la Feria de la Amistad," 5.

83. "Esta es la Feria de la Amistad," 5.

84. "Esta es la Feria de la Amistad," 5.

85. Valko, "Nuestro personaje del día, don Santiago Udina Martell," *Diario*, October 14–15, 1963, 5.

86. Valko, "Nuestro personaje," 5.

87. Valko, "Nuestro personaje," 5.

88. "La nuestra feria: Santiago de Cruylles," *Diario*, August 20, 1963, 1.

89. "La nuestra feria," 1.

90. "Mr. James Griffin," *Diario*, August 21, 1963, 2.

91. Esteve, "Nuestro personaje del día: Enrique Guitart," *Diario*, August 23, 1963, 2.

92. Esteve, "Nuestro personaje," 2.

93. "El viñedo en el Penedès," *Diario*, August 30, 1963, 5.

94. "El viñedo en el Penedès," 5.

95. "El viñedo en el Penedès," 5.

6. MAKING FRIENDS WITH WINE

1. Report on *IIº Salon Internacional de la Alimentación*, 1967, AGA, Sección Sindicatos, Caja 5477.

2. Report on *IIº Salon Internacional*.

3. Report on *IIº Salon Internacional*.

4. Martínes-Carrión and Medina-Albaladejo, "Change and Development," 85–87.

5. Rodriguez Salcedo, "Public Relations," 289–91.

6. *Wine and Spirit Trade Review*, June 5, 1964, 31.

7. *Wine and Spirit Trade Review*, September 4, 1964, 7.

8. García de Quevedo de la Barrera, *Economía de Jerez*, 166.

9. García de Quevedo de la Barrera, *Economía de Jerez*, 170.

10. García de Quevedo de la Barrera, *Economía de Jerez*, 171.

11. García de Quevedo de la Barrera, *Economía de Jerez*, 186–87.

12. García de Quevedo de la Barrera, *Economía de Jerez*, 189.

13. García de Quevedo de la Barrera, *Economía de Jerez*, 186–87.

14. García de Quevedo de la Barrera, *Economía de Jerez*, 186–87.

15. Director general of the Ministry of Commerce to National Syndicate, September 17, 1964, AGA, Sección Sindicatos, Caja 5479.

16. M. Albizu Alba to the Ministry of Commerce, September 19, 1964, AGA, Sección Sindicatos, Caja 5479.

17. "El 30 de septiembre de 1964 España debe denuciar el acuerdo comercial con Francia," *La Semana Vitivinícola,* August 29 1964, 14.

18. ". . . Y algo más que se conviene saber, para decirles," *La Semana Vitivinícola* 945 (September 19, 1964): n.p.

19. ". . . Y algo más."

20. Rodolfo Argamentería García to national vice-secretary of economic management, October 2, 1964, AGA, Sección Sindicatos, Caja 5479.

21. Argamentería García to national vice-secretary, October 2, 1964.

22. Argamentería García to national vice-secretary, October 2, 1964.

23. General director of trade policy, October 20, 1964, AGA, Sección Sindicatos, Caja 5479.

24. General director of trade policy, October 20, 1964.

25. General director of trade policy, October 20, 1964.

26. Nicolás Castejón y Paz-Pardo to the Campaign General for the Propaganda of Spanish Wine in France, July 28, 1966, AGA, Sección Sindicatos, Caja 5479.

27. Comité de Propaganda de Vinos Españoles en Francia, Plans, August 11, 1964, AGA, Sección Sindicatos, Caja 5479, 1.

28. Comité de Propaganda de Vinos, 2.

29. Comité de Propaganda de Vinos, 3.

30. Nicolás Castejón y Paz-Pardo to don Enrique Barceló Carles, September 9, 1966, AGA, Sección Sindicatos, Caja 5479.

31. García de Quevedo de la Barrera, *Economía de Jerez*, 238.

32. García de Quevedo de la Barrera, *Economía de Jerez*, 238.

33. García de Quevedo de la Barrera, *Economía de Jerez*, 239.

34. *Wine & Spirit Trade Review*, October 16, 1964, 4.

35. *Wine & Spirit Trade Review*, October 16, 1964, 55.

36. *Wine & Spirit Trade Review*, November 27, 1964, 55.

37. *Wine & Spirit Trade Review*, May 15, 1964, 2.

38. *Wine & Spirit Trade Review*, May 15, 1964, 2.

39. *Wine & Spirit Trade Review*, September 11, 1964, 45.

40. García de Quevedo de la Barrera, *Economía de Jerez*, 207.

41. García de Quevedo de la Barrera, *Economía de Jerez,* 209.

42. García de Quevedo de la Barrera, *Economía de Jerez,* 324.

43. Girón Sierra, "El Marco de Jerez," 186.

44. Lunzer, *Reports of Patent,* 1.

45. Lunzer, *Reports of Patent,* 6.

46. Lunzer, *Reports of Patent,* 6.

47. Lunzer, *Reports of Patent,* 7–8.

48. Lunzer, *Reports of Patent,* 8.

49. Lunzer, *Reports of Patent,* 8.

50. Lunzer, *Reports of Patent,* 8.

51. Lunzer, *Reports of Patent,* 3.

52. Lunzer, *Reports of Patent,* 4.

53. Lunzer, *Reports of Patent,* 4.

54. Lunzer, *Reports of Patent,* 4.

55. Lunzer, *Reports of Patent,* 4–5.

56. Lunzer, *Reports of Patent,* 5.

57. Lunzer, *Reports of Patent,* 5.

58. Lunzer, *Reports of Patent,* 10.

59. Lunzer, *Reports of Patent,* 10.

60. Lunzer, *Reports of Patent,* 11.

61. Lunzer, *Reports of Patent,* 11.

62. Lunzer, *Reports of Patent,* 11.

63. Lunzer, *Reports of Patent,* 11.

64. Lunzer, *Reports of Patent,* 13.

65. Lunzer, *Reports of Patent,* 16.

66. Lunzer, *Reports of Patent,* 17.

67. Lunzer, *Reports of Patent,* 17.

68. Lunzer, *Reports of Patent,* 18.

69. Lunzer, *Reports of Patent,* 18.

70. Lunzer, *Reports of Patent,* 19.

71. Lunzer, *Reports of Patent,* 21.

72. Lunzer, *Reports of Patent,* 32.

73. Víctor Audera to Pío Miguel Irurzun, March 3, 1970, AGA: Sección Sindicatos, Caja 5476.

74. Víctor Audera to Pío Miguel Irurzun, March 3, 1970.

75. Víctor Audera to Pío Miguel Irurzun, March 3, 1970.

76. García de Quevedo de la Barrera, *Economía de Jerez,* 241–42.

77. Antonio Riaño to the director general of commercial policy, March 3, 1970, AGA: Sección Sindicatos, Caja 5476.

78. Antonio Riaño to director general, March 3, 1970.

79. Antonio Riaño to director general, March 3, 1970.

80. Antonio Riaño to director general, March 3, 1970.

81. Antonio Riaño to director general, March 3, 1970.

82. Antonio Riaño to director general, March 3, 1970.

83. Juan Antonio Domingo and José Antonio Lopez Cascante, to director general of commercial policy, March 23, 1970, AGA: Sección Sindicatos, Caja 5478.

84. Antonio Domingo and Lopez Cascante to director general, March 23, 1970.

85. José Antonio Lopez Cascante to the Spanish National Syndicate of Wine, Beer, and Beverages, May 8, 1970, AGA: Sección Sindicatos, Caja 5478.

86. Luis Medina to director general for commercial policy and General Commission of Festival, June 30, 1970, AGA: Sección Sindicatos, Caja 5478.

87. Medina to director general, June 30, 1970.

88. Medina to director general, June 30, 1970.

89. Medina to director general, June 30, 1970.

90. Medina to director general, June 30, 1970.

91. "Presupuesto aproximado de lo que podría costar la degustación de vinos españoles en Dinmarca," April 7, 1970, AGA: Sección Sindicatos, Caja 5478.

92. "Los vinos españoles, a la conquista de Europa," *Arriba*, November 6, 1966, AGA: Sección Sindicatos, Caja 5477.

93. Pío Miguel Irurzun to director general of commercial policy, July 23, 1968, AGA: Sección Sindicatos, Caja 5478.

94. Pío Miguel Irurzun to director general of commercial policy, November 30, 1968, AGA: Sección Sindicatos, Caja 5459.

95. García de Quevedo de la Barrera, *Economía de Jerez*, 229.

96. García de Quevedo de la Barrera, *Economía de Jerez*, 229.

97. García de Quevedo de la Barrera, *Economía de Jerez*, 258.

98. García de Quevedo de la Barrera, *Economía de Jerez*, 263.

99. Pío Miguel Irurzun to Russell G. Hopkins, November 28, 1969, AGA: Sección Sindicatos, Caja 5476.

100. "Misión comercial a España de importadores en los Estados Unidos de vinos y licores," 1969, AGA: Sección Sindicatos, Caja 5476.

101. García de Quevedo de la Barrera, *Economía de Jerez*, 232.

102. Pío Miguel Irurzun to director general of commercial policy, April 29, 1969, AGA: Sección Sindicatos, Caja 5479.

103. Pío Miguel Irurzun, April 29, 1969.

7. SPANISH WINE TODAY

1. Heckle, *Traveler's Wine Guide*, inside front cover.

2. Heckle, *Traveler's Wine Guide*, xiv–xv.

3. Matelles-Lazo, "Consumo del enoturismo," 48.

4. Young, *Wine Routes*, 35.

5. Molina et al., "Market Segmentation," 192.

6. Serrano Miracle, "El turismo del vino," 19.

7. VVAA, *El cava*, 199.

8. Thach and Cuellar, "Trends and Implications," 17.

9. Thach and Cuellar, "Trends and Implications," 17.

10. Medina, Serrano, and Tresserras, "Introducción," 11.

11. Thach and Cuellar, "Trends and Implications," 1, 9.

12. Thach and Cuellar, "Trends and Implications," 11.

13. Thach and Cuellar, "Trends and Implications," 16.

14. Thach and Cuellar, "Trends and Implications," 16.

15. Molina et al., "Market Segmentation," 193.

16. Mason and O'Mahony, "On the Trail," 500.

17. Millán Vázquez et al., "Análisis de la ofreta," 185.

18. Mason and O'Mahony, "On the Trail," 501–2.

19. Duarte Alonso, "Saborea (Tasting) Lanzarote," 69.

20. Ceisel, "*El sabor de Galicia*," 136.

21. Bessière, "Local Development and Heritage," 22.

22. Bessière, "Local Development and Heritage," 23.

23. Bessière, "Local Development and Heritage," 25.

24. Matelles-Lazo, "Consumo del enoturismo," 47.

25. Escolar and Fernández Morueco, "Vino, turismo e innovación," 144.

26. Escolar and Fernández Morueco, "Vino, turismo e innovación," 149.

27. "Conoce las rutas del vino de España," Rutas Vino de España, https://www
.wineroutesofspain.com/ver/2457/Rutas-del-vino-.html (accessed December 7, 2022).

28. Medina, Serrano, and Tresserras, "Introducción," 11.

29. Millán Vázquez, Agudo, Molina, "Análisis," 184.

30. Escolar and Fernández Morueco, "Vino, turismo e innovación," 143.

31. Hernández, "Rutas del vino," 17–18.

32. Millán and Agudo, "Las rutas del vino," 63.

33. Molina et al., "Market Segmentation," 216.

34. Molina et al., "Market Segmentation," 216.

35. Duarte Alonso, "Saborea (Tasting) Lanzarote," 77.

36. Blanco Quesada, "Enoturismo, una propuesta," 5.

37. Alonso, "Comercializar el enoturismo," 11.

38. Nuñez Pinto, "El vino es patrimonio," 30.

39. Nuñez Pinto, "El vino es patrimonio," 30.

40. See Tolosa, *Barcelona Wine*.

41. Tolosa, *Marketing*, 11–32.

42. Tolosa, *Marketing*, 33–48.

43. Tolosa, *Marketing*, 49–56.

44. Tolosa, *Marketing*, 57–68.

45. Tolosa, *Marketing*, 69–78.

46. Tolosa, *Marketing*, 79–90.

47. Tolosa, *Marketing*, 91–104.

48. Tolosa, *Marketing*, 105–20.

49. Tolosa, *Marketing*, 121–32.

50. Tolosa, *Marketing*, 133–48.

51. Tolosa, *Marketing*, 149–75.

52. Doxat and González Gordon, *Sherry*, 204.

53. Doxat and González Gordon, *Sherry*, 235–37.

54. Radford, *New Spain*, 189.

55. Radford, *New Spain*, 189.

56. Radford, *New Spain*, 190.

57. Maldonado Rosso, *Las Rutas del Vino*, 319.

58. Baiocchi, *Sherry*, 2.

59. Baiocchi, *Sherry*, 2.

60. Doxat and González Gordon, *Sherry*, 204.

61. Baiocchi, *Sherry*, 4, 44.

62. Baiocchi, *Sherry*, 77.

63. Heckle, *Traveler's Wine Guide*, 130–31.

64. Baiocchi, *Sherry*, 64–65.

65. See Doxat and González Gordon, *Sherry*, chap. 9.

66. Ben O'Donnell, "Does Wine Evangelism Work? Part 2," *Wine Spectator*, April 13, 2019, https://www.winespectator.com/articles/does-wine-evangelism-work-part-2-48328#.

67. O'Donnell, "Wine Evangelism."

68. Baiocchi, *Sherry*, 85.

69. See Baiocchi, *Sherry*, 160–229.

70. Radford, *New Spain*, 126.

71. Wallner, *Cava*, 13.

72. Wallner, *Cava*, 17.

73. Wallner, *Cava*, 17.

74. Wallner, *Cava*, 17.

75. VVAA, *El cava*, 40–41.

76. See VVAA, *El cava*, 42–63.

77. Wallner, *Cava*, 51–53.

78. Wallner, *Cava*, 46.

79. *Wines and Cavas of Catalonia*, 56.

80. Wallner, *Cava*, 57.

81. Wallner, *Cava*, 57.

82. Wallner, *Cava*, 61–77.

83. Radford, *New Spain*, inside front cover.

84. Miguel Torres, in Radford, *New Spain*, 6.

85. Radford, *New Spain*, 11.

86. Heckle, *Traveler's Wine Guide*, xvii–xviii.

87. Young, *Wine Routes*, 11.

88. Davidson, "*Terroir* and Catalonia," 40, 47.

89. *Wines and Cavas of Catalonia*, 179.

90. *Wines and Cavas of Catalonia*, 33–34.

91. *Wines and Cavas of Catalonia*, 235–37.

92. *Wines and Cavas of Catalonia*, 75.

93. Heckle, *Traveler's Wine Guide*, 25–26.

94. Heckle, *Traveler's Wine Guide*, 20.

95. Tolosa Planet and Larreina Díaz, *Vinos y bodegas*, 17, 19.

96. Tolosa Planet and Larreina Díaz, *Vinos y bodegas*, 32–33.

97. Radford, *New Spain*, 54–55.

98. Radford, *New Spain*, 56.

99. Radford, *New Spain*, 60–61.

100. Heckle, *Traveler's Wine Guide*, 158.

101. Heckle, *Traveler's Wine Guide*, 156.

102. Thach and Cuellar, "Trends and Implications," 16.

103. Thach and Cuellar, "Trends and Implications," 19.

CONCLUSION

1. Thomas Matthews, "Spain's Extreme Virtues," *Wine Spectator*, October 15, 2018, https://top100.winespectator.com/2018/article/extreme-virtues/.

2. Matthews, "Spain's Extreme Virtues."

3. Matthews, "Spain's Extreme Virtues."

4. Matthews, "Spain's Extreme Virtues."

BIBLIOGRAPHY

ARCHIVES/MANUSCRIPTS

ABGB Archivo Bodegas Gonzáles Byass, Jerez de la Frontera
ABMM Archivo Bodegas Marqués de Murrieta, Logroño
AGA Archivo General de la Administración, Alcalá de Henares
AMJF Archivo Municipal de Jerez de la Frontera
ARB Archivo Raventós i Blanc, Sant Sadurní d'Anoia
CRJ Consejo Regulador Jerez-Xerez-Sherry, Jerez de la Frontera
MAPA Ministerio de Agricultura, Pesca y Alimentación. Archivo Central, Madrid
Vinseum, Vilafranca de Penedès

CAVA VISITS

Blancher, Sant Sadurní d'Anoia, 2015
Codorníu, Sant Sadurní d'Anoia, 2017
Freixenet, Sant Sadurní d'Anoia, 2017
Mascaró, Vilafranca de Penedès, 2015
Montesquius, Sant Sadurní d'Anoia, 2017
Parés Baltà, Plá de Penedès, 2015
Pere Ventura, Sant Sadurní d'Anoia, 2017
Raventós i Blanc, Sant Sadurní d'Anoia, 2017
Recaredo, Sant Sadurní d'Anoia, 2017

SHERRY VISITS

Cayetano del Pino y Cía, Jerez de la Frontera, 2019
Diez Mérito, Jerez de la Frontera, 2019
El Maestro Sierra, Jerez de la Frontera, interview with doña María del Carmen Borrego
    Plá, 2015, 2017
Faustino González, Jerez de la Frontera, 2019

Fernández-Gao, Jerez de la Frontera, 2019
Fundador, Jerez de la Frontera, 2015
Gonzáles Byass, Jerez de la Frontera, 2015, 2017
Lustau, Jerez de la Frontera, 2015
Rey Fernando de Castilla, Jerez de la Frontera, 2017
Sánchez Romate Hermanos, Jerez de la Frontera, 2017
Tío Pepe, Jerez de la Frontera, 2015, 2017
Tradiciones, Jerez de la Frontera, 2015, 2017
Sandeman, Jerez de la Frontera, 2015

WINE VISITS

CVNE, Haro, 2015
Franco-Españolas, Logroño, 2015
Lagar de Cervera, O Rosal, 2015
Marqués de Murrieta, Logroño, 2015
Marqués de Riscal, Elciego, 2015
Muga, Haro, 2015
Ramón Bilbao, Haro, 2015
Santiago Ruiz, A Guarda, interview with doña Rosa Ruíz, 2015
Torres, Plá de Penedès, 2015
Vivanco, Briones, 2015

PUBLISHED WORKS

Albala, Ken. "To Your Health: Wine as Food and Medicine in Mid-Sixteenth-Century Italy." In *Alcohol: A Social and Cultural History*, edited by Mack P. Holt, 11–23. Oxford: Berg, 2006.

Alonso, Christina. "Comercializar el enoturismo." *Terruños* 25 (2015):10–13.

Alonso Fernandez, Francisco. "The State of Alcoholism in Spain Covering Its Epidemiological and Aetiological Aspects." *British Journal of Addiction* 71 (1976): 235–42.

Amor, Fernando. "Sobre el azuframiento de la viñas." *Revista de la Agricultura Práctica, Economía Rural, Horticultura y Jardinería* 8, no. 11 (November 1, 1859): 206.

Anderson, Lara. *Control and Resistance: Food Discourse in Franco Spain*. Toronto: University of Toronto Press, 2020.

———. *Cooking up the Nation: Spanish Culinary Texts and Culinary Nationalization in the late Nineteenth and Early Twentieth Century*. Suffolk: Tamesis, 2013.

———. "A Recipe for a Modern Nation: Miguel Primo de Rivera and Spanish Food Culture." *Revista de Estudios Hispanicos* 52 (2018): 75–99.

Armesto López, Xosé, and Belén Gómez Martín. "Tourism and Quality Agro-Food Products: An Opportunity for the Spanish Countryside." *Tijdschrift voor Economische en Sociale Geografie* 97, no. 2 (2006): 166–77.

Badia-Miró, Marc, Enric Tello, Francesc Valls, and Ramon Garrabou. "The Grape Phylloxera Plague as a Natural Experiment: The Upkeep of Vineyards in Catalonia (Spain),
1858–1955." *Australian Economic History Review* 50, no. 1 (2010): 39–61.

Baiocchi, Talia. *Sherry: The World's Best-Kept Secret*. Berkeley CA: Ten Speed, 2014.

Bessière, Jacinthe. "Local Development and Heritage: Traditional Food and Cuisine as
Tourist Attractions in Rural Areas." *Sociologia Ruralis* 38, no. 1 (1998): 21–34.

Blanco Quesada, María. "Enoturismo, una propuesta de valor en la estrategia de promo-
ción internacional de Turespaña." *Terruños* 25 (2015): 4–9.

Bohling, Joseph. "'Drink Better, but Less': The Rise of France's Appellation System in the
European Community." *French Historical Studies* 37, no. 3 (2014): 501–30.

Bonfanti, Angelo, Paola Castellani, and Chiara Rossato. "Developing Territorial Identity:
The Experience of Historical Italian Companies." *International Journal of Management Cases* 17, no. 4 (2015): 45–58.

Catalogue des exposants du comité Xérès a l'exposition universelle de Bordeaux 1895. Bordeaux: Imprimierie G. Gounouilhou, 1895.

Cavicchi, Alessio, Cristina Santini, and Eleonora Belletti. "Preserving the Authenticity of
Food and Wine Festivals: The Case of Italy." *Il Capitale Culturale* 8 (2013): 251–71.

Cazorla-Sánchez, Antonio. "Family Matters: Ministerial Elites and the Articulation of the
Francoist Dictatorship." *Portuguese Journal of Social Science* 3, no. 2 (2004): 73–89.

Ceisel, Christina M. "*El sabor de Galicia*: Wine as Performance in Galicia, Spain." In *Wine
and Culture: Vineyard to Glass*, edited by Rachel E. Black and Robert C. Ulin, 125–
44. London: Bloomsbury Academic, 2013.

Chang, Seohee. "The Spillover Effects of Wine and Harvest Festivals on Other Festivals."
Tourism Analysis 19 (2014): 689–99.

Christensen, Bradley, Martin Kenney, and Donald Patton. "Regional Identity Can Add
Value to Agricultural Products." *California Agriculture* 69, no. 2 (2015): 85–91.

Colomé Ferrer, Josep, and Francesc Valls-Junyent. "Las consecuencias demográficas de la
crisis Filoxérica en la Región Vitícola del Penedès." *Historia Agraria* 57 (2012): 47–77.

Cuevas, José de las. *Biografía del vino de Jerez*. Jerez de la Frontera: Jerez Industrial SA,
1949.

Davidson, Robert A. "*Terroir* and Catalonia." *Journal of Catalan Studies* 10 (2007): 39–53.

Diarios de la Exposición y Feria Oficial de la Viña y del Vino. Vilafranca de Penedès, 1943,
1953, 1963. Vinseum.

Duarte Alonso, Abel. "Saborea (Tasting) Lanzarote: Building the Foundation of a New
Food and Wine Event through Collaborative Efforts." *Tourism and Planning Development* 11, no. 1 (2014): 68–85.

———. "Stakeholders, Collaboration, Food, and Wine: The Case of Jumilla's Gastronomic Days." *Journal of Convention & Event Tourism* 17, no. 3 (2016): 173–91.

Duarte Alonso, Abel, and Alessandro Bressan. "Stakeholders' Perspectives on the Evolu-
tion and Benefits of a Traditional Wine Festival: The Case of the Grape Festival in
Impruneta, Italy." *Journal of Convention & Event Tourism* 14 (2013): 309–30.

"El azufre empleado como medio para la curación de la enfermedad de las viñas." *Revista de Agricultura, Economía Rural, Horticultura y Jardinería* 6, no. 6 (1857): 171–72.

Escolar, Belén Miranda, and Ricardo Fernández Morueco. "Vino, turismo e innovación: Las *Rutas del vino de España*, una estrategia integrada de desarrollo rural." *Estudios de Economía Aplicada*, 29, no. 1 (2011): 129–64.

España en forma. Madrid: Artes Gráficas EMA, 1963/64.

Espigado Tocino, Gloria. "Exportación y fraude en el comercio del vino: Los informes del Consul Norteamericano en Cádiz (1866–1867)." *Revista Historia de Jerez* 1 (1995): 29–41.

Farré Huguet, Jordi. "Del arte a la ciencia del vino." In *La máquinas de papel: Simposio sobre la publicidad de la maquinería agrícola y del la bodega desde siglo XIX*, edited by Fundación Joaquin Díaz, 21–67. Urueña: Noviembre 2015.

Fernández-Pérez, Paloma. "Challenging the Loss of an Empire: González and Byass of Jerez." *Business History* 41, no. 4 (1999): 72–87.

Filippo Fontefrancesco, Michele. "Of Grape, Feast, and Community: An Ethnographic Note on the Making of the Grape Harvest Festival in an Italian Town in the Piedmont." *Journal of Ethnology and Folkloristics* 8, no. 1 (2014): 75–90.

Foxá, Miguel de. "Del cultivo de la vid de la elaboración de vinos." *Revista de Agricultura, Economía Rural, Horticultura y Jardinería* 9, no. 8 (August 1, 1860): 169–72.

———. "Del cultivo de la vid de la elaboración de vinos." *Revista de Agricultura, Economía Rural, Horticultura y Jardinería* 9, no. 9 (September 1, 1860): 193–97.

———. "Del cultivo de la vid de la elaboración de vinos." *Revista de Agricultura, Economía Rural, Horticultura y Jardinería* 9, no. 10 (October 1, 1860): 229–32.

———. "Noticias acerca del oidium y del azuframiento." *Revista de Agricultura, Economía Rural, Horticultura y Jardinería* 9, no. 5 (May 1, 1860): 101–4.

Galen on Food. Translated by Mark Grant. New York: Routledge, 2000.

García de Quevedo de la Barrera, José. *Economía de Jerez*. Jerez de la Frontera: Gráficas del Exportador, 1970.

Girón Sierra, Álvaro. "El marco de Jerez cabalgando entre dos crisis (1974–1980)." In *Actas del Congreso Científico: El vino de Jerez en los 80 años de la denominación de origen, 1935–2015*, edited by César Saldaña, 175–90. Jerez de la Frontera: Consejo Regulador de las Denominaciones de Origen "Jerez-Xérès-Sherry," "Mazanilla-Sanlúcar de Barrameda" y "Vinagre de Jerez," 2000.

Gómez, Mar, and Arturo Molina. "Wine Tourism in Spain: Denomination of Origin Effects on Brand Equity." *International Journal of Tourism Research* 14 (2012): 353–68.

González Gordon, Manuel M. *Sherry: The Noble Wine*. London: Quiller, 1990.

Gonzàlez Turmo, Isabel. *Sevilla banquetes, tapas, cartas y menus, 1863–1995: Antropología de la alimentación*. Sevilla: Área de Cultura del Ayuntamiento de Sevilla, 1996.

Granett, Jeffrey, M. Andrew Walker, Laszlo Kocsis, and Amir Omer. "Biology and Management of Grape Phylloxera." *Annual Review of Entomology* 46 (2001): 387–412.

Grieco, Allen J. "Medieval and Renaissance Wine: Taste, Dietary Theory, and How to Choose the 'Right' Wine." *Mediaevalia* 30, no. 1 (2009): 15–42.

Guy, Kolleen M. "Rituals of Pleasure in the Land of Treasures: Wine Consumption and the Making of French Identity in the Late Nineteenth Century." In *Food Nations: Selling Taste in Consumer Societies*, edited by Warren Belasco and Philip Scranton, 34–47. New York: Routledge, 2002.

———. *When Champagne Became French: Wine and the Making of National Identity*. Baltimore MD: Johns Hopkins University Press, 2003.

Haine, W. Scott. "Drink, Sociability, and Social Class in France, 1789–1945: The Emergence of the Proletarian Public Space." In *Alcohol: A Social and Cultural History*, edited by Mack P. Holt, 121–44. Oxford: Berg, 2006.

Harrington, Robert J. "Defining Gastronomic Identity: The Impact of Environment and Culture on Prevailing Components, Textures, and Flavors in Wine and Food." *Journal of Culinary Science & Technology* 4, nos. 2–3 (2005): 129–52.

Heckle, Harold. *A Traveler's Wine Guide to Spain*. Northampton MA: Interlink, 2012.

Hernández, Rosario. "Rutas del vino de España, la apuesta de ACEVIN por el enoturismo." *Terruños* 25 (2015): 14–20.

Holmberg, Lars. "Wine Fraud." *International Journal of Wine Research* 2 (2010): 105–13.

Jiménez Garcia, José Luis. "Una(s) mirada(s) al Jerez de entresiglos: Industria y publicidad entre tradición y el progreso." In *La máquinas de papel: Simposio sobre la publicidad de la maquinería agrícola y del la bodega desde siglo XIX*, edited by Fundación Joaquin Díaz, 84–106. Urueña: Noviembre 2015.

Johnson Morgan, Melissa. "Food Festivals, Food Marketing, and the Re-invention of a Rural Community." *Journal of New Business Ideas & Trends* 13, no. 2 (2015): 57–72.

Kneale, James, and Shaun French. "Moderate Drinking before the Unit: Medicine and Life Assurance in Britain and the U.S. ca. 1860–1930." *Drugs: Education, Prevention, and Policy* 22, no. 2 (2015): 111–17.

Laferté, Gilles. "The Folklorization of French Farming: Marketing Luxury Wine in the Interwar Years." *French Historical Studies* 34, no. 4 (2011): 679–712.

Llansó, Jaime. "De la vinificación o sea la tansformación del mosto en vino." *Revista de Agricultura, Economía Rural, Horticultura y Jardinería* 8, no. 3 (March 1, 1859): 59–63.

———. "Sección práctica." *Revista de Agricultura, Economía Rural, Horticultura y Jardinería* 7, no. 9 (September 1, 1858): 218–22.

Lunzer, Ralph. *Reports of Patent, Design, and Trade Mark Cases, Vine Product Limited & Others v. Mackenzie & Company Limited & Others*. London: Patent Office, 1969.

Maldonado Rosso, Javier. "Cadiz." In *Las rutas del vino en Andalucía*, edited by Javier Maldonado Rosso, 319–39. Sevilla: Fundación José Lara, 2006.

Manjarrés y de Bofarull, Ramón de. "Revista agrícola de la esposicion de Paris, en 1855." *Revista de Agricultura, Economía Rural, Horticultura y Jardinería* 4, no. 10 (April 1, 1856): 297–304, 328–35.

Martínes-Carrión, José Miguel, and Francisco José Medina-Albaladejo. "Change and Development in the Spanish Wine Sector, 1950–2009." *Journal of Wine Research* 21, no. 1 (2010): 77–95.

Mason, Robb, and Barry O'Mahony. "On the Trail of Food and Wine: The Tourist Search for Meaningful Experience." *Annals of Leisure Research* 10 (2007): 498–517.

Matelles-Lazo, Mónica. "Consumo del enoturismo en la D.O. Ribera del Duero." *Revista de comunicación vivat academia* 15, no. 123 (2013): 41–71.

Medina, F. Xavier, Damià Serrano, and Jordi Tresserras, eds. *Turismo del vino: Análisis de casos internacionales.* Barcelona: Editorial UOC, 2011.

Millán, María Genoveva, and Eva M. Agudo. "Las rutas del vino en España: Estudio de la Denominación de Origen Montilla-Moriles." In *Turismo del vino: Análisis de casos internacionales*, edited by F. Xavier Medina, Damià Serrano, and Jordi Tresserras, 61–80. Barcelona: Editorial UOC, 2011.

Millán Vázquez, María Genoveva, Eva María Agudo Gutiérrez, and Emilio Morales Fernández. "Análisis de la ofreta y la demanda de oleoturismo en el sur de España: Un estudio caso." *Cuadernos de Desarrollo Rural* 8, no. 67 (2011): 181–202.

Miller, Montserrat. *Feeding Barcelona, 1714–1975: Public Market Halls, Social Networks, and Consumer Culture.* Baton Rouge: Louisiana State University Press, 2015.

Mintz, Sidney W. "Food and Eating: Some Persistent Questions," In *Food Nations: Selling Taste in Consumer Societies*, edited by Warren Belasco and Philip Scranton, 24–33. New York: Routledge, 2002.

———. *Tasting Food, Tasting Freedom: Excursions into Eating, Culture, and the Past.* Boston: Beacon, 1996.

Molina, Arturo, Mar Gómez, Belén González-Diaz, and Águeda Esteban. "Market Segmentation in Wine Tourism: Strategies for Wineries and Destinations in Spain." *Journal of Wine Research* 26, no. 3 (2015): 192–224.

Molleví Bortoló, Gemma, and David Serrano Giné. "El impacto de la filoxera en Andalucia según la diplomacia francesa." *Cuadernos Geográficos* 40, no. 1 (2007): 133–48.

Munholland, Kim. "*Mon docteur le vin*: Wine and Health in France, 1900–1950." In *Alcohol: A Social and Cultural History*, edited by Mack P. Holt, 77–90. Oxford: Berg, 2006.

Nadeau, Carolyn A. "*Moscatel morisco*: The Role of Wine in the Formation of Morisco Identity." *Bulletin of Hispanic Studies* 90 (2013): 153–65.

Nuñez Pinto, Lola. "El vino es patrimonio." *Terruños* 25 (2015): 26–30.

Parkhurst Ferguson, Priscilla. *Accounting for Taste: The Triumph of French Cuisine.* Chicago: University of Chicago Press, 2004.

———. *Word of Mouth: What We Talk about When We Talk about Food.* Berkeley: University of California Press, 2014.

Parada y Barreto, Don Adolfo. *Discurso en la primer conferencia filoxérica dada el 20 de julio de 1879 en la ciudad de Jerez de la Frontera.* Madrid: Moreno y Rojas, 1880.

Phillips, Rod. "Wine and Adulteration." *History Today* 50 (2000): 31–37.

Piqueras Haba, Juan. *From the American Pests to Cooperativism, 1850–2007.* Vilafranca de Penedès: Edicions i Propostes Culturals Andana, SL, 2010.

Planas, Jordi. "State Intervention in the Wine Markets in the Early 20th Century: Why Was It So Different in France and Spain." *Journal of Iberian and Latin American Economic History* 35, no. 2 (2016): 175–206.

Plasencia, Pedro. *Los vinos de España: Vistos por los viajeros europeos.* Madrid: Ministerio de Argricultura, Pesca, y Alimentación, 1995.

Pozo Andrés, María del Mar del, and Teresa Rabazas Romero. "Exploring New Concepts of Popular Education: Politics, Religion, and Citizenship in the Suburban Schools of Madrid, 1940–1975." *Paedagogica Historica* 47, nos. 1–2 (2011): 221–42.

Puig, Núria. "El mercado vinícola española en el siglo XX: Reguladores y regulados entre 1932 y 1970." In *Actas del I encuentro de historiadores de la vitivinicultura española*, edited by Javier Maldonado Rosso and Alberto Ramos Santana, 243–49. Puerto de Santa María: Ayuntamiento de El Puerto de Santa María, 2000.

Radford, John. *The New Spain: A Complete Guide to Contemporary Spanish Wine.* London: Octopus, 1998.

Raventós, María del Mar. "Codorníu, la historia de una familia que elabora vinos hace quinientos años." *Universia Business Review* 3 (2011): 126–31.

Revista de Agricultura Práctica, Economía Rural, Horticultura y Jardinería. El Instituto Agrícola Catalan de San Isidro, 1856–60. Vinseum.

Rodriguez Salcedo, Natalia. "Public Relations before 'Public Relations' in Spain: An Early History (1881–1960)." *Journal of Communication Management* 12, no. 4 (2008): 279–93.

Serrano Miracle, Damià. "El turismo del vino: La lectura espacial de un binomio estratégico." In *Turismo del vino: Análisis de casos internacionales*, edited by F. Xavier Medina, Damià Serrano, and Jordi Tresserres, 19–34. Barcelona: Editorial UOC, 2011.

Simpson, James. "Adapting to International Markets: Sherry, 1820–1900." *DUORO— Estudos & Documentios* 7, no. 13 (2002): 207–22.

———. *Creating Wine: The Emergence of a World Industry, 1840–1914.* Princeton NJ: Princeton University Press, 2011.

———. "La producción de vinos en Jerez de la Frontera, 1850–1900." In *La nueva historia económica en España*, edited by Pablo Martín Aceña and Leonardo Prados de la Escosura, 166–89. Madrid: Tecnos, 1985.

———. "Selling to Reluctant Drinkers: The British Wine Market, 1860–1914." *Economic History Review* 57, no. 1 (2014): 80–108.

———. "Too Little Regulation? The British Market for Sherry, 1840–90." *Business History* 45, no. 3 (2007): 367–82.

Soler Becerro, Raimon. "From Trade to Industry: The Wine Production Sector of the Penedès Denomination of Origin, 1940–2000." Working Papers in Economics 266, Universitat de Barcelona, Espai de Recerca en Economia, 2011.

Stanziani, Alessandro. "Information, Quality, and Legal Rules: Wine Adulteration in Nineteenth Century France." *Business History* 51, no. 2 (2009): 268–91.

Stilling Blichfeldt, Bodil, and Henrik Halkier. "Mussels, Tourism, and Community Development: A Case Study of Place Branding through Food Festivals in Rural North Jutland, Denmark." *European Planning Studies* 22, no. 8 (2014): 1587–603.

Thach, Liz, and Steven Cuellar. "Trends and Implications for Spanish Wine Sales in the U.S. Market." *International Journal of Wine Business Research* 19 (2007): 63–78.

Timón Tiemblo, María Pía. "El patrimonio inmaterial de la viña y el vino: Usos, conocimientos, rituals y simbolismo." In *La máquinas de papel: Simposio sobre la publicidad de la maquinería agrícola y del la bodega desde siglo XIX*, edited by Fundación Joaquin Díaz, 4–20. Urueña: Noviembre 2015.

Tolosa, Lluís. *Barcelona Wine: Enjoy Wine Tourism in the City*. Barcelona: LTA Ediciones & Tolosa Wine, 2015.

———. *Guia d'enoturisme de Catalunya*. Barcelona: Tolosa Wine, 2018.

———. *Guia d'enoturisme del Penedès*. Barcelona: Tolosa Wine, 2016.

———. *Marketing del enoturismo: 12 errores habituales, 12 propuestas alternativas*. Barcelona: Tolosa Wine, 2017.

———. *Vinos de España*. Barcelona: Tolosa Wine, 2020.

Tolosa Planet, Luís, and Mikel Larreina Díaz. *Vinos y bodegas de Rioja*. Rioja: LT&A Ediciones, 2005.

Trubek, Amy B. *The Taste of Place: A Cultural Journey into Terroir*. Berkeley: University of California Press, 2008.

Ulin, Robert C. "*Terroir* and Locality: An Anthropological Perspective." In *Wine and Culture: Vineyard to Glass*, edited by Rachel E. Black and Robert C. Ulin, 67–88. London: Bloomsbury, 2013.

Ulin Robert C., and Rachel E. Black. "Rethinking Terroir." In *Wine and Culture: Vineyard to Glass*, edited by Rachel E. Black and Robert C. Ulin, 11–14. London: Bloomsbury, 2013.

Valls-Junyent, Francesc. *La Catalunya atlantica: Aiguardent i teixits a l'arrencada industrial catalana*. Vic: Eumo Editorial, 2003.

———. "Compitiendo con el *champagne*: La industria española de los vinos espumosos antes de la Guerra Civil." *Revista Historia Industrial* 33 (2007): 47–79.

Varriano, John. "Wine and Death *Carpe Diem* or *Vanitas*." *Mediaevalia* 30, no. 1 (2009): 5–14.

Visita de S.M. el rey don Alfonso XIII a las Cavas Codorníu, April 17, 1904, Archivo Raventós i Blanc, Sant Sadurní d'Anoia.

VVAA. *El cava y sus elaboradores*. Barcelona: RT&A Ediciones, 1996.

Wallner, Anne. *Cava: Sparkling Happiness*. London: Grenadine, 2012.

The Wines and Cavas of Catalonia: The Designations of Origen: History, Heritage, and Landscape. Vilafranca de Penedès: Ediciones i Propostes Culturals Andana, 2011.

Young, Alan. *Wine Routes of the Penedès and Catalonia*. San Francisco: International Wine Academy, 2000.

INDEX

Spanish Pavilion, 129, 130
Spanish Society for Wine and
    Winemaking, 54
Spanish Superior Council of Agriculture,
    Industry, and Commerce, 16, 30–32,
    34, 36
Spansk Vinefestival (Copenhagen, 1970),
    131, 152–56, 159–60
sugar, in wine production, 20–21, 24, 47,
    176
sulfur, as oidium cure, 39, 40, 41–43
surveys, for wine sales, 30–36, 73, 76–77
Switzerland, 156–57

tariffs, in wine trade, 28, 49, 130, 134–35,
    136, 138–39, 150–51, 153
Tarragona (province), 35, 47
taxes, in wine trade, 28, 56, 95, 150–51,
    155–56
technology, in wine production, 46–47, 50,
    71–72, 180–81, 182
Televisión Española (TVE), 76
Tello, Enric, 47
tempranillo grapes, 179
terroir, 10, 22–25
Thach, Liz, 163, 182
Thudichum, John Louis William, 28
Time Magazine, 163
Times, 28
Tolosa, Lluís: Marketing del enoturismo,
    167–70
Torelló, Pelegrí, 92–93
Torres, Miguel, 178
totalitarianism, 13, 97
tourists and tourism: authenticity impor-
    tant for, 109–10; and cava industry, 175,
    178; economy helped by, 156; festivals
    attracting, 97; trade helped by, 135–36,
    137–38; wine tours for, 99–101, 109–11,
    161–62, 164–70
Trade Mark Act (1875), 147–48

A Traveler's Wine Guide to Spain (Heckle),
    161
Treaty of Rome (1957), 130
Trubek, Amy, 23
Tucker, Edward, 38–39
TVE (Televisión Española), 76

Udina Martell, Santiago, 123, 124–25
Ulin, Robert C., 2, 22
United Kingdom. See Britain, imports of;
    sherry, lawsuit over
United States, and wine trade, 1–2, 102,
    157–58, 162–63, 174, 182
unity, fairs promoting, 108, 115–16
Universal Exhibition of Products of
    Agriculture, Industry, and Fine Arts
    (Paris, 1855), 16–19, 23

Valdespino, 139
Valencia (region), 35
Valls, Fransesc, 47
Velázquez, Diego: Los borrachos, 101–2
venenciadores, 99–100, 130
Vergne, de la, Mr., 42
Vilafranca de Penedès, Barcelona, 33, 105,
    107, 110, 115–16, 122
Vine Products Limited, 143, 148
Vine Products v. Mackenzie & Co. Ltd, 159.
    See also sherry, lawsuit over
vines, 24–25, 40–43, 44–45, 46–47, 68–69
vineyards: physical qualities of, 14; reputa-
    tion of, 55; restrictions on, 72; statistics
    on, 32–35; wine plagues affecting, 11,
    37–38, 39, 40–41, 42, 43–44, 46
Vintage Magazine, 163

Walker, M. Andrew, 44–45
Walker, Mr. (British citizen), 147
Wallner, Anne, 175–76, 177
water, in wine production, 44–45, 49–50,
    52

IN THE AT TABLE SERIES

*Educated Tastes: Food, Drink,
and Connoisseur Culture*
Edited and with an introduction
by Jeremy Strong

*In Food We Trust: The Politics of
Purity in American Food Regulation*
Courtney I. P. Thomas

*¡Vino! The History and
Identity of Spanish Wine*
Karl J. Trybus

*The Banana: Empires, Trade
Wars, and Globalization*
James Wiley

*Fried Walleye and Cherry Pie:
Midwestern Writers on Food*
Edited and with an introduction
by Peggy Wolff

*Predictable Pleasures: Food and the
Pursuit of Balance in Rural Yucatán*
Lauren A. Wynne

AVAILABLE IN BISON BOOKS EDITIONS

The Food and Cooking of Eastern Europe
Lesley Chamberlain
With a new introduction by the author

The Food and Cooking of Russia
Lesley Chamberlain
With a new introduction by the author

*The World on a Plate: A Tour through
the History of America's Ethnic Cuisine*
Joel Denker

Jewish American Food Culture
Jonathan Deutsch and Rachel D. Saks

*The Recipe Reader: Narratives,
Contexts, Traditions*
Edited by Janet Floyd and Laurel Forster

*A Chef's Tale: A Memoir of
Food, France, and America*
Pierre Franey
With Richard Flaste and Bryan Miller
With a new introduction
by Eugenia Bone

*Masters of American Cookery:
M. F. K. Fisher, James Beard,
Craig Claiborne, Julia Child*
Betty Fussell
With a preface by the author

My Kitchen Wars: A Memoir
Betty Fussell
With a new introduction
by Laura Shapiro

Good Things
Jane Grigson

Jane Grigson's Fruit Book
Jane Grigson
With a new introduction
by Sara Dickerman

Jane Grigson's Vegetable Book
Jane Grigson
With a new introduction
by Amy Sherman

*Dining with Marcel Proust:
A Practical Guide to French
Cuisine of the Belle Epoque*
Shirley King
Foreword by James Beard

*Pampille's Table: Recipes and
Writings from the French
Countryside from Marthe Daudet's*
Les Bons Plats de France
Translated and adapted by Shirley King

*Moveable Feasts: The History,
Science, and Lore of Food*
Gregory McNamee

To order or obtain more information on these or other University
of Nebraska Press titles, visit nebraskapress.unl.edu.